"This is an important book and essential reading for students, practitioners, and policymakers alike! It carefully – and critically – explains how new data sources and innovative methodologies can be used to advance our knowledge of offending across the life course. What results is truly a blueprint for the ongoing development of evidence-based crime prevention policy and practice."

Andrew Day, *Professor of Criminology, University of Melbourne*

"This book charts an ambitious and essential way forward for developmental and life-course criminology (DLC) theory, research, and practice. The edited text provides numerous innovative examples of how DLC researchers can collaborate across disciplines and with community members and policymakers to enhance crime prevention."

Abigail A. Fagan, *Professor, Department of Sociology and Criminology & Law, University of Florida*

"This timely volume offers diverse and novel perspectives to inform the future of developmental/life-course criminology. The content challenges and extends DLC approaches, and helpfully canvasses both theoretical and practical developments in the field. It will appeal to scholars and practitioners in diverse fields including criminology, law, social work, and psychology."

Dr Susan Baidawi, *Senior Lecturer in Social Work, Monash University*

"I am confident that this exceptional edited collection will become an essential resource for developmental life-course criminologists. In addition to contributions that wrestle with important and contemporary theoretical debates, there are chapters that are highly relevant to real-world settings and practice. These relatively untapped domains range from a thorough examination of the benefits and limitations of using administrative data for DLC research to integrating the voices of Indigenous populations and those with lived experience into DLC research."

Professor Darrick Jolliffe, *Professor of Criminology, Royal Holloway, University of London and Co-Editor-in-Chief, Journal of Developmental and Life Course Criminology*

Frontiers in Developmental and Life-Course Criminology

Frontiers in Developmental and Life-Course Criminology advances the field of developmental and life-course criminology (DLC) by highlighting some recent methodological innovations, and exploring the ways in which DLC criminologists are helping to bridge the gap between science and service by their engagement with policymakers and government and non-government agencies.

The book is united by three related themes: the use of new data sources including government administrative data systems, the development of intervention and prevention strategies grounded in DLC research, and resilience, prosocial behaviour, and strengths-based approaches.

This book opens up new possibilities for the future of DLC research, orienting the DLC field as one that prioritises the achievement of better outcomes for individuals and society.

Catia Malvaso is a Senior Research Fellow in the School of Public Health and School of Psychology at the University of Adelaide.

Tara Renae McGee is a Professor in the School of Criminology and Criminal Justice at Griffith University and is the Deputy Director of the Transforming Corrections to Transform Lives (TCTL) Centre.

Ross Homel is a Foundation Professor of Criminology at Griffith University.

Criminology at the Edge

Edited by
Benoit Leclerc
Ross Homel
Clifford Shearing
Griffith University, Australia

This interdisciplinary series explores innovative developments and imagined futures for criminology.

Over the last few decades, criminology has become known for its rigorous research methods and innovative analyses as well as for the development and testing of traditional and new theories. Criminology, as an inherently multidisciplinary enterprise concerned with a very wide range of urgent community, national, and global problems, is also characterised by its dedication to *knowledge translation*, thereby helping to realise the goal of creating safe and just societies.

The objective of this series is to expand the boundaries of criminological thought and research and facilitate dissemination of the fruits of both philosophically oriented and empirically grounded discussions of some of the most important emerging trends within criminology. Innovative thinkers working on problems of criminological significance will be encouraged to take risks as they imagine a criminology for the 21st Century.

The Future of Rational Choice for Crime Prevention
Edited by Danielle M. Reynald and Benoit Leclerc

Criminology and the Anthropocene
Edited by Cameron Holley and Clifford Shearing

Big Data
Benoit Leclerc and Jesse Cale

Criminology and Climate
Insurance, Finance and the Regulation of Harmscapes
Edited by Cameron Holley, Liam Phelan and Clifford Shearing

Frontiers in Developmental and Life-Course Criminology
Methodological Innovation and Social Benefit
Catia Malvaso, Tara Renae McGee and Ross Homel

For more information about this series, please visit: https://www.routledge.com/Criminology-at-the-Edge/book-series/CATE

Frontiers in Developmental and Life-Course Criminology

Methodological Innovation and Social Benefit

Edited by Catia Malvaso, Tara Renae McGee, and Ross Homel

Routledge
Taylor & Francis Group
LONDON AND NEW YORK

First published 2024
by Routledge
4 Park Square, Milton Park, Abingdon, Oxon OX14 4RN

and by Routledge
605 Third Avenue, New York, NY 10158

Routledge is an imprint of the Taylor & Francis Group, an informa business

British Library Cataloguing-in-Publication Data
A catalogue record for this book is available from the British Library

Library of Congress Cataloging-in-Publication Data
Names: Malvaso, Catia, editor. | McGee, Tara Renae, editor. | Homel, Ross, editor.
Title: Frontiers in developmental and life-course criminology: methodological innovation and social benefit/edited by Catia Malvaso, Tara Renae McGee and Ross Homel.
Description: Abingdon, Oxon; New York, NY: Routledge, 2024. | Includes
bibliographical references and index. | Summary: "This book opens up new possibilities for the future of DLC research, orienting the DLC field as one that prioritises the achievement of better outcomes for individuals and society"—Provided by publisher.
Identifiers: LCCN 2023027480 (print) | LCCN 2023027481 (ebook) | ISBN 9781032279275 (hardback) | ISBN 9781032279381 (paperback) | ISBN 9781003294740 (ebook)
Subjects: LCSH: Criminology.
Classification: LCC HV6025 .F85 2024 (print) | LCC HV6025 (ebook) | DDC 364—dc23/eng/20230726
LC record available at https://lccn.loc.gov/2023027480
LC ebook record available at https://lccn.loc.gov/2023027481

ISBN: 9781032279275 (hbk)
ISBN: 9781032279381 (pbk)
ISBN: 9781003294740 (ebk)

DOI: 10.4324/9781003294740

Typeset in Sabon
by Deanta Global Publishing Services, Chennai, India

Contents

SECTION 2
Innovations in Collecting, Analysing, and Interpreting DLC Data: Showcasing Visual, Interactive, and Indigenous Methodologies

SECTION 3
Examples of DLC Research Informing Translation Activities and Driving Advances in Policy and Practice

Author Biographies

Troy Allard is a Senior Lecturer in the School of Criminology and Criminal Justice at Griffith University and has 20 years' experience working in the field of youth justice. His research interests focus on improving understanding about the causes of serious and persistent offending and 'what works' to efficiently reduce this offending. He has considerable experience evaluating new approaches and using complex administrative data to promote effective and efficient policies and practices. Troy is currently Co-Lead of the Queensland Cross-sector Research Collaboration (QCRC) and member of the Research Consultative Forum for the Queensland Sentencing Advisory Council.

Jacqueline Allen is a Senior Lecturer in the School of Criminology and Criminal Justice at Griffith University. Dr Allen's research is about the development of antisocial behaviour and mental health problems from childhood to young adulthood. She is also committed to translating research findings into strategies to prevent youth antisocial behaviour and mental health problems and to boost wellbeing. Also of special interest is the statistical modelling of complex longitudinal processes and innovative use of administrative data.

Chantelle Baguley is a Postdoctoral Research Fellow on the Maternal Incarceration Project (ARC Discovery) within the Griffith Criminology Institute at Griffith University. Her research focuses on measuring the risk factors that incarcerated mothers experience throughout their lives, and how their experiences of these risk factors change after important life events. She has an interest in conducting research that advances methodological techniques and has strong policy implications.

Sara Branch calls herself a "pracademic." She has a background in Organisational Psychology and has focused much of her practice-research on researching workplace bullying, facilitating change, and supporting partnerships. Her current work focuses on applying organisational theory to enhance processes for collective action (and change) within communities and organisations. Over her time on the CREATE-ing Pathways and Pathways to Prevention projects, Sara worked with a wide range of project partners, inclusive of federal and state government departments and a range of non-government organisations. Sara was the recipient of the Australian Award for University Teaching for innovative and practical approach to the enhancement of the quality of teaching and learning.

Catherine Chittleborough is an epidemiologist in BetterStart Health and Development Research, and Deputy Head, School of Public Health. She returned to the University of Adelaide in 2011 following a decade with SA Health and a two-year postdoctoral position at the University of Bristol. Her current research focuses on how we can reduce inequalities in, and improve overall population levels of, child health and development. She has an interest in applying causal epidemiological techniques to these questions and making use of population data from longitudinal cohorts and data linkage studies. She also teaches undergraduate public health and epidemiology.

Jessica M. Craig is an Associate Professor in the Department of Criminal Justice at the University of North Texas. She received her Bachelor of Science in Sociology and Psychology from Texas A&M University in 2011. She received both her Master of Science (2013) and Ph.D. (2015) in Criminology from the University of Texas at Dallas. Dr Craig's research interests include juvenile justice and life-course criminology. For instance, she has focused on the role of child maltreatment and other traumatic events in predicting delinquent and criminal behaviour. She is also interested in the role of protective factors that may diminish the consequences of these adverse experiences. Her other research projects have centred on delinquency, testing criminological theories, and the use of advanced research methodologies.

Susan Dennison is a Professor in the School of Criminology and Criminal Justice and the Griffith Criminology Institute at Griffith University. She is the Director of the Transforming Corrections to Transform Lives Centre, leading a transformative system of practice to better support mothers who experience incarceration, and their children, break down intergenerational cycles of disadvantage and incarceration, and generate new knowledge for evidence-based programmes. She is a former Australian Research Council Future Fellow and across multiple funded projects has investigated how childhood adversity, particularly maltreatment and parental incarceration, affects young people's outcomes. She emphasises translating research to policy and practice.

Li Eriksson is a Senior Lecturer in the School of Criminology and Criminal Justice at Griffith University. She was awarded her PhD in 2013 for her research examining differences between males who kill their intimate partners and males who kill others. Her research forms part of the Australian Homicide Project, which is a national ARC Discovery project examining developmental and situational pathways to homicide. Her research interests include violence, intimate partner homicide, filicide, and criminological theory. Prior to joining Griffith University, Li worked as a Research Analyst for the Swedish National Council of Crime Prevention.

Kathleen Falster is an epidemiologist leading research to inform and evaluate policy and service initiatives to improve child population health. Kathleen leads and collaborates on projects that build and analyse linked health and social data to create the "intelligence" needed to inform system responses to public health problems affecting children and young people, with a focus on disadvantaged populations and inequities. Currently, Kathleen's research focuses on children involved with child protection services, evaluation of a sustained nurse-home visiting program, and contributing population-level evidence on Aboriginal child health to mixed methods projects led by Aboriginal academics and/or Aboriginal Community Controlled Service collaborations.

David P. Farrington, OBE, is an Emeritus Professor of Psychological Criminology at the Institute of Criminology, Cambridge University. He received the Stockholm Prize in Criminology in 2013. He was President of the American Society of Criminology in 1998–99 (the first person from outside North America to be elected to this office). He is the first and only person to receive the four major awards of the American Society of Criminology: the Edwin Sutherland Award in 2002 for outstanding contributions to criminology, the Sellin-Glueck Award in 1984 for international contributions to criminology, the August Vollmer Award in 2014 for outstanding contributions to the prevention of delinquency, and the Herbert Bloch Award in 2018 for outstanding service contributions to criminology. In addition to 918 published journal articles and book chapters on criminological and psychological topics, he has published 134 books, monographs, and government publications and 164 shorter publications (total = 1,216).

Kate Freiberg, Adjunct Associate Professor at Griffith University, is Research and Development Manager at RealWell. Her work draws together developmental psychology and prevention science. She maintains a strong focus on the development of accessible resources and methodologies to support frontline professionals, child-serving organisations, and policymakers who strive to achieve better outcomes for children and families living in challenging environments.

Angela Gialamas is a Lecturer and epidemiologist working in the BetterStart Development Research Group, School of Public Health, at the University of Adelaide. Her research focuses on examining how parental investments and early childhood education and care influence developmental outcomes with the aim of identifying interventions to improve child health and development, particularly among disadvantaged populations. She uses advanced epidemiological methods (e.g., effect measure modification, multiple imputation, inverse probability treatment weighting, and propensity score methods) in her research to allow for more robust conclusions about causation.

Danielle Arlanda Harris, ATSAF, is the Deputy Director-Research of the Griffith Youth Forensic Service and a Senior Lecturer in the School of Criminology and Criminal Justice at Griffith University. Her research examines sexual aggression through a developmental and life-course perspective, examining onset, specialisation, versatility, desistance, and related public policy. Her study of sex offenders in Massachusetts was funded by the Guggenheim Foundation, and her current work is funded by Westpac Bank. She received the 2019 Australia and New Zealand Society of Criminology Award for her book, *Desistance from Sexual Offending: Narratives of Retirement, Regulation, and Recovery*.

David John Harris, SFHEA, teaches design at the Queensland College of Art, Griffith University and is curator of the University of Queensland Physics Museum. He is a Senior Fellow of the Higher Education Academy. As a designer, he has worked for clients such as universities, academic journals, and corporations. As a freelance journalist and writer, he has written for many major science magazines and journals around the world, primarily in the United States, Australia, and the United Kingdom, as well as leading universities, scientific societies, and think tanks. His art has been exhibited in a variety of galleries, public art exhibitions, and institutions around the world including in the United States, Australia, Europe, and online venues.

Ross Homel, AO, is a Foundation Professor of Criminology at Griffith University. He is a highly cited social scientist and has won many awards for his research on the prevention of crime, violence, and injuries and the promotion of positive development for children and young people in socially disadvantaged communities. These include the 2010 Sellin-Glueck Award from the American Society of Criminology. In 2008 he was appointed an Officer in the General Division of the Order of Australia "for service to education, particularly in the field of criminology, through research into the causes of crime, early intervention and prevention methods."

Hugh Hunkin is a postdoctoral researcher and registered psychologist working across the School of Psychology and School of Public Health at the University of Adelaide. Hugh is a part of the BetterStart Health and Development Research Group. His work currently involves a large systematic review evaluating two family-based treatments aimed at improving youth functioning and reducing reoffending, as part of Dr Catia Malvaso's

Discovery Early Career Researcher Award funding. Hugh's research interests largely relate to mental health across the lifespan.

Emily Hurren is a Lecturer in the School of Criminology and Criminal Justice at Griffith University. She is a member of the Griffith Criminology Institute and the Queensland Cross-Sector Research Collaboration (QCRC). Her research interests include child maltreatment, youth offending, and domestic and family violence.

Sjharn Leeson is a Doctoral Candidate at the School of Criminology and Criminal Justice, Griffith University. She holds a Bachelor of Laws (Honours) / Bachelor of Social Science (Criminology) (Bond University), and a Master of Criminology (Bond University). Her Master's dissertation explored the incarceration rates of women across Australia, the United Kingdom, and the United States. Her doctoral research is focused on the incarceration of First Peoples women in the Northern Territory and Western Australia, and the way prison quality, a form of prison performance measurement, may require adjustment to appropriately account for intersectionality and the far-reaching impacts of colonisation.

Krystal Lockwood is a Gumbaynggirr and Dunghutti woman. She is a Lecturer in the School of Criminology and Criminal Justice at Griffith University. Her research focuses on the way evidence is used in the criminal justice system, particularly in the way evidence can impact, influence, or hinder steps to achieving social justice. She aims to use her work to address the over-representation of Indigenous peoples throughout criminal justice systems.

John Lynch is a Professor of Epidemiology and Public Health at the University of Adelaide, South Australia. He is a Visiting Professor of Epidemiology in the Population Health Sciences at the University of Bristol. He spent 20 years studying and working in North America and, before returning to Australia in 2009, held professorial positions at the University of Michigan and at McGill University. In 2019 he won Research Australia's Data Innovation Award for developing the South Australian Better Evidence Better Outcomes Linked Data (BEBOLD) platform. From 2014 to 2018 he received "Highly Cited Researcher" status, placing him in the top 1% of cited scientists internationally in his field.

Molly McCarthy is a Lecturer in Criminology at the School of Social Sciences at Monash University and an Adjunct Senior Research Fellow at the Griffith Criminology Institute. Dr McCarthy brings an interdisciplinary lens to her work, with a background in public health research and early career experience as a psychologist working in child and youth mental health. Her current work is focused on understanding changing trends in youth offending, and more broadly on examining drivers of chronic or persistent youth offending. Dr McCarthy's work also examines predictors of coercive policing practices and the intersection of policing and disadvantaged communities.

Tara Renae McGee is a Professor in the School of Criminology and Criminal Justice at Griffith University. McGee is the Deputy Director of the Transforming Corrections to Transform Lives (TCTL) Centre; a multi-year, multi-site, multi-million-dollar programme of work to support incarcerated mothers and their children. She is also a CI (ARC Discovery) on the Mater University Study of Pregnancy (MUSP), where her focus is on prospective longitudinal study of violence and antisocial behaviour in three generations. She is former foundation co-editor of the *Journal of Developmental and Life-Course Criminology* (Springer) (2015–2021). McGee is also the former President of the Australian and New Zealand Society of Criminology (2017–2020).

Katherine McLachlan, PhD, has extensive experience working across criminal justice and social welfare agencies focused on child protection and child exploitation, youth justice, police intelligence, crime policy and research, victim support, and corrections. In 2015, she was appointed by the Minister for Correctional Services as the victim representative on the Parole Board of South Australia and was re-appointed in 2018 and 2021. She is an award-winning teacher who joined Flinders University Criminology in 2022 and has a professional interest in victimology, trauma-informed practice, sentencing, and violence against women and children. She is currently writing her first book based on her PhD research.

Catia Malvaso is a Senior Research Fellow in the School of Public Health and School of Psychology at the University of Adelaide. Her research is informed by an interdisciplinary perspective spanning psychology, public health, and criminology. She leads a programme of research which aims to identify prevention and early investment opportunities to disrupt pathways from maltreatment to offending behaviour. In 2020, Catia was awarded an Early Career Researcher Prize from the American Society of Criminology, and in 2021 a Tall Poppy Award for excellence in research achievement and community engagement from the Australian Institute of Policy and Science.

Paul Mazerolle, PhD, is the President and Vice Chancellor of the University of New Brunswick. His research examines processes that shape offending behaviour across the life course. His primary focus is in building knowledge on violence to inform theories, advance understanding, and improve policy and practices to reduce or prevent violence.

Alicia Montgomerie is a Senior Research Associate in the School of Public Health, University of Adelaide, South Australia, as a part of the BetterStart

Health and Development research group. Alicia is an epidemiologist who specialises in manipulating and analysing large population-based linked administrative data. Over the last five years, Alicia has worked as lead analyst on the Better Evidence Better Outcomes Link Data (BEBOLD) platform, one of the most comprehensive population-based linked administrative research databases in Australia, that spans data from health, education, justice, child protection, homelessness, and welfare.

James Ogilvie is a Lecturer in the School of Criminology and Criminal Justice, Griffith University. His current research is focused on examining the intersection of mental illness and offending using population-level linked administrative datasets from criminal justice and health agencies. His broader research interests are on the causes of youth offending and the development, implementation, and evaluation of interventions to reduce reoffending. Dr Ogilvie previously worked for 10 years as a practitioner (psychologist) with the Griffith Youth Forensic Service (GYFS) to deliver assessment and treatment services for young people who have engaged in sexually harmful behaviour.

Odette Pearson is a Kuku Yalanji/Torres Strait Islander woman, co-theme leader for the Wardliparingga Aboriginal Health Equity Research and Strategy theme at SAMHRI. Her experience and training in Aboriginal health policy, systems, and inequity comprises a comprehensive skillset relevant to existing and emerging complexities of Aboriginal health and wellbeing. Odette seeks to understand how institutional policies and practices drive health and social inequities experienced by Indigenous populations. Integral to her research is the inclusion of Aboriginal communities in defining their health and wellbeing and how Indigenous data can be governed in the future to derive greater benefit for the population.

Rhiannon Pilkington is a Senior Research Fellow in the School of Public Health, University of Adelaide, South Australia, and part of the BetterStart Health and Development research group led by Professor John Lynch. She is an epidemiologist with expertise in translational research, data analytics, and linked administrative data. Her research focuses on improving the evidence that informs how we can ensure every child, young person, and family receives the support they need. Dr Pilkington works with government and non-government organisations across Australia, using their data to bring a public health perspective to service design and delivery to support better outcomes for populations in disadvantaged circumstances.

Janet Ransley is Professor and Director of the Griffith Criminology Institute and a co-investigator on the Transforming Corrections to Transform Lives Centre. She is also a co-CI on an ARC Linkage project on an early warning system for police health and performance and on a UK College of Policing–funded project on predicting police misconduct. She has led multiple other projects on criminal justice integrity, practices, and policies with a focus on reducing crime and related harms.

Carleen Thompson is a Senior Lecturer in the School of Criminology and Criminal Justice and the Griffith Criminology Institute at Griffith University, Australia. She is Co-Lead of the Queensland Cross-Sector Research Collaboration (QCRC) and a Project Investigator in the Transforming Corrections to Transform Lives Centre. Carleen's research aims to improve understanding of the causes and progression of antisocial behaviour to drive evidence-based intervention planning that reduces offending and other harmful behaviours. Carleen has extensive experience using her research to help policymakers and practitioners more effectively target interventions on the basis of offenders' risks and needs.

Stacy Tzoumakis is a Senior Research Fellow at the Griffith Criminology Institute, Griffith University, Australia. Her work focuses on understanding the development of mental health, antisocial behaviour, and offending over the life course. She is particularly interested in considering gender differences in risk and protective factors for maltreatment and offending. Her research is interdisciplinary, and she has published in criminology, social work, family studies, psychology, law, education, psychiatry, and epidemiology. She has been involved in several longitudinal studies in Canada and Australia, including large intergenerational population-based record linkage studies in NSW and QLD.

Corrie Williams is a Research Fellow with the Transforming Corrections to Transform Lives Centre at Griffith University. Her research interests include the development of prosocial behaviour and promoting strength-based approaches to support children and families who are involved in the justice system. Before academia, Corrie worked as a youth justice case worker and analyst, gaining valuable insights into the challenges young people face in the justice system. Her experience in the field drives her commitment to improving outcomes for those impacted by the system.

Abbreviations

ACEs	Adverse Childhood Experiences
BEBOLD	Better Evidence Better Outcomes Linked Data Platform
CEBC	California Evidence-Based Clearinghouse
CJS	Criminal Justice System
CREATE	Collaborative; Relationships-driven; Early in the pathway; Accountable; Training-focused; Evidence-based
CDC	Centers for Disease Control and Prevention (US)
CSDD	Cambridge Study of Delinquent Development
CTC	Communities That Care
DLC	Developmental and Life-Course Criminology
EIF	Early Intervention Foundation
ITT	Intention to Treat
LHP	Life History Plot
MST	Multi-Systemic Therapy
MUSP	Mater-University of Queensland Study of Pregnancy
NFP	Nurse Family Partnership
RCT	Randomised Controlled Trial
TMLE	Targeted Minimum Loss Estimation
UK	United Kingdom
US	United States

Chapter 1

Introduction

Catia Malvaso, Tara Renae McGee, and Ross Homel

Frontiers in Developmental and Life-Course Criminology: Methodological Innovation and Social Benefit

Developmental and life-course criminologists study the initiation of antisocial and offending behaviour and how and why such behaviours change over time. Drawing on many well-established theories of human behaviour such as strain theory, labelling theory, and rational choice perspectives, developmental and life-course criminology (DLC) research suggests that the causes of crime are a combination of individual characteristics such as impulsiveness, in interaction with environmental characteristics at many levels of the social ecology including parenting, families, schools, and neighbourhoods.

The complexity of these interactions gives rise to diverse patterns of offending behaviour, the study of which is central to DLC. The goal is to better understand how people's lives unfold within a broad social and economic context, and what factors might lead people to be more or less likely to engage in criminal and other antisocial behaviours. Key areas of theoretical focus and empirical investigation in DLC include: onset (when and why people start offending); persistence (why people continue offending); frequency (at what ages people commit the most offences); participation (at what ages more people commit offences); and desistance (processes leading to the eventual termination of offending). This knowledge is viewed as foundational to identifying opportunities to intervene as early as possible to prevent the onset of offending or at least reduce the frequency and severity of criminal behaviour over the life course. Equally important to DLC researchers with an interest in strength-based prevention and positive youth development are interventions to promote prosocial behaviour and resilience, which as Corrie Williams argues in Chapter 13 may not necessarily improve even if offending is eliminated or reduced. We need to know more about the assumed links between antisocial and prosocial behaviours.

In this volume we have assembled a collection of brief original papers designed to illustrate some new possibilities for the future of DLC research, orienting the DLC field as one that prioritises the achievement of better

DOI: 10.4324/9781003294740-1

outcomes for individuals and society. Strategies canvassed in the book include:

- Harnessing new opportunities and techniques for understanding offending patterns over time and generating the evidence needed to inform crime reduction and promote positive development (e.g., Chapters 5, 10, 12, and 13)
- The exploration of new methodologies, for example for studying within-person change (Chapters 4 and 6) or measurement in diverse or challenging populations (e.g., Chapters 7 and 8)
- The use of population-level linked administrative data to produce more generalisable, policy-relevant results faster than traditional cohort studies and facilitating methodological and theoretical innovation (Chapters 2 and 3)
- Experimentation with new approaches to research translation through such techniques as co-creation (Chapter 9), the integration of DLC understandings of childhood trauma into the sentencing of life-course persistent offenders (Chapter 11), and the construction of "intermediary spaces" between the worlds of science and service (Chapter 14)
- The integration of DLC perspectives with insights from other disciplines to ensure that the prevention of crime is accorded top priority (e.g., Chapters 3 and 14)

We are in addition extremely grateful to Professor David Farrington, OBE, for his incisive commentary in Chapter 15. David not only identifies key priorities for DLC research such as the need to move from simple correlation or prediction via risk and protective factors to the establishment of *causal* pathways, he also highlights a range of distinctive contributions of this book to methodological innovation and developmental crime prevention.

Background

The impetus for this volume of the Criminology at the Edge series arose from the relatively recent formation of a DLC Thematic Group as part of the Australian and New Zealand Society of Criminology (ANZSOC). Thematic groups enable ANZSOC members to connect with peers who have specific expertise or interest in particular topics or current issues in the broader criminology field. Catia Malvaso and Tara McGee established and were the inaugural co-chairs of the DLC Thematic Group in 2019, with the aims to: (1) advance DLC and the study of criminal careers; (2) bring together ANZSOC members interested in discussing and supporting DLC research in criminology; (3) facilitate and encourage interaction and dissemination of DLC research among ANZSOC members, practitioners, funding agencies, policy-making bodies, and other relevant groups; and (4) organise and promote ANZSOC conference sessions related to issues in DLC research.

The group hosted its first public-facing event in December 2020 in the form of an online research symposium sponsored by ANZSOC and the Griffith Criminology Institute, Griffith University. Group members presented their research across four sessions: (1) research using administrative data; (2) using visual criminology to display DLC data; (3) translational research; and (4) new directions in the field. A diverse audience tuned into the event from across Australia, the United States, and the United Kingdom. Registrants included researchers at all stages of their academic careers from undergraduate students to leading professors, as well as government and non-government sector employees in both frontline practice and policy-making roles. After the success of this event the co-convenors submitted a proposal to Routledge's Criminology at the Edge series to disseminate the ideas presented at the symposium and to incorporate new submissions from the group's members and their national and international collaborators.

Content

Apart from this introductory chapter and the commentary, this volume comprises 13 chapters which have been organised into four sections:

1. *Responding to Challenges in the DLC Field: Opportunities to Advance Theory, Research, and Practice*

This section introduces some of the most pressing challenges faced by DLC researchers and identifies some of the opportunities available to address these challenges. A hallmark of DLC research is the study of criminal careers and the effects of risk or protective factors and life events using prospective longitudinal surveys. As articulated by Farrington (2015), these studies involve repeated measures of the same individuals over time and enable the natural history of offending to be studied. This includes information about developmental sequences and within-individual change that help us draw conclusions about potential causal effects. However, it is also recognised that there are several challenges and barriers associated with prospective longitudinal studies including, but not limited to, attrition, validity, cost, and the generalisability of findings.

In Chapter 2 Carleen Thompson and colleagues discuss three challenges currently facing the DLC field arising from its reliance on prospective longitudinal studies. These challenges are: (a) replication and differentiation of studies to establish validity, generalisability, and nuance; (b) understanding better the influence of historical contexts and social changes on offending behaviours; and (c) examining at greater depth the processes of within-individual continuity and change. The authors argue that the use of linked administrative data platforms offers a powerful strategy for addressing these challenges. Synthesis of learnings from longitudinal research and administrative data sets has the potential to stimulate methodological and theoretical innovation and open up new opportunities to bridge the gaps between research, policy, and practice.

Recent progress in population-level linked administrative data platforms in Australia have created new opportunities to expand what we know about the pathways of individuals who have contact with the criminal justice system and, importantly, how these platforms can be used to evaluate the implementation and effectiveness of intervention programmes designed to prevent and/or reduce offending behaviour. In Chapter 3, Rhiannon Pilkington and colleagues draw on their recent meta-analytic review of two prominent delinquency prevention programmes – multi-systemic therapy and functional family therapy – to explore challenges in producing high-quality evidence using traditional randomised controlled trial methods. The authors propose a new and innovative approach to evaluation that leverages population-level administrative linked data platforms and quasi-experimental methods.

In Chapter 4, Jacqueline Allen and Corrie Williams provide a thought-provoking discussion of one of the challenges facing DLC researchers: the distinction between theory and methods about between-person versus within-person changes in offending pathways. While DLC theories have provided detailed frameworks for understanding within-person changes (with more to be done), quantitative methods purporting to study such changes tend to emphasise between-person changes. The authors tackle this issue by drawing on literature and methods from neighbouring fields such as psychology, statistics, and economics to highlight new ways to disentangle between- and within-person effects, with a particular focus on longitudinal data. This chapter offers a creative way forward for both theorists and quantitative researchers working towards the identification of crime prevention strategies.

2. *Innovations in Collecting, Analysing, and Interpreting DLC Data: Showcasing Visual, Interactive, and Indigenous Methodologies*

This section comprises four chapters that showcase innovations in the collection, analysis, and interpretation of data that can advance DLC theory and research. These innovations have arisen in part from some of the known limitations of prospective longitudinal cohort studies in studying offending behaviour, in particular around the detailed sequencing of complex, inter-related life events and risk and protective factors that influence offending pathways. Particular challenges have been identified in using these studies to examine offending behaviours which have a low incidence rate within the population (Sutton 2010); to explore patterns within racial, ethnic, and cultural minority populations who continue to be over-represented in criminal justice systems around the world (Piquero, 2015); and to collect data from younger children in order to inform prevention strategies early in the life course (Homel et al., 2015). Each of the four chapters in this section highlights advances in collecting, analysing, and interpreting DLC data to address these challenges.

In Chapter 5, David Harris and Danielle Harris provide a new perspective on criminal careers research using information graphics and data visualisation methods. They demonstrate how graphics can be used to facilitate deeper interrogation of DLC concepts of interest, including onset, frequency, escalation, persistence, abstinence, desistance, and temporal ordering of events. Importantly, the chapter highlights opportunities for new collaborations between DLC researchers and creative artists and designers that can facilitate better problem-solving and communication of complex offending behaviours and pathways.

Chapter 6 by Li Eriksson and colleagues details the use of life event calendars to study offending behaviours such as homicide which have a low incidence rate within the population and hence are difficult to study using longitudinal cohort studies. The authors explain how life event calendars can increase data accuracy, facilitate participatory research, and can be used to examine dynamic and inter-related sequences of life events and their potential associations with offending behaviours over time. The chapter provides guidance on the implementation of the life event calendar approach including ways to overcome barriers to implementation.

In Chapter 7, Krystal Lockwood and colleagues consider the implications of traditional DLC research methodologies when studying the experiences of Australia's First Peoples, highlighting the cultural inappropriateness and relative lack of meaning of life event calendars. It is widely recognised that racial, ethnic, and cultural minority populations across the world are over-represented in the criminal justice system and that these experiences continue to exacerbate the impacts of intergenerational trauma in individuals, families, and communities. This chapter offers a way to incorporate Indigenous research methodologies into the study of criminal behaviour, highlighting how transforming the life event methodology into more meaningful conversations that accommodate fluid concepts of time can lead to more culturally appropriate data collection strategies. This includes the reconceptualisation of "life events" as "life stories" and enhancing participatory and collaborative approaches to data collection, analysis, and interpretation.

This section concludes with Chapter 8, in which Kate Freiberg and Ross Homel describe the development of a digital game-based measure of social-emotional wellbeing for middle childhood: Rumble's Quest. The authors detail the unique partnerships that underpinned the measure's conception, creation, and eventual deployment in both research and practice. They demonstrate how data collected through assessments generated by an engaging computer game can maximise the chances that children's expressed needs will be addressed by schools, families, and communities and provide valid and reliable data at the school or community level as a basis for planning interventions for early crime prevention and healthy child development.

3. *Examples of DLC Research Informing Translation Activities and Driving Advances in Policy and Practice*

One of the criticisms of the DLC field is that important research findings have seldom been communicated in a way that informs policy and practice reforms, beyond cursory discussions of risk and protective factors (France & Homel, 2014). This section highlights three important examples of how key findings from DLC research can be translated to inform policy discussions, the development of intervention programmes, and changes in practice.

In Chapter 9, Corrie Williams and colleagues describe how DLC research has been foundational to the development of the Transforming Corrections to Transform Lives (TCTL) Project, which is a major initiative led by university researchers in partnership with philanthropy and government. The authors introduce the concept of co-creation and its novel application in a correctional systems context, illustrating how DLC researchers can move beyond the field's traditional methodological approaches to achieve greater social impact.

Catia Malvaso and colleagues in Chapter 10 discuss how the popular Adverse Childhood Experiences (ACEs) framework offers a new angle on how to bridge the gaps between research, policy, and practice, particularly in the area of youth crime prevention. The authors begin by highlighting some of the unintended consequences of assumptions made about the ACEs framework and the implications for criminal justice system policy and practice. They then suggest ways that DLC researchers can generate and translate the high-quality evidence needed to inform treatment, early investment, and prevention efforts in relation to ACEs-offending pathways.

In Chapter 11, Katherine McLachlan applies theory and evidence from DLC research in a new setting: adult sentencing of individuals engaging in persistent offending behaviours from adolescence into adulthood. Drawing on research in an Australian jurisdiction, this chapter highlights opportunities for judicial decision-makers to utilise DLC research on the impacts of traumatic life events in sentencing practices. McLachlan offers a theoretical viewpoint on how and why "trauma-informed" sentencing practices can contribute to desistance in offending behaviour.

4. *Placing Prevention at the Forefront of DLC*

Bridging gaps between research, policy, and practice is a challenge in all areas of criminological inquiry. Although one of the main tenets of DLC research is to identify risk and protective factors that may be targeted in prevention initiatives, it has not always been clear how the evidence about these factors can be used to inform the development and implementation of prevention initiatives. In this section, three examples of ways DLC research can inform developmental crime prevention efforts are showcased.

In Chapter 12, Catia Malvaso focuses on the child maltreatment-youth offending link, describing how the integration of DLC, psychology, and public health perspectives can provide insights into what is needed to effectively design and conduct research and translate findings into evidence that can be used to inform the prevention of offending behaviour across the life course. The chapter builds on the important finding that while most young people caught up in the youth justice system have also had contact with the child protection system, most children who have been maltreated do not go on to offend. Malvaso discusses how whole-of-population linked administrative data augmented by in-depth longitudinal cohort and survey studies can be used to provide a comprehensive understanding of maltreatment-offending pathways, proposing three stages of epidemiological evidence generation based on description of the maltreatment-offending link, prediction of which children will enter the justice system, and the estimation of the causal effect of maltreatment on offending.

In Chapter 13 Corrie Williams highlights the need for a renewed stream of strengths-focused DLC research that examines the role of prosocial behaviour more deeply in order to better inform developmental crime prevention efforts, particularly in the social services sector. Williams discusses the need for stronger theoretical and empirical foundations in this area to generate the information that policymakers need to take developmental crime prevention approaches to scale.

In Chapter 14, the final chapter of this section, Ross Homel and colleagues address one of the biggest challenges not just in DLC research but in criminology more broadly: the primary prevention of youth crime. Drawing on the findings of a programme of research in a number of disadvantaged communities participating in the Federal Government's Communities for Children programme, the authors highlight how insights and methods from the very successful Communities That Care prevention system can be used to build capacity for sustainable, scalable, place-based youth crime prevention.

Common Themes Throughout This Book

Two clear cross-cutting themes emerge across these 13 chapters. First, DLC researchers are pushing boundaries in the field by strengthening and in some cases moving beyond the use of prospective longitudinal studies to not only better understand offending pathways but also to identify opportunities to alter these pathways. There are a number of ways that this is occurring, including through the utilisation of: *new data sources* (e.g., population-level linked administrative data platforms); *diverse data collection methods* (e.g., life event calendars, gamed-based technologies); *different epistemological approaches* (e.g., Indigenous research methods); and *enhanced collaborations across diverse fields* (e.g., public health, psychology, design and visual arts).

Second, DLC researchers are moving beyond cursory discussions of the implications of risk and protective factors in informing the development of preventive and rehabilitative initiatives. Numerous examples are presented in this book of the care being taken to translate DLC research into evidence-informed innovations in policy and practice. This emerges in terms of advancing theory (e.g., the influence of within-individual changes and the importance of strengths-based perspectives), in the development of policy (e.g., the importance of recognising the impacts of child maltreatment and adversity in offending pathways), and in developing rehabilitative and preventive programmes (e.g., in correctional and community settings).

In his commentary in Chapter 15 David Farrington identifies these themes and observes that the book contains content important for DLC's "coming of age." It does this by, for example, proposing fresh approaches to the fundamental challenge of establishing causal influences and through its consistent emphasis on strengthening the nexus between DLC research and prevention policies and practices.

As editors we are delighted that the chapters in this volume constitute such a thought-provoking collection of ideas, providing a platform for the examination of key DLC concepts, translational and other challenges, and methodological advances in the field. We are as one with David Farrington in the sentiment expressed in his concluding sentences: "Hopefully, this book will encourage more application of effective techniques to prevent offending. That would be in everyone's interests!"

References

Farrington, D. P. (2015). Prospective longitudinal research on the development of offending. *Australian and New Zealand Journal of Criminology*, *48*(3), 314–335. https://doi.org/10.1177/0004865815590461.

France, A., & Homel, R. (2014). *Pathways and crime prevention: Theory, policy and practice*. New York: Routledge.

Homel, R., Freiberg, K., & Branch, S. (2015). CREATE-ing capacity to take developmental crime prevention to scale: A community-based approach within a national framework. *Australian and New Zealand Journal of Criminology*, *48*(3), 367–385.

Piquero, A. R. (2015). Understanding race/ethnicity differences in offending across the life course: Gaps and opportunities. *Journal of Developmental and Life-Course Criminology*, *1*(1), 21–32.

Sutton, J. E. (2010). A review of the life-events calendar method for criminological research. *Journal of Criminal Justice*, *38*(5), 1038–1044. Retrieved from http://www.sciencedirect.com/science/article/B6V75-50RMPJ0-2/2/4b75b66b7d80e1eedb3c4166a60b6f1c.

Chapter 2

Linked Administrative Data

Providing Unique Solutions to Key Challenges in Developmental and Life-Course Criminology

Carleen Thompson, Emily Hurren, Molly McCarthy, James Ogilvie, Troy Allard, Stacy Tzoumakis, and Susan Dennison

We dedicate this chapter to our former mentor, colleague, and friend, Emeritus Professor Anna Stewart (1955–2021). Anna was an early advocate for the use of linked administrative data in developmental and life-course criminology research. She believed in the capacity of research using linked administrative data to enhance service delivery systems to better the lives of children, young people, and their families. Thank you, Anna, for showing us the way.

Introduction

To advance developmental and life-course criminology (DLC), field leaders have called for more: (a) replication and differentiation studies; (b) consideration of the impact of historical context and jurisdictional system changes; and (c) examination of within-individual change. These are largely appeals for adherence to fundamental scientific principles and the consideration of foundational life-course concepts, yet they remain key challenges for the field. We argue that linked administrative datasets provide unique solutions to these challenges and can support traditional longitudinal cohort survey designs to propel the DLC field forward.

In this chapter we detail the three aforementioned challenges facing the DLC field and the limitations to addressing them using traditional longitudinal cohort surveys. Next, we provide an overview of the core features and advantages of linked administrative datasets for addressing these challenges. We describe how linked administrative data facilitate methodological and theoretical innovation and can assist in bridging the gap between research, policy, and practice. We conclude with a discussion of limitations associated with these data and recommendations for the appropriate use of this powerful methodology in future DLC research.

Key Contemporary Challenges for DLC Criminology

Contemporary Challenge One: Replication and Differentiation Studies

Replication and differentiation studies of many key DLC findings are still required to establish validity, generalisability, and nuance (Farrington et al.,

DOI: 10.4324/9781003294740-2

2019). There is general acceptance of the scientific value of replication, differentiation, and cross-national studies for confirming/disconfirming the validity of findings and theoretical postulates, and for establishing generalisability (and distinctiveness) across place, space, and subgroups of individuals. However, obtaining appropriate longitudinal data to enable these explorations remains a challenge.

To date, a reasonably small set of traditional longitudinal cohort survey studies have played a pivotal role in driving the DLC knowledge-base and theoretical foundations (for detail, see: Farrington et al., 2019; McGee & Farrington, 2019; Piquero, 2022). While these cohort studies are impressive in terms of depth and longevity of data collection efforts, given the considerable financial and "time" costs associated with data collection, they are often purposefully and necessarily limited in sample size and/or representativeness (e.g., high-risk samples, all males; Stewart et al., 2015). Often, this renders samples too small to disaggregate across key groups (e.g., gender, race, or offender/offence types) or to explore generalisability and nuances within and across subgroups (Broidy et al., 2015). These cohorts may also be limited to select geographical locations, preventing exploration of jurisdictional or place-based differences (e.g., national context).

While there is no question that these core studies have laid the foundations for current DLC knowledge, the need for new longitudinal cohorts to propel the field forward is widely recognised (Farrington et al., 2019). Large representative samples are required to establish replicability across subgroups (Stewart et al., 2015), cross-national comparisons are required to explore generalisability and the role of national context (McGee & Farrington, 2019), and new cohorts that reflect contemporary social, environmental, and technological conditions are required for replication in current contexts (McGee & Farrington, 2019). However, using traditional longitudinal survey designs to address these needs is expensive and time consuming.

Contemporary Challenge Two: Understanding the Influence of Social Change and Historical Context on Offending Patterns

Laub and Sampson (2020) argue that examining the influence of macrolevel social change on offending patterns is one of the "biggest frontiers" for DLC. To illustrate the importance of such macrolevel social change, consider the major decline in crime that has been observed in the past 20–30 years, predominantly driven by a decline in the number of young people participating in offending behaviour as a normative part of adolescence (McCarthy, 2021). This has been referred to as the "most important criminological phenomenon of modern times" (Farrell et al., 2014, p. 421) and has obvious implications for DLC theorising.

The past 50 years have heralded notable changes in social and economic influences on developmental transitions and trajectories, including declining rates of marriage, increased educational attainment, a growth in precarious work, and rising income inequality (Laub & Sampson, 2020). In more recent decades, young people have faced a transformed social landscape, with the growth of widespread internet access and social media leading to dramatic changes in routine activities, including reductions in unstructured, unsupervised time (Svensson & Oberwittler, 2020). Changes in parenting practices and supervision, alcohol consumption (Baumer et al., 2020), and recognition and response to mental illness (Finkelhor & Johnson, 2017) have also been documented. Furthermore, the developmental stage of adolescence is now longer for some, with delayed engagement in adult-like activities such as driving, having sex, and drinking alcohol (Laub & Sampson, 2020). These evolutions in social and developmental contexts have critical implications for developmental transitions and offending trajectories in the contemporary world. Hence, it is imperative to explore which DLC theoretical processes transcend these (and future) historical contexts, if/how the drivers of such processes differ, and whether theoretical refinement is necessary (McGee & Farrington, 2019).

Although the need to situate individuals' development within historical time and place is a fundamental life-course principle (Elder, 1998), longitudinal surveys of single cohorts are not equipped to examine the influence of these changes on offending transitions and trajectories. Multiple cohorts over distinct time periods are required to detect and delineate the influence of social changes on offending patterns (Laub & Sampson, 2020). Given these challenges, it is perhaps unsurprising that such explorations remain rare and have been referred to as the missing link in DLC research (Sampson, 2015).

Contemporary Challenge Three: Examination of Within-Individual Change

A central objective of DLC is to identify, examine, and explain continuity and change in criminal behaviour over time (Laub & Sampson, 2020). Existing research highlights the variability in offending pathways and intercorrelated risk factors associated with offending (Farrington et al., 2019). For example, trajectory modelling shows varied offending pathways concealed within the aggregate age-crime curve, differentiated by age of onset, frequency, and longevity of offending (Nagin & Odgers, 2010). Further, documented offending risk factors span biosocial (e.g., interaction between autonomic arousal and social context), individual (e.g., mental illness), family (e.g., maltreatment), and social (e.g., peer influence) factors (Farrington et al., 2019). However, significant knowledge gaps remain, including how risk factors and developmental correlates of offending differentially relate to the onset and progression of varied trajectories of offending, establishing causal pathways to and from offending, and sequencing offending pathways when they coincide with other challenges, such as mental illness and child maltreatment (for further discussion of these issues see Chapters 4 and 10).

Traditional longitudinal cohort survey studies that have formed the foundation of seminal works in establishing DLC undoubtedly have distinct advantages for exploring within-individual change, given the depth of data collected and control over variable choice and measurement. However, these methodologies also have unavoidable limitations, such as small and selected samples, attrition, and low response rates. Such selection biases can reduce the capacity to establish causality and prevent exploration of heterogeneous developmental outcomes, including on the basis of timing or sequencing of risk and protective factors. A second difficulty is an inability to explore rare events, subtypes/subgroups of individuals or offences and/or developmental sequences that may prove important for understanding pathways among those responsible for disproportionately high levels of offending/harm. Third, they preclude complex modelling methods to examine heterogeneous offending pathways as they coincide with other experiences over the life course. Finally, reliance on retrospective recall during intermittent waves of data collection means sequencing of events may be unclear and/or influenced by errors or biases in memory or willingness to disclose, potentially hampering examinations of within-individual change and impeding understanding of time points critical for early intervention (see Chapters 6 and 7 for discussions of the use of life event calendars to address these challenges). While there is agreement that more within-individual research is needed in the DLC field to establish sequencing, causality, and timing (Farrington et al., 2019), the scope, focus, and complexity of such research is restricted to what is possible with the data available.

Addressing Challenges: The Case for Linked Administrative Data

The three key challenges outlined above are well recognised in the DLC field. What is less well recognised, or at least underestimated, is the largely untapped value of linked administrative data for establishing contemporary longitudinal cohorts to provide solutions to these challenges. This is a timely consideration, given Laub and Sampson's (2020) recent warning regarding the uncertain future of longitudinal surveys due in part to cost, attrition, and response rates. In this section we briefly outline the core features of linked administrative datasets and then illustrate why these features make such datasets ideal for addressing contemporary DLC challenges as well as bridging gaps between research, policy, and practice.

Core Features of Linked Administrative Datasets

Administrative data are collected in the daily operations of an organisation. They can be linked for individuals both within and across distinct organisational datasets and across the life course. When large, longitudinal linked administrative datasets are constructed, they facilitate life-course examinations of population-based samples and birth cohorts. For instance, a birth cohort can be convened that includes information on all contacts with multiple government systems during a particular time period (such as police, corrections, child protection, health, education, employment, census data, etc.). Large population-based samples provide increased statistical power to detect heterogeneous patterns in offending pathways and enable examination of under-represented subgroups of the population. Furthermore, the inclusion of multiple systems and sources of administrative data enables comprehensive depictions of system engagement over the life course. Since linked administrative data capitalises on existing data collected by government agencies, the substantial financial costs, data collection time, and "lag" time waiting for cohorts to age that are associated with traditional prospective longitudinal survey designs are also minimised. Data are collected continuously, in real time, and are not reliant on retrospective recall. Though new prospective longitudinal cohort survey studies are unquestionably important for generating evidence and testing theory (Farrington et al., 2019), the core features of large linked administrative datasets make them unique and powerful for addressing the identified three contemporary challenges facing DLC.

Addressing Challenge One: Using Linked Administrative Data to Conduct Replication and Differentiation Studies to Establish Generalisability and Explore Nuances

The unrealised potential for linked administrative data to enable direct and conceptual replication studies was noted over two decades ago (Drake & Jonson-Reid, 1999). Since these datasets capitalise on existing data routinely collected by service systems, they are not burdened by the cost and time restrictions of traditional methodologies. This has distinct advantages for replications within and across jurisdictions and facilitates cross-national comparisons. New cohorts can be extracted with relative ease to support cost-effective, timely, and comprehensive replications to facilitate validation, refinement, and/or expansion of DLC theories.

International collaborations can enable comparisons of broadly similar linked administrative datasets to support cross-national comparisons of contemporary population-based samples. For example, a cross-national comparison of individuals born in 1984 in Queensland and the Netherlands revealed marked similarities in rates of adult-onset offending, though noteworthy gender and racial differences (Thompson et al., 2019). Importantly, cross-national datasets for such comparative research can be continuously expanded in terms of data scope and geographical locations. Given the dearth of cross-national comparisons, linked data used in this way are valuable for advancing understanding of universal pathways to and from offending as well as the interplay between cultural, social, and policy contexts and offending.

Linked administrative datasets also have distinct advantages for establishing the replicability of DLC findings within and across subgroups. Large representative population-based samples facilitate the exploration of the full spectrum of offending pathways and patterns, including nuances within and across subgroups. Comparatively small segments of the population and relatively uncommon or rare events can be examined to determine the replicability and distinctiveness of key findings across subgroups that are often challenging in more limited datasets due to being statistically underpowered (e.g., gender, race, intersectionality of gender and race, developmental periods, types of crimes, chronic and/or persistent offenders). Uncovering these differences and/or similarities is essential for theory building and refining and for articulating heterogeneity in life-course offending patterns. For example, population-based linked administrative data enabled Matthews et al. (2022) to examine the cumulative effects of both child welfare and youth justice contact on heterogeneous adult offending trajectories, identifying important intersectional variations across sex and Indigenous status.

Addressing Challenge Two: Using Linked Administrative Data to Better Understand the Influence of Social Change and Historical Context on Offending Patterns

Administrative data enable flexibility in terms of population parameters, including selection of time points and cohorts, rendering it an ideal source of information for understanding macrolevel social changes (e.g., the "universal crime drop"). Administrative datasets from various systems, such as child protection, mental health, education, and employment, can be linked to provide insights into how shifting social contexts may contribute to changing offending patterns (Stewart et al., 2015), and whether such changes apply equally to subgroups of the population. Moreover, new cohorts (and variables) can be extracted and incorporated at regular intervals, and updated extracts can be obtained for existing cohorts (and variables) as they age, to support ongoing and long-term explorations of social change and associated cohort differences. Linked administrative data can therefore be a useful resource to obtain contemporary longitudinal data on multiple cohorts that reflects societal change in offending patterns and ensures current DLC theories are fit for the contemporary social world (Laub & Sampson, 2020; Piquero, 2022).

Addressing Challenge Three: Using Linked Administrative Data to Examine Within-Individual Change

The continuous collection of data for large population-based samples in linked administrative datasets, and associated increases in statistical power, has several advantages for investigating within-individual change. First, these datasets are representative and thus do not suffer from selection biases that may impact the capacity to establish causality. Counterfactual models can be established to better understand factors driving continuity and change over the life course. Second, continuous and objective data collection means that findings are not influenced by retrospective recall biases regarding the timing and/or occurrence of variables of interest.

Third, large population-based datasets that span multiple service systems enable the use of sophisticated statistical techniques to explore complex patterns of within-individual change as well as variability in offending pathways. For example, investigating how the timing of developmental risks, stages, and events differentially relate to the onset and progression of diverse offending trajectories. Linked data across multiple agencies provide an avenue for modelling patterns in how multiple issues interrelate and are sequenced over time (e.g., criminal justice, health, education, and child protection experiences), with these integrated datasets particularly suited for multi- or joint-trajectory modelling methods to examine the co-occurrence of offending with other outcomes. Examining different agency/system records in parallel can highlight the impact of specific events on long-term offending outcomes, such as employment, marriage, victimisation, imprisonment, and childbirth. Furthermore, with increased power, rare and heterogeneous developmental sequences can be explored to elucidate and examine the cascade of behavioural and health problems that emerge, including among the small subset of the most severe offenders (DeLisi, 2018). People who persist in offending are often users of multiple systems and may continue to offend in part because of ineffective interventions or service responses (Rivenbark et al., 2018). Linking individual-level information across multiple administrative data sources holds significant promise in advancing understanding of diverse patterns in the temporal sequencing or ordering of onset for offending and other developmental outcomes, thus improving our theoretical understanding of life-course offending patterns and pathways.

The Innovative Use of Linked Administrative Data for Social Benefit: Connections Between Research, Policy, and Practice

A key feature of working with linked administrative data for DLC research is that it strengthens the policy relevance of research by working closely with government stakeholders. The application, collation, research, and reporting from these datasets require regular communication and ongoing relationships with data custodians, including policymakers and practitioners in key service systems. These relationships bring researchers into closer contact with current policy and practice concerns and challenges and enhance the potential for translational research and knowledge transfer through both formal and informal dissemination of research findings. These relationships can also create feedback loops, whereby researchers can remain abreast of issues or policy developments, and tailor research that responds to current policy and practice challenges. These relationships can form the basis of ongoing industry-research partnerships to support more responsive and effective solutions to complex social issues such as offending. Linked datasets provide the potential for a more panoramic view of patterns of service use and associated costs for different subpopulations of offending individuals across multiple systems (Herz et al., 2019), which have important implications for guiding the timing and targeting of interventions within and across service systems. Moreover, linked administrative datasets can support quasi-experimental evaluations of programmes and prevention initiatives to promote efficacious policy and practice (for which see Chapter 3). Together, this type of work can make research more translational and policy-relevant, break down silos across service sectors, and facilitate the growth of evidence-based policy and practice for crime prevention.

Limitations, Considerations, and Lessons Learned

While we acknowledge that linked administrative datasets cannot fully replace traditional longitudinal cohort surveys and other complementary data collection methods, they can play a strong supporting role in advancing understanding of offending pathways. Through our experience using these data, this is the type of knowledge needed to design, implement, and evaluate crime prevention efforts. Despite this, there are six limitations or considerations we believe are important for DLC researchers to heed when using linked administrative data. First and foremost, administrative data are not collected for the purpose of research, thus researchers have limited control over which variables are available. Consequently, the scope of replication studies, examinations of within-individual change, and theoretical constructs that can be tested are limited to the data collected by agencies. While the breadth and depth of data collected is rapidly improving (e.g., standardised assessment tools), answers to some theoretical questions will not be possible using linked administrative data. Hybrid datasets, which can combine administrative data with survey data, may be a promising area of development for future DLC studies.

Second, it is essential to acknowledge administrative data represent system contacts and do not provide any illustration of the lived experience of individuals. Underreporting is an issue across many administrative datasets. Certain offences are known to be underreported (e.g., domestic violence, sexual assault, and child maltreatment), due in part to the unwillingness of victims to report offences that may be associated with stigma or lead to unwelcome contact with statutory services. However, there may be other drivers of underreporting that are more difficult to assess, such as trust in institutions, and policy or legislative arrangements which limit recognition or recording of particular types of offences or problematic behaviour. Arguably though, administrative datasets may provide greater access to "hard to reach" individuals and communities than do longitudinal cohort surveys, which require researchers to maintain long-term contact with individuals.

Third, since researchers do not collect these data themselves, they have limited control over its quality. Related to this, researchers using administrative data may in the first instance be accessing data with which they have limited familiarity. It is critical for researchers to develop a thorough understanding of the data they receive, to avoid incorrect and unsupported inferences and to ensure that their findings reflect accurately the phenomena they seek to represent. This is facilitated by strong and enduring relationships with data custodians. At the same time, this also provides opportunities for researchers to play a role in improving government system data collections.

Fourth, system contacts are a complex reflection of individuals' actions and different systems' responses to their actions (Matthews et al., 2022). Some groups may be overrepresented in systems for complex reasons, such as entrenched social disadvantage and system biases (e.g., Cunneen, 2020). These issues need to be carefully considered when interpreting findings. Fifth, the time, effort, and skills required to clean and understand these data, as well as maintain relationships with relevant custodians to ensure appropriate use and translation of research, are significant but often underestimated.

Sixth, use of these data is not without debate, including the ethics of data use when the individuals to which it pertains have not and cannot provide consent. By extension, legal requirements for data use may vary across data custodians, which can lead to complexity for researchers who are using datasets from multiple organisations. Researchers must familiarise themselves with these debates, including Indigenous Data Sovereignty, which relates to the rights of Indigenous peoples to govern the collection, ownership, analysis, and application of data as a cultural and economic asset (Walter et al., 2021). The need for administrative data methodologies to be coupled with other data collection methods is particularly relevant for research for the benefit of Indigenous peoples. For example, administrative data alone cannot account for Indigenous epistemologies, or cultural risk and protective factors. Hence, researchers using administrative data should also incorporate data sources that can include the voices and experiences of Indigenous peoples (discussed in Chapter 6).

Conclusion

DLC research faces key challenges in terms of ongoing replication, exploration of heterogeneity and/or uniformity in pathways and precursors of within-individual change, and exploration of how notable social changes may have influenced patterns of offending behaviour. While linked administrative datasets cannot replace traditional longitudinal cohort survey designs, they can provide unique solutions to contemporary DLC challenges and are a powerful supplement to support traditional designs to advance the DLC field. Linked administrative data can enable cost-effective, timely, and comprehensive replication and expansion of DLC theories, ensuring that DLC research transcends the changing social world and bridges the gap between science and service. DLC as a discipline should embrace and expand the use of linked administrative datasets to ensure that life-course theories remain fit for purpose for explaining offending behaviour in contemporary and changing social contexts.

References

Baumer, E. P., Cundiff, K., & Luo, L. (2020). The contemporary transformation of American youth: An analysis of change in the prevalence of delinquency, 1991–2015. *Criminology*, *59*(1), 109–136.

Broidy, L. M., Stewart, A. L., Thompson, C. M., Chrzanowski, A., Allard, T., & Dennison, S. M. (2015). Life course offending pathways across gender and race/ethnicity. *Journal of Developmental and Life-Course Criminology, 1*(2), 118–149. https://doi.org/10.1007/s40865-015-0008-z

Cunneen, C. (2020). *Conflict, politics and crime: Aboriginal communities and the police*. Routledge. Retrieved from https://doi.org/10.4324/9781003115243.

DeLisi, M. (2018). The big data potential of epidemiological studies for criminology and forensics. *Journal of Forensic and Legal Medicine*, *57*, 24–27. https://doi.org/10.1016/j.jflm.2016.09.004.

Drake, B., & Jonson-Reid, M. (1999). Some thoughts on the increasing use of administrative data in child maltreatment research. *Child Maltreatment, 4*(4), 308–315.

Elder Jr, G. H. (1998). The life course as developmental theory. *Child development, 69*(1), 1–12.

Farrell, G., Tilley, N., & Tseloni, A. (2014). Why the crime drop? *Crime and Justice*, *43*(1), 421–490. https://doi.org/10.1086/678081.

Farrington, D. P., Kazemian, L., & Piquero, A. R. (2019). Conclusions and implications for developmental and life-course criminology. In D. P. Farrington, L. Kazemian, & A. R. Piquero (Eds.), *The Oxford handbook of developmental and life-course criminology* (pp. 749–756). Oxford: Oxford University Press.

Finkelhor, D., & Johnson, M. (2017). Has psychiatric medication reduced crime and delinquency? *Trauma, Violence, and Abuse*, *18*(3), 339–347.

Herz, D. C., Dierkhising, C. B., Raithel, J., Schretzman, M., Guiltinan, S., Goerge, R. M., ... Abbott, S. (2019). Dual system youth and their pathways: A comparison of incidence, characteristics and system experiences using linked administrative data. *Journal of Youth and Adolescence*, *48*(12), 2432–2450. https://doi.org/10.1007/s10964-019-01090-3.

Laub, J. H., & Sampson, R. J. (2020). Life-course and developmental criminology: Looking back and moving forward – ASC division of developmental and life-course criminology inaugural David P. Farrington Lecture, 2017. *Journal of Developmental and Life-Course Criminology*, *6*(2), 158–171.

Matthews, B., McVie, S., Thompson, C., & Stewart, A. (2022). From childhood system contact to adult criminal conviction: Investigating intersectional inequalities using Queensland administrative data. *Journal of Developmental and Life-Course Criminology*, *8*(3), 1–41.

McCarthy, M. (2021). How universal is the youth crime drop? Disentangling recent trends in youth offending through a socio-economic lens. *Victims and Offenders*, *16*(6), 796–818. https://doi.org/10.1080/10439463.2020.1869235.

McGee, T. R., & Farrington, D. P. (2019). Developmental and life-course explanations of offending. *Psychology, Crime and Law*, *25*(6), 609–625.

Nagin, D. S., & Odgers, C. L. (2010). Group-based trajectory modeling (nearly) two decades later. *Journal of Quantitative Criminology*, *26*(4), 445–453. https://doi.org/10.1007/s10940-010-9113-7.

Piquero, A. (2022). "We study the past to understand the present; we understand the present to guide the future": The time capsule of developmental and life-course criminology. *Journal of Criminal Justice*. Advanced online publication. https://doi.org/10.1016/j.jcrimjus.2022.101932.

Rivenbark, J. G., Odgers, C. L., Caspi, A., Harrington, H., Hogan, S., Houts, R. M., ... Moffitt, T. E. (2018). The high societal costs of childhood conduct problems: Evidence from administrative records up to age 38 in a longitudinal birth cohort. *Journal of Child Psychology and Psychiatry*, *59*(6), 703–710.

Sampson, R. J. (2015). Crime and the life course in a changing world: Insights from Chicago and implications for global criminology. *Asian Criminology*, *10*(4), 277–286.

Stewart, A., Dennison, S., Allard, T., Thompson, C., Broidy, L., & Chrzanowski, A. (2015). Administrative data linkage as a tool for developmental and life-course criminology: The Queensland linkage project. *Australian and New Zealand Journal of Criminology*, *48*(3), 409–428. https://doi.org/10.1177/0004865815589830.

Svensson, R., & Oberwittler, D. (2020). Changing routine activities and the decline of youth crime: A repeated cross-sectional analysis of self-reported delinquency in Sweden, 1999–2017. *Criminology*. Advanced online publication. https://doi.org/10.1111/1745-9125.12273.

Thompson, C., van de Weijer, S., Stewart, A., & Broidy, L. (2019, November 13-16). *A cross-national comparison of adult-onset offending: Implications for theory and criminal justice policy*. [Paper presentation]. 2019 American Society of Criminology Conference. San Francisco, USA.

Walter, M., Lovett, R., Maher, B., Williamson, B., Prehn, J., Bodkin-Andrews, G., & Lee, V. (2021). Indigenous data sovereignty in the era of big data and open data. *Australian Journal of Social Issues*, *56*(2), 143–156. https://doi.org/10.1002/ajs4.141.

Chapter 3

How will we obtain High-Quality Evidence to Inform Youth Crime Prevention and Reduction?

Rhiannon Pilkington, Catia Malvaso, Alicia Montgomerie, Kathleen Falster, Catherine Chittleborough, Odette Pearson, Angela Gialamas, Hugh Hunkin, and John Lynch

Introduction

Understanding what works to prevent and reduce offending behaviour relies on the generation of high-quality evidence to provide insights into intervention effectiveness. Generating high-quality evidence is not straightforward (Lynch, 2017). For example, even in well-developed research fields such as nurse home visiting, less than 50% of the evidence is of moderate to high quality, even when coming from Randomised Control Trials (RCTs) (HomVEE, 2022). This chapter explores the challenges to generating high-quality evidence of programme effectiveness through RCTs. We use a recent systematic review and meta-analysis (Littell et al., 2021) as well as our own research, to illustrate the barriers to understanding what works to prevent a range of outcomes among youth justice–involved populations. We discuss a complementary approach to evidence generation based on quasi-experimental methods that leverage and build on existing administrative linked data platforms. The increasing availability of linked administrative data is an opportunity to improve the quality of the evidence base we rely on to prevent offending behaviour and improve outcomes for young people. For researchers, this may require a new way of working that focuses on establishing, nurturing, and maintaining authentic research partnerships.

Generating High-Quality Evidence of What Works

The traditional view of evidence generation holds RCTs as the gold-standard study design to identify causal effects of treatments (Deaton & Cartwright, 2018; Frieden, 2017; Jones & Podolsky, 2015). There are many good reasons for this. In large, well-designed, appropriately powered RCTs with high treatment fidelity and adherence, high participant retention, and valid outcome measurement, randomisation can evenly distribute intervention and control group background characteristics. This helps ensure that the intervention and control groups have the same potential outcomes (as defined by the RCT protocol) whether they are treated or not, thereby making it

DOI: 10.4324/9781003294740-3

possible to confidently attribute causation to the intervention being tested. However, meeting the conditions for what might be considered a high-quality RCT can be extremely challenging. This is particularly true when studying treatment effectiveness in populations experiencing disadvantage, as is common in the social sciences, where we suggest the subject matter of interest (e.g., delinquency among youth justice populations, child maltreatment) creates additional challenges to those experienced in medical research. Table 3.1 illustrates a number of challenges that we have commonly seen in RCTs aiming to prevent or reduce youth crime, out-of-home care placement, or child maltreatment.

Of course, there are other challenges experienced across RCTs more broadly. These include, first of all, timeliness. A common criticism of RCTs is that they take too long to plan, implement, and analyse and therefore are often poorly positioned to support decision-making in often short policy-relevant timeframes (Bothwell et al., 2016; Frieden, 2017). Second, RCTs are expensive. A challenge for all trials is obtaining appropriate levels of funding to support designs with sufficient power (through recruitment and retention) to detect relevant effects, and where there are effects post-intervention, having the funding to support longer-term follow-up. A review of neuroscience meta-analyses found that only 20–30% of individual studies were adequately powered, raising ethical questions about research inefficiencies and the wasted effort and burden on participants in undertaking small underpowered trials (Button et al., 2013). A third challenge relates to data collection to support the estimation of per-protocol effects. RCTs typically estimate the intention-to-treat (ITT) effect of assignment to intervention irrespective of drop-out or dose of intervention received. This effect can be confusing to interpret as in the absence of perfect randomisation compliance and treatment adherence, the effect represents a mix of intervention doses (Hernán & Robins, 2017). Whether the ITT effect estimate corresponds to a relevant question or can help guide decision-making depends on whether events such as level of adherence to a treatment would occur in the same way in the real world. On the other hand, the per-protocol effect provides an estimate of the effect of treatment if everyone had adhered to the protocol of the study. There is evidence that patients and researchers highly value being able to understand the effect of a treatment *when it is adhered to* (i.e. the per-protocol effect) as opposed to the effect of treatment assignment (i.e. the intention-to-treat effect) (Murray et al., 2018). In a complex social services space like crime prevention and reduction, it is imperative we build capacity to understand the effect of the intervention when delivered as prescribed in the model of care (i.e. the per-protocol effect). The data needs for this cannot be underestimated as it requires collecting information on post-randomisation factors prognostic for adherence and requires researchers upskilling in advanced analysis such as g-methods that can account for time-varying confounding by factors affecting adherence (Hernán & Robins, 2017). We consider that the gains to be made in obtaining useful information from costly and time-consuming RCTs make the endeavour worthwhile.

Table 3.1 Challenges to undertaking high-quality RCTs that may be amplified in the social sciences

Recruitment, retention, and follow-up	High levels of disadvantage and complex circumstances experienced by target populations may pose additional challenges to recruitment and retention, given the lack of capacity to add an intervention into already challenging life circumstances. Related to this, multiply disadvantaged populations may be more difficult to re-contact for subsequent follow-up data collection periods. This is in contrast to a drug trial related to cancer where patients may be highly motivated to participate in an RCT, or where primary outcomes are obtained through registry data that do not require re-contacting participants (e.g., mortality obtained through death registrations).
A mismatch between target and trial populations	The target population of trials focused on preventing offending behaviour (i.e., the population to which the treatment would be offered in the real world) includes young people often experiencing a range of challenging mental and physical health, familial, and environmental conditions (e.g., see Chapter 10, this volume). Currently, it is difficult to assess how closely recruited trial populations represent the target population, as studies usually report univariable baseline characteristics – e.g., what proportion experience substance abuse, mental health challenges, low income – as opposed to combinations of these characteristics that might more closely reflect the multiply disadvantaged circumstances of the target population. Systematic differences between trial and target populations can impact on the external validity of trial results.
Randomisation	Many randomised controlled trials in the social sciences are embedded in service delivery (i.e., are pragmatic), requiring assistance from non-research staff with participant recruitment and consent, eligibility assessment, and randomisation. Concerns from staff regarding the ethics of randomising participants to treatment or control can lead to failure to adhere to the random allocation sequence, or "switching" post-randomisation where it is most commonly seen that participants randomised to control are "switched" by staff to the intervention. When not part of the treatment protocol (as may for example occur in a cancer treatment trial), crossover between treatment and control poses challenges to producing unbiased estimates of the effect of treatment compared to treatment-as-usual.
Participant blinding	When the treatment involves intensive family- or individual-based therapy, it is often not possible (or very difficult) to blind participants to treatment assignment. Therefore, outcome-related behaviours and self-reporting of outcomes may be impacted by individual awareness of group assignment. In reviews investigating the impact of blinding on effect sizes in RCTs of alternative medicines or osteoarthritis treatments, it was found lack of participant blinding resulted in increased and more beneficial effect sizes for participant reported outcomes (Hrobjartsson et al., 2014; Nüesch et al., 2009). The researchers theorised that this exaggeration in effects was caused by a combination of self-report bias, differential attrition (e.g., much higher attrition among unblinded control), and differential co-intervention (e.g., knowledge of assignment to control prompts control group members to seek additional intervention not considered a part of treatment-as-usual) (Hrobjartsson et al., 2014).

(Continued)

Table 3.1 Continued

Outcome measurement	Measurement of outcomes such as offending or child maltreatment is often obtained through self-report. There is nothing innately wrong with obtaining self-report measures, and often this is the only way to collect data on some outcomes (e.g., family functioning). However, when combined with participant awareness of treatment assignment, a reliance on only self-report outcome measures may introduce bias.

The Example of the Multi-Systemic Therapy Programme

Multi-Systemic Therapy (MST) was originally developed to help support and rehabilitate children and young people with antisocial behaviour, particularly those involved with the justice system. MST is intended to be family and community-based, and a holistic therapeutic model of treatment. The aim is to work with the individual, as well as with their family, school, and community. MST has been adapted as an intervention that can also address child abuse and neglect, in family preservation efforts (Henggeler, 2001). In recent years, nuances in the status of MST as one of the most impactful "evidence-based" programmes have begun to emerge. We explore some of the contrasting assessments of the MST evidence base and what these might mean for how we think about generating high-quality evidence of programme impact.

Two well-known evidence clearinghouses, the Early Intervention Foundation and the California Evidence-Based Clearinghouse, both rate MST as meeting the highest evidence standards of "evidence of effectiveness" and "well supported," respectively (Early Intervention Foundation Guidebook, 2023; The California Evidence-Based Clearinghouse for Child Welfare, 2021). While the clearinghouses' evidence standards differ, broadly speaking this determination has been based on there being two or more evaluations with control groups illustrating positive impacts for at least one year post-intervention. The EIF also reports on mixed findings for the program, citing studies conducted in Sweden (Sundell et al., 2008) and the UK (Fonagy et al., 2018) which overall suggested MST did not improve outcomes relative to usual care. Neither the EIF nor the CEBC reports on individual study "risk of bias" assessments, although the EIF considers 33 criteria related to design, sample, measurement, analysis, and impact.

In stark contrast to these assessments of MST, a Campbell Collaboration review led by Littell and colleagues (2021) concluded "the benefits of MST are not well established" (p.58) and that findings were inconsistent across studies and mostly favourable within the US. Littell and colleagues adapted the first version of the gold-standard Cochrane tool for risk-of-bias in RCTs

(Higgins et al., 2011). Problems with inadequate reporting were identified, as there was often insufficient information on randomisation and allocation concealment, and it was sometimes difficult to identify the number of participants randomised. Every study except one was rated as high risk of bias on at least one domain. The 2018 START trial undertaken by Fonagy et al. in the UK was deemed to be the best example of a high-quality, well-conducted RCT. The START trial found no evidence that MST was beneficial for reducing out-of-home placements or criminal behaviour 18 months post-randomisation. A more recently published follow-up of the START trial at five years has extended on this reporting that MST was not superior to "management-as-usual" (Fonagy et al., 2020).

It is difficult to reconcile these starkly contrasting views of the impact of MST, and it raises questions around the need to consider applying the gold-standard risk-of-bias review tools and study quality assessments at the study design and reporting phase. These difficulties are exacerbated because different evidence clearinghouses use different methods for assessing "what works" (Axford et al., 2022). When we used the Cochrane Risk of Bias tool (Sterne et al., 2019) in our own systematic review and meta-analysis of MST and Functional Family Therapy (currently underway, registered on Prospero https://www.crd.york.ac.uk/PROSPERO/; record ID CRD42021279736), we echoed some of the findings from the Littell review (2021). Of the 56 RCTs included, over 90% were rated high risk of bias or had some concern on the Cochrane Risk of Bias tool, again highlighting the complexity and challenges inherent in attempting to generate high-quality evidence from RCTs with complex, disadvantaged populations.

The Importance of the Local Context

The most consistent explanation for the variation in findings on the effectiveness of MST is differences in the US and UK local contexts (Early Intervention Foundation Guidebook, 2023; Fonagy et al., 2018; Fonagy et al., 2020; Littell et al., 2021). There are substantial differences in the welfare, justice, health, and education systems that constitute "usual care" in the US trials compared to the recent UK trial (also see Hazel, 2008). It is broadly accepted that in the context of MST the usual care condition in US RCTs is less effective than usual care in the UK and that this is a strong contributor to the lack of replicated positive outcomes across contexts. In direct support of this, Littell (2021) reported that control groups in US studies had worse outcomes and received fewer services than control groups in other high-income countries (such as UK and Sweden). MST is not the first programme for which trials conducted in the US show positive impacts that are not replicated in other Western countries with stronger welfare systems. The Nurse Family Partnership (NFP) is another example of this phenomenon. Successive US NFP trials showed positive impacts on a range of outcomes (Kitzman et al.,

1997; Olds et al., 1986; Olds et al., 2002). These findings were not replicated in the large, high-quality Building Blocks trial conducted in the UK (Robling et al., 2016). The challenges in transporting evidence from the US to countries with better developed welfare systems (i.e., usual care) have been discussed by one of the founders of the NFP model (Olds, 2016). Olds stresses that study findings need to be understood within the context of usual care and that we need to ensure this is part of considering how best to allocate limited resources to support improved outcomes for populations experiencing disadvantage. A further cogent point is made by Homel (2021) that if "usual care" is just as effective as more expensive programmes, then understanding "care as usual" is a potential pathway to scaling usual systems that contribute to crime prevention (Homel, 2021).

Beyond the local system context, we also need to consider differences in the relevant populations. MST and NFP are just two examples where it is apparent that broader local conditions substantially limit intervention impacts on short- and longer-term outcomes (Lynch, 2017). In Australia, we know that nearly half of the youth justice population are identified as being of Aboriginal or Torres Strait Islander origin (Australian Institute of Health and Welfare, 2022). Aboriginal and Torres Strait Islander children are overrepresented due to the enduring impact of colonisation, legacies of systemic racism, oppression, and systems set up to remove and assimilate Indigenous peoples. This contributes to intergenerational trauma and multiple economic and social disadvantages experienced by current generations. When any researcher or organisation is considering the use of data on Aboriginal and Torres Strait Islander communities, it is imperative that the principles of Indigenous Data Sovereignty are enacted. Indigenous Data Sovereignty is the right of Indigenous peoples to exercise ownership over Indigenous data through its creation, collection, access, analysis, interpretation, management, dissemination, and re-use. Formal Indigenous governance systems must be in place to ensure that the "when, how, and why" of data use reflects the interests, values, and culture of Indigenous people (Maiam nayri Wingara Indigenous Data Sovereignty Collective, 2018; Walter et al., 2021). Taking this approach to research with Indigenous Australians will help avoid perpetuating and repeating harms of the past, and contribute to building trust, and translating research in a way that contributes to better outcomes (Braunack-Mayer et al., 2017). These same tenets should be applied when policymakers are considering importing programmes from different international contexts to Australia.

As we look for how we can better support young people and prevent youth crime, we need to resist the temptation to search for that *one* off-the-shelf programme that will be the solution to what is often the product of complex, chronic, and disadvantaged circumstances. Instead, we propose considering how we can use local data to design programmes based on population needs in the local service context, leverage existing knowledge about best practice, and create genuine partnerships with communities through meaningful and respectful participation and consultation processes to support service co-design (e.g., Bateman et al., 2022). We suggest this local approach is key to ensuring government investments have the best chance of achieving positive outcomes for different population groups (see Chapter 14 in this volume for one approach to this challenge).

An Opportunity in Criminology Research to Explore Complementary Approaches to Generating High-Quality Evidence

Collective efforts to prevent and reduce youth crime are challenged by the complex nature of the problem, but also by the difficulties in producing high-quality evidence of effectiveness that we have explored in this chapter. Promoting RCTs without considering the merits of complementary research methods and data sources is hampering our ability to understand what works (Frieden, 2017; Lynch, 2017). We will always need RCTs, but they are not always fit for purpose. If the goal is research evidence that can be used to inform decision-making, then we have the opportunity to consider how existing administrative data sources can be augmented with data from relevant services and programmes to support the timely generation of "good-enough evidence" of real-world programme effectiveness (Lynch, 2017).

Government and non-government systems and services collect a substantial amount of administrative data related to service processes, client contact with services, and client outcomes. Many of these systems (such as justice and housing) operate largely independently of each other, reflected in the siloed nature of the data holdings. However, the opening up of administrative data and the advent of data linkage as a privacy protecting method through which data can be "joined-up" present opportunities to build an "intelligent information infrastructure" (Malvaso et al., 2020; Chapter 2, this volume). While different data linkage models exist in developed Western countries (Ford et al., 2009; Foust et al., 2022), the basic structure is the same: an independent authority authorised under the relevant legislation uses personal information (e.g., name, date of birth, sex, address) to link formerly siloed service records to one unique ID that represents an individual. Collectively, the authorship team for this chapter have over three decades of experience in research using linked administrative data.

One example of this approach is the South Australian de-identified administrative linked data platform called the Better Evidence, Better Outcomes, Linked Data (BEBOLD) platform. Led by author Professor John Lynch, BEBOLD has been developed over a decade and includes whole-of-population data on more than 500,000 children in SA from 1991 onwards as well as their parents and carers. Data sources include: birth information from perinatal statistics and birth registrations; health information from emergency departments, hospitalisations, community mental health, adult drug and alcohol agencies, and an adolescent wellbeing and engagement census; education information from wholistic child development measures in the first year of formal schooling, standardised academic achievement tests, school absences; welfare services information from child protection, public housing, homelessness services, and Centrelink (welfare support via cash transfer); and justice information from youth justice and adult corrections. With extensive ethical and data custodian governance processes and approvals in place, BEBOLD is an enduring and updateable de-identified linked data platform with the capacity to add new data sources and birth cohorts.

The BEBOLD platform is the foundation of an intelligent information infrastructure. Our goal is to support improved outcomes for children, young people, and families in disadvantaged circumstances through more coordinated targeting of scarce resources with the capability to conduct routine evaluations using quasi-experimental methods. The existing platform can be used to support research into policy-relevant populations (e.g., size, characteristics) and their patterns of service use across different agencies (e.g., the crossover between public housing and child protection system contact; Malvaso et al., 2022). The data can be used to help understand the needs of local populations, but it is only by augmenting the existing platform with service data from both government and non-government organisations working to prevent and reduce youth crime that a richer picture of the impact of service investments can be drawn (Pilkington et al., 2019). By working closely with the relevant service agencies, and under the appropriate ethical and broader governance arrangements, we can join-up programme data with BEBOLD to support high-quality quasi-experimental observational data analysis that complements RCT evidence (Hernan, 2021).

In the absence of RCTs, the goal is to compare outcomes among the intervention and control groups in a way that emulates a randomised trial. Figure 3.1 depicts the identification of programme clients within the whole-population data platform and the use of covariables to identify an appropriate comparison group. Methodological advances have shown that valid causal inferences can be drawn from deliberately emulating RCTs using observational data (Hernán & Robins, 2016). The target trial framework has been formalised by causal inference experts Miguel Hernan and James Robins from the Harvard School of Public Health (Hernán & Robins, 2016). The purpose of the target trial framework is to explicitly design and emulate the target trial to minimise the risk of common biases that may produce misleading results from observational data analysis. This approach relies on counterfactual reasoning and is consistent with the counterfactual theory of causality (Robins, 1986). Use of the framework may also help with the identification of crucial data items that permit estimation of both the intention-to-treat effect (ITT: the effect of being assigned to an intervention, irrespective of the dose received) and the per-protocol effect (the effect of receiving the intervention as specified by the model of

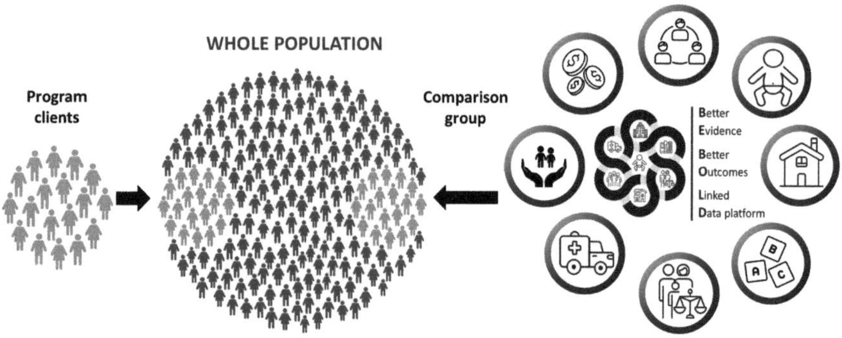

Figure 3.1 The linking of de-identified programme information to support the comparison of programme clients with a "matched" comparison group

care or protocol). The whole-population data platform provides the foundational data for constructing intervention eligibility criteria and for identifying a rich set of covariables to create comparison groups that are exchangeable. This requires methods such as inverse probability weights (propensity scores) to estimate causal effects using targeted minimum loss estimation (TMLE). TMLE methods share similarities with regression standardisation and g-computation but are doubly robust for estimating the average treatment effect in observational studies (Schuler & Rose, 2017). We have illustrated the use of such methods and the target trial framework using administrative linked data for an investigation of the longer-term impact of the South Australian Family Home Visiting programme (Moreno-Betancur et al., 2023).

Beyond understanding programme impact, augmenting linked data platforms with service data enables investigators to assess whether secondary and tertiary prevention programmes reached all those eligible for the intervention. Even if an intervention or suite of interventions is effective, if population reach is limited, these interventions cannot drive population-level improvements. In other words, we will never "turn the curve." Additionally, with consent, this data infrastructure could provide the opportunity to follow up participants of longitudinal cohort studies and pragmatic RCTs over longer time periods. This would increase insights into "real-world" outcomes not available within the timeframes supported by limited funding for RCTs. Many high-quality trials are now routinely linking to justice administrative data to do just this (e.g., Fonagy et al., 2018), although there is also the opportunity to support such trials with a broader data platform to assist with estimating per-protocol effects (i.e., the effect of treatment adherence).

Our experience of building BEBOLD with the aim of achieving public good through the use of public data also speaks to the need to consider how academics work with government and non-government stakeholders.

Using service data to support evaluation and innovation of service provision requires collaborative partnerships with stakeholders. This entails substantial investment of time and, of course, buy-in from the relevant stakeholders. We have found that there is little interest in the traditional model of academic-government partnerships where knowledge generation and translation take three to five years through some form of partnership or linkage grant. This way of working is simply not fit for purpose in a policy climate of data-driven reform. Researchers get left behind as policy partners are forced to make decisions in the absence of locally relevant, high-quality evidence. Our partnerships with various parts of government and with non-government agencies have been underpinned by our capacity and willingness to respond rapidly to government priorities. We work closely with multiple non-government organisations to support data collection that will be the basis of evaluations using quasi-experimental methods in years to come. This sort of investment has implications for how different kinds of research outputs are valued in universities and funding agencies, pointing to the need for more up-to-date, sophisticated, and comprehensive typologies of research to ensure that academics engaged in non-traditional research are appropriately supported. This is especially true for early and mid-career researchers where the emphasis remains on traditional academic outputs.

While creating renewable and intelligent data platforms is clearly desirable, funding structures also need to support this enterprise. National funding structures are still largely locked into one-off funding processes as discrete projects are created, have defined end dates, and sometimes data are destroyed. We need more funding directed to sustainable data platforms that can be deployed to answer multiple questions. Our approach challenges current funding structures to foster sustainable, purpose-built linked data platforms. Without a strategically designed and appropriately funded system-wide intelligent information infrastructure, there will be limited ability to measure the success of investments to improve justice outcomes for young people in Australia.

References

Australian Institute of Health and Welfare. (2022). *Youth justice in Australia 2020–21*. Canberra: Australian Government. Retrieved from https://www.aihw.gov.au/getmedia/10da194d-5756-4933-be0a-29d41743d79b/aihw-juv-138.pdf.aspx?inline=true.

Axford, N., Morpeth, L., Bjornstad, G., Hobbs, T., & Berry, V. (2022). "What works" registries of interventions to improve child and youth psychosocial outcomes: A critical appraisal. *Children and Youth Services Review*, *137*, 106469. https://doi.org/10.1016/j.childyouth.2022.106469.

Bateman, S., Arnold-Chamney, M., Jesudason, S., Lester, R., McDonald, S., O'Donnell, K., ... Kelly, J. (2022). Real ways of working together: Co-creating meaningful Aboriginal community consultations to advance kidney care. *Australian and New*

Zealand Journal of Public Health, *46*(5), 614–621. https://doi.org/10.1111/1753-6405.13280.

Bothwell, L. E., Greene, J. A., Podolsky, S. H., & Jones, D. S. (2016). Assessing the gold standard — Lessons from the history of RCTs. *The New England Journal of Medicine*, *374*(22), 2175–2181. https://doi.org/10.1056/NEJMms1604593.

Braunack-Mayer, A. J., Gibson, O. R., & The, C. M. G. (2017). Including minority populations in research: We must do better. *Medical Journal of Australia*, *207*(1), 22–23. https://doi.org/10.5694/mja17.00305.

Button, K. S., Ioannidis, J. P. A., Mokrysz, C., Nosek, B. A., Flint, J., Robinson, E. S. J., & Munafò, M. R. (2013). Power failure: Why small sample size undermines the reliability of neuroscience. *Nature Reviews. Neuroscience*, *14*(5), 365–376. https://doi.org/10.1038/nrn3475.

Deaton, A., & Cartwright, N. (2018). Understanding and misunderstanding randomized controlled trials. *Social Science and Medicine (1982)*, *210*, 2–21. https://doi.org/10.1016/j.socscimed.2017.12.005.

Early Intervention Foundation Guidebook. (2023, February 2018). *Multisystemic Therapy*. Retrieved March 1, 2021, from https://guidebook.eif.org.uk/programme/multisystemic-therapy.

Fonagy, P., Butler, S., Cottrell, D., Scott, S., Pilling, S., Eisler, I., … Goodyer, I. M. (2018). Multisystemic therapy versus management as usual in the treatment of adolescent antisocial behaviour (START): A pragmatic, randomised controlled, superiority trial. *The Lancet Psychiatry*, *5*(2), 119–133. https://doi.org/10.1016/S2215-0366(18)30001-4.

Fonagy, P., Butler, S., Cottrell, D., Scott, S., Pilling, S., Eisler, I., … Goodyer, I. M. (2020). Multisystemic therapy versus management as usual in the treatment of adolescent antisocial behaviour (START): 5-year follow-up of a pragmatic, randomised, controlled, superiority trial. *The Lancet Psychiatry*, *7*(5), 420–430. https://doi.org/10.1016/S2215-0366(20)30131-0.

Ford, D. V., Jones, K. H., Verplancke, J.-P., Lyons, R. A., John, G., Brown, G., … Leake, K. (2009). The SAIL Databank: Building a national architecture for e-health research and evaluation. *BMC Health Services Research*, *9*(1), 157–157. https://doi.org/10.1186/1472-6963-9-157.

Foust, R., Hoonhout, J., Eastman, A., Prindle, J., Rebbe, R., Nghiem, H., … McCroskey, J. (2022). Children's data network: Harnessing the scientific potential of linked, administrative data to inform children's programs and policies. *International Journal of Population Data Science*, *6*(3). https://doi.org/10.23889/ijpds.v6i3.1702.

Frieden, T. R. (2017). Evidence for health decision making — Beyond randomized, controlled trials. *The New England Journal of Medicine*, *377*(5), 465–475. https://doi.org/10.1056/NEJMra1614394 (The Changing Face of Clinical Trials).

Hazel, N. (2008). *Cross-national comparison of youth justice*. Manchester: University of Salford. Retrieved from http://usir.salford.ac.uk/id/eprint/50528/1/Cross_national_final.pdf.

Henggeler, S. W. (2001). Multisystemic therapy. *Residential Treatment for Children and Youth*, *18*(3), 75–85. https://doi.org/10.1300/J007v18n03_07.

Hernan, M. A. (2021). Methods of public health research — Strengthening causal inference from observational data. *The New England Journal of Medicine*, *385*(15), 1345–1348. https://doi.org/10.1056/NEJMp2113319.

Hernán, M. A., & Robins, J. M. (2016). Using big data to emulate a target trial when a randomized trial is not available. *American Journal of Epidemiology, 183*(8), 758–764. https://doi.org/10.1093/aje/kwv254.

Hernán, M. A., & Robins, J. M. (2017). Per-protocol analyses of pragmatic trials. *The New England Journal of Medicine, 377*(14), 1391–1398. https://doi.org/10.1056/NEJMsm1605385.

Higgins, J. P. T., Altman, D. G., Gøtzsche, P. C., Jüni, P., Moher, D., & Oxman, A. D. (2011). The Cochrane Collaboration's tool for assessing risk of bias in randomised trials. *BMJ, 343*, d5928. https://doi.org/10.1136/bmj.d5928.

Hom, V. E. E. (2022). *Early childhood home visiting models reviewing evidence of effectiveness* (OPRE Report #2022-284). Administration for Children & Families.

Homel, R. (2021). Developmental crime prevention in the twenty-first century: Generating better evidence embedded in large-scale delivery systems. *Journal of Developmental and Life-Course Criminology*, 7(1), 112–125. https://doi.org/10.1007/s40865-021-00163-x.

Hrobjartsson, A., Emanuelsson, F., Thomsen, A. S. S., Hilden, J., & Brorson, S. (2014). Bias due to lack of patient blinding in clinical trials. A systematic review of trials randomizing patients to blind and nonblind sub-studies. *International Journal of Epidemiology, 43*(4), 1272–1283. https://doi.org/10.1093/ije/dyu115.

Jones, D. S., & Podolsky, S. H. (2015). The history and fate of the gold standard. *The Lancet (British edition), 385*(9977), 1502–1503. https://doi.org/10.1016/S0140-6736(15)60742-5.

Kitzman, H., Olds, D. L., Henderson Jr. C. R., Hanks, C., Cole, R., Tatelbaum, R., ... Barnard, K. (1997). Effect of prenatal and infancy home visitation by nurses on pregnancy outcomes, childhood injuries, and repeated childbearing: A randomized controlled trial. *JAMA: The journal of the American Medical Association, 278*(8), 644–652. https://doi.org/10.1001/jama.278.8.644.

Littell, J. H., Pigott, T. D., Nilsen, K. H., Green, S. J., & Montgomery, O. L. K. (2021). Multisystemic Therapy® for social, emotional, and behavioural problems in youth age 10 to 17: An updated systematic review and meta-analysis. *Campbell Systematic Review, 17*(4). https://doi.org/10.1002/cl2.1158.

Lynch, J. (2017). What can early interventions really achieve, and how will we know? *Family Matters, 99*, 15–22.

Malvaso, C., Montgomerie, A., Pilkington, R. M., Baker, E., & Lynch, J. W. (2022). Examining the intersection of child protection and public housing: Development, health and justice outcomes using linked administrative data. *BMJ, (Open), 12*(6), e057284. https://doi.org/10.1136/bmjopen-2021-057284.

Malvaso, C., Pilkington, R., Montgomerie, A., Delfabbro, P., & Lynch, J. (2020, August). A public health approach to preventing child maltreatment: An intelligent information infrastructure to help us know what works. *Child Abuse and Neglect, 106*, 104466–104469. https://doi.org/10.1016/j.chiabu.2020.104466.

Moreno-Betancur, M., Lynch, J. W., Pilkington, R. M., Schuch, H. S., Gialamas, A., Sawyer, M. G., ... Gurrin, L. C. (2023). Emulating a target trial of intensive nurse home visiting in the policy-relevant population using linked administrative data. *International Journal of Epidemiology, 52*(1), 119–131. https://doi.org/10.1093/ije/dyac092.

Murray, E. J., Caniglia, E. C., Swanson, S. A., Hernández-Díaz, S., & Hernán, M. A. (2018). Patients and investigators prefer measures of absolute risk in subgroups for pragmatic randomized trials. *Journal of Clinical Epidemiology*, *103*, 10–21. https://doi.org/10.1016/j.jclinepi.2018.06.009.

Nüesch, E., Reichenbach, S., Trelle, S., Rutjes, A. W. S., Liewald, K., Sterchi, R., ... Jüni, P. (2009). The importance of allocation concealment and patient blinding in osteoarthritis trials: A meta-epidemiologic study. *Arthritis and Rheumatism*, *61*(12), 1633–1641. https://doi.org/10.1002/art.24894.

Olds, D. (2016). Building evidence to improve maternal and child health. *The Lancet (British edition)*, *387*(10014), 105–107. https://doi.org/10.1016/S0140-6736(15)00476-6.

Olds, D. L., Henderson Jr., C. R., Tatelbaum, R., & Chamberlin, R. (1986). Improving the delivery of prenatal care and outcomes of pregnancy: A randomized trial of nurse home visitation. *Pediatrics (Evanston)*, *77*(1), 16–28. https://doi.org/10.1542/peds.77.1.16.

Olds, D. L., Robinson, J., O'Brien, R., Luckey, D. W., Pettitt, L. M., Henderson, C. R. Jr., ... Talmi, A. (2002). Home visiting by paraprofessionals and by nurses: A randomized, controlled trial. *Pediatrics (Evanston)*, *110*(3), 486–496. https://doi.org/10.1542/peds.110.3.486.

Pilkington, R., Montgomerie, A., Grant, J., Gialamas, A., Malvaso, C., Smithers, L., ... Lynch, J. (2019). *An innovative linked data platform to improve the wellbeing of children: The South Australian Early Childhood Data Project*. Canberra: Australian Institute of Health and Welfare.

Robins, J. (1986). A new approach to causal inference in mortality studies with a sustained exposure period—Application to control of the healthy worker survivor effect. *Mathematical Modelling*, *7*(9), 1393–1512. https://doi.org/10.1016/0270-0255(86)90088-6.

Robling, M. D., Bekkers, M.-J. P., Bell, K. P., Butler, C. C. P., Cannings-John, R. P., Channon, S. D., ... Torgerson, D. P. (2016). Effectiveness of a nurse-led intensive home-visitation programme for first-time teenage mothers (Building Blocks): A pragmatic randomised controlled trial. *The Lancet (British edition)*, *387*(10014), 146–155. https://doi.org/10.1016/S0140-6736(15)00392-X.

Schuler, M. S., & Rose, S. (2017). Targeted maximum likelihood estimation for causal inference in observational studies. *American Journal of Epidemiology*, *185*(1), 65–73. https://doi.org/10.1093/aje/kww165.

Maiam nayri Wingara Indigenous Data Sovereignty Collective. (2018). *Indigenous data sovereignty communique*. Retrieved from https://static1.squarespace.com/static/5b3043afb40b9d20411f3512/t/63ed934fe861fa061ebb9202/1676514134724/Communique-Indigenous-Data-Sovereignty-Summit.pdf.

Sterne, J. A. C., Savović, J., Page, M. J., Elbers, R. G., Blencowe, N. S., Boutron, I., ... Higgins, J. P. T. (2019). RoB 2: a revised tool for assessing risk of bias in randomised trials. *BMJ*, *366*, l4898. https://doi.org/10.1136/bmj.l4898.

Sundell, K., Hansson, K., Löfholm, C. A., Olsson, T., Gustle, L.-H., & Kadesjö, C. (2008). The transportability of multisystemic therapy to Sweden: Short-term results from a randomized trial of conduct-disordered youths. *Journal of Family Psychology*, *22*(4), 550–560. https://doi.org/10.1037/a0012790.

The California Evidence-Based Clearinghouse for Child Welfare. (2021, October 2021). *Multisystemic Therapy (MST)*. Retrieved March 1, 2021, from https://www.cebc4cw.org/program/multisystemic-therapy/.

Walter, M., Lovett, R., Maher, B., Williamson, B., Prehn, J., Bodkin-Andrews, G., & Lee, V. (2021). Indigenous data sovereignty in the era of big data and open data. *The Australian Journal of Social Issues*, *56*(2), 143–156. https://doi.org/10.1002/ajs4.141.

Chapter 4

Within-Person Change and Theories of Developmental and Life-Course Criminology

Jacqueline Allen and Corrie Williams

Introduction

Developmental and life-course criminology (DLC) is fundamentally concerned with questions about how people change. For instance, researchers ask: how does offending change as people move through adolescence and into young adulthood? Does an increase in alcohol use at age 14 lead to an increase in aggressive behaviour by age 16? What can account for why people stop offending? These sorts of questions are often about within-person change: they ask what may happen within a given person, rather than focusing on differences across a set of people.

Major theories in developmental and life-course criminology (DLC) have provided frameworks for understanding how and why within-person change occurs. Theories tend to explicitly or implicitly contain two broad sets of propositions about within-person effects. The first is concerned mostly with describing change. Specifically, it is proposed that people's behaviour does change over time, that there is variability in the nature of this change, and that this variability may be explained. For example, how does offending change during adolescence, how much variability or heterogeneity is there in this within-person change, and what kinds of risk factors may account for this variability? The second is concerned mostly with the dynamics of how behaviours, experiences, and contexts vary together over time at the within-person level. That is, changes in one aspect of people's lives lead to changes in other aspects of people's lives or behaviours, in a manner that may be cumulative or cascading. For example, it is well known that adolescents who have more deviant peers tend to report more delinquent behaviour (Haynie & Osgood, 2005), but how does a person's delinquent behaviour change if deviant peer associations change? Might changes in delinquency also drive changes in peer associations?

Despite the compelling propositions offered in DLC theory about how changes within people over time can explain antisocial and offending behaviour, DLC research often uses statistical models that tend to emphasise between-person differences (Farrington, 2002). This mismatch between what

DOI: 10.4324/9781003294740-4

theory proposes and how effects are tested can lead to missed opportunities to explore the complexities of how people change. Although people's lives are highly variable, deducing systematic patterns in their pathways will lead to a better understanding of the fundamentals of human behaviour, and how this may lead to the prevention of crime.

In this chapter, we aim to showcase the potential of within-person methods to answer critical questions about the development of offending and antisocial behaviour and to push the DLC field forward. We argue that there is no one particular model or method that provides all the answers about within-person change and that researchers should think creatively about both methods and theory to answer big questions in DLC. Therefore, we also aim to inspire DLC researchers to be bold in asking questions about within-person change.

In the next section we give examples of how each of the two broad propositions about within-person change are described and tested in DLC research and in some selected DLC theories. We highlight the complexity of the questions about within-person change that can be posed. For each of the two aspects of within-person change, we also provide a brief critical overview of some statistical models that can be used. In the concluding section we discuss the opportunities and challenges of a within-person perspective for theory and research in DLC.

Developmental and Life-Course Criminology Research, Theory, and Within-Person Change

Describing Change

The first broad proposition about within-person change is that people's behaviour does change over time and that this change may be explained by other variables. DLC theory as a whole is concerned with describing and understanding changes in antisocial behaviour (Farrington, 2015). However, within-person change in even one type of behaviour, such as antisocial behaviour, is quite challenging to model statistically. This may be illustrated by considering two methods for modelling change, the *latent growth model* and the *latent class growth model.*

Latent growth models (Grimm & Ram, 2012) describe how people change on a variable or variables over repeated measurement occasions. This change (or growth) can be represented as an increase or decrease in a straight line, or the growth can be curvilinear in form, such as rising and then falling. Latent growth models are very useful for answering questions about what change is like, and what predicts change. For instance, Mason and colleagues (2010) found that problem behaviours at age 10 predicted an increasing trajectory of delinquency in adolescence. Latent class growth models are like latent growth models in that growth or change in behaviour is modelled (Feldman et al., 2009). However, any variability in change is accounted for by allowing distinct subgroups (or classes) of individuals to exist in the data. These subgroups have different patterns of growth, so that growth for members of one class may increase in a straight line, while another may start high and then decline gradually. Often called *semiparametric group-based models* following Daniel Nagin's influential work (Nagin & Land, 1993), these approaches are extremely popular in DLC (Jennings & Reingle, 2012). Many researchers have examined factors associated with variation in the development of antisocial behaviour over time using latent class growth models (Russell & Odgers, 2016).

Although both latent growth models and latent class growth models are very useful for describing change, their interpretation often tends to emphasise between-person differences. This is particularly true for latent class growth models which tend to focus on variables that explain membership in trajectory classes (e.g., Wiesner et al., 2007) and generally do not model any variation within these trajectory classes. Another limitation of growth models is that they are not well-suited to examining the dynamics of within-person change as it relates to more than one variable, a problem to which we now turn.

Understanding the Dynamics of Change

Developmental and life-course researchers are very often interested in the dynamics of change. This may be described as how changes in one variable may lead to changes in something else, usually with a causal ordering in mind. For example, Woodin and colleagues (2016) examined how relational peer aggression, physical peer aggression, and heavy drinking reinforced each other across adolescence, with these behaviours subsequently leading to romantic relational aggression.

In DLC, these sorts of questions have often been addressed using *cross-lagged panel models*. Usually including two or three variables measured repeatedly over time, these approaches model stability with autoregressive paths, which means that the same variables are linked across waves, and also include links between different variables across subsequent waves, which are called *cross-lags*. However, cross-lagged models have been criticised because they do not appropriately represent within-person changes. In an influential paper, Hamaker and colleagues (2015) argued that the cross-lagged effects reflect a combination of stable, trait-like individual differences and within-person changes. As it is not possible to separate out the within- and between-person effects from a conventional cross-lagged panel model, these models are increasingly viewed as not very useful for understanding within-person processes. For example, in the study by Woodin and colleagues (2016) it is hard to say whether adolescents who were more aggressive were also heavier drinkers in general (between-person differences), or whether drinking at one time point led to a within-person increase in aggression at the next time point.

There are a number of newer models that do allow researchers to separate out between-person differences from within-person effects. One of these is the *random-intercept cross-lagged panel model* (Hamaker et al., 2015; Mulder & Hamaker, 2020), which is increasingly used in DLC. For instance, Mercer and colleagues (2017) tested the relationships between delinquency and identity in a sample of adolescents followed for five years. Hypotheses were drawn from several theories. Results showed that adolescents who were more delinquent than others tended to have more identity confusion (between-person differences). However, there was also evidence that within-person increases in delinquency predicted increases in identity confusion, and to a certain extent, change in the direction of less identity confusion was also related to decreases in delinquency.

While new approaches to cross-lagged panel models have the potential to aid understanding of how changes are linked within people over time, they do have a number of limitations. One of the most important is a difficulty in testing longer-run hypotheses that incorporate both between-person differences and within-person processes (Shamsollahi et al., 2022). An example of these complex questions is found in two DLC theories, David Farrington's Integrated Cognitive Antisocial Potential (ICAP) Theory (Farrington, 2005) and Per-Olof Wikström's Situational Action Theory (Wikström, 2006). Both theories explain the commission of crime via complex interactions between characteristics of people and characteristics of situations. Both long-term (between-person) propensities to break rules or commit crime matter, but so do short-term factors (opportunities, intoxication) that may fluctuate at the within-person level. Therefore within-person processes underlying actual offending may be influenced by longer-term characteristics of people and by past experiences, and experience of different short-term situations may also change the longer-term trajectory of criminal behaviour. In general, tests of these theories have used between-person methods to focus on the role of long-term propensities or between-person factors (Farrington & McGee, 2019; Pauwels et al., 2018). Some studies have supported the hypothesised situational, within-person drivers of offending (Bernasco et al., 2013; Gerth, 2022). However, the longer-run interplay between people's stable propensities, their within-person fluctuations, and offending has not been tested and would be difficult to test within the confines of a cross-lagged model.

Opportunities and Challenges for Developmental and Life-Course Criminology

The previous sections highlighted the complexity of examining questions about within-person change within DLC theory and research. We touched on a few statistical models that are prevalent, or becoming prevalent, in the social and behavioural sciences, and that can provide insights into within-person processes. However, none of these models, on their own, is suitable for testing many of the big questions that arise from DLC theory. One reason for this is that DLC theory is often concerned with cascades of experiences, situations, and behaviour that unfold over many years. For instance, early neuro-developmental difficulties may lead to problems with peer relationships, leading to peer rejection and problem behaviour in school, leading to disengagement and delinquent behaviour in adolescence (Homel & Thomsen, 2017). This sort of developmental cascade could not be tested in a within-person fashion using cross-lagged models such as the random-intercept cross-lagged panel model, which require the same variables to be measured at each time point.

However, DLC researchers interested in within-person change do not need one model to rule them all. Instead, researchers should think creatively about both theory and methods. First, it is important to be explicit about hypotheses (Hamaker et al., 2018). For instance, does theory suggest that the research question is about the within-person level or the between-person level? Over what kind of timescale does theory suggest that the phenomena under study should be observed? Is the question about describing developmental change, or understanding dynamics of change? These are difficult questions that have implications both for data collection and the approach to modelling.

Second, researchers could consider how a within-person perspective might provide the opportunity to test new hypotheses from DLC theories, including those theories that have a conceptual emphasis on between-persons processes. As an example, the Social Development Model (Catalano & Hawkins, 1996) contends that the development of both prosocial and antisocial behaviour follow the same socialisation process, involving perceived opportunities for involvement in behaviour with others, skills for participation in these activities, and the perception of rewards for participation. Ultimately, the socialisation process results in prosocial or antisocial bonding and values, which are key predictors of behaviour. Empirical tests supporting the Social Development Model have utilised structural equation models linking these constructs over time (e.g., Herrenkohl et al., 2001), which tend to emphasise differences between people. However, it is also possible to dig deeper into the processes implied by the theory that may occur at the individual level. The Social Development Model predicts that strong prosocial bonding in earlier developmental periods should increase the likelihood of a person perceiving opportunities for prosocial behaviour in the next developmental period. It might be possible to consider within-person accumulation in perceived opportunities for behaviour over a year or two in one developmental period and ask how this is related to between-person differences in bonding in an earlier period. Another possibility would be to compare the dynamic interplay between key theoretical variables such as perceived opportunities for prosocial or antisocial activities, perceived reward for involvement, and prosocial or antisocial values in different developmental periods.

Third, researchers could consider how hypotheses about the relationship between short-term, within-person processes and longer-run, between-person processes might be tested by considering both macro- and micro time scales. One way to approach this would be by incorporating "measurement bursts" of experience (Sliwinski et al., 2010) into conventional longitudinal studies. In these designs (Brown et al., 2022), a small subgroup of participants completes frequent assessments of a small number of measures over a relatively short period. This may be a one-off, or the burst may be repeated at some later period. There are several emerging statistical methods, such as *dynamic structural equation modelling* (Asparouhov et al., 2018), that are designed to examine how two or more variables fluctuate together in the short term, such as over hours or days. Such methods can be used to link the dynamic processes assessed by a measurement burst to between-person factors. For instance, short-term antisocial potential in Farrington's ICAP theory (2005) arises from factors such as routine activities, anger, and perceptions of risk and reward in specific situations. The confluence of these could be assessed in the short term via smartphone surveys, or even through emerging methodologies in which smart devices can record situational factors such as alcohol consumption, environmental light levels, and the presence of other people nearby (Ruiter & Bernasco, 2018). It might then be possible to test how short-term fluctuations in antisocial potential are related to long-term antisocial potential (refer to Balkaya-Ince et al., 2020, for an empirical example of this approach). Although there are considerable privacy issues with smartphone technologies, especially for passive data collection, research into the feasibility and acceptability of this methodology with adolescents and hard-to-reach populations is promising (Modecki et al., 2019; Sugie, 2018).

Finally, there are some substantive areas of investigation in the DLC field that might be enhanced through a focus on within-person processes. One of these is a better understanding of the process of cumulative risk. The role of cumulative risk in the development of delinquency and offending is well known – the more risk factors a child or adolescent has, the higher the likelihood of poor outcomes compared to a person with a lower number of risk factors (Ttofi et al., 2016). This is a between-persons comparison. However, it is also important to understand the intra-individual processes involved in the accumulation of that risk. What kinds of dynamic interplay between people and situations at particular developmental stages might "push" a child along a pathway of cumulative risk? Are there long-run consequences of particular very early events? A second area for investigation could be the unpacking of turning points, as described in the work of Rob Sampson and John Laub (Laub & Sampson, 2003; Sampson & Laub, 1993). Rather than considering events such as marriage and employment as single points in time, some of the models described here may assist in understanding turning points as part of a longer-term, dynamic process (Nguyen & Loughran, 2018).

Conclusion

In this chapter we argued that understanding within-person change and within-person processes is central to understanding the development of antisocial behaviour, a key concern of DLC theory. However, we noted that DLC research often uses models that emphasise between-person differences. Our aim was to showcase the potential of within-person methods to answer key questions in the DLC field and suggest how researchers may use these methods creatively to address existing and new hypotheses.

In the first section we presented an overview of different ways that within-person change and within-person effects are conceptualised and tested in DLC research and theory, focusing on two broad propositions about within-person change: first, that changes in people's behaviour over time can be described, and variability in that change may be explained; and second, that there are dynamic relationships between people's behaviour, experiences, and contexts that unfold over time and can explain antisocial behaviour. We briefly discussed some statistical models that can be used to understand these sorts of within-person processes.

In the final section we proposed that the key to using within-person methods to advance DLC lies in creative thinking about theory, hypotheses, data collection, and statistical modelling. Human behaviour is enormously complicated. Researchers tend to have only a small number of blurry photographs of people living their lives. Yet, the DLC field has generated a huge amount of knowledge about the causes, development, and prevention of delinquency and offending. We hope that ongoing methodological developments, along with increasing use of open-access software such as R, may lead to new insights into the dynamics of people's behaviour in the contexts of their unfolding lives. Most importantly, improved understanding of the within-person processes involved in delinquency and offending should lead to strategies to prevent crime and enhance wellbeing.

References

Asparouhov, T., Hamaker, E. L., & Muthén, B. (2018). Dynamic structural equation models. *Structural Equation Modeling: A Multidisciplinary Journal*, *25*(3), 359–388. https://doi.org/10.1080/10705511.2017.1406803.

Balkaya-Ince, M., Cheah, C. S. L., Kiang, L., & Tahseen, M. (2020). Exploring daily mediating pathways of religious identity in the associations between maternal religious socialization and Muslim American adolescents' civic engagement. *Developmental Psychology*, *56*(8), 1446–1457. https://doi.org/10.1037/dev0000856.

Bernasco, W., Ruiter, S., Bruinsma, G. J. N., Pauwels, L. J. R., & Weerman, F. M. (2013). Situational causes of offending: A fixed-effects analysis of space-time budget data. *Criminology*, *51*(4), 895–926. https://doi.org/10.1111/1745-9125.12023.

Brown, R., Speyer, L. G., Eisner, M., Ribeaud, D., & Murray, A. L. (2022). Exploring the effect of ADHD traits on the moment-to-moment interplay between provocation and aggression: Evidence from dynamic structural equation modelling. https://doi.org/10.31234/osf.io/d27ta.

Catalano, R. F., & Hawkins, D. J. (1996). The social development model: A theory of antisocial behavior. In D. J. Hawkins (Ed.), *Delinquency and crime: Current theories* (pp. 149–197). Cambridge: Cambridge University Press.

Farrington, D. P. (2002). Building developmental and life-course theories of offending. In F. T. Cullen, J. Wright, & K. Blevins (Eds.), *Taking stock: The status of criminological theory*. Transaction Publishers.

Farrington, D. P. (2005). The integrated cognitive antisocial potential (ICAP) theory. In D. P. Farrington (Ed.), *Integrated developmental and life-course theories of offending: Advances in criminological theory* (Vol. 14, pp. 73–92). Transaction Publishers.

Farrington, D. P. (2015). Prospective longitudinal research on the development of offending. *Australian and New Zealand Journal of Criminology*, *48*(3), 314–335. https://doi.org/10.1177/0004865815590461.

Farrington, D. P., & McGee, T. R. (2019). The integrated cognitive antisocial potential (ICAP) theory: New empirical tests. In D. P. Farrington, L. Kazemian, & A. R. Piquero (Eds.), *The Oxford handbook of developmental and life-course criminology* (pp. 173–192). Oxford: Oxford University Press. https://doi.org/10.1093/oxfordhb/9780190201371.013.11.

Feldman, B. J., Masyn, K. E., & Conger, R. D. (2009). New approaches to studying problem behaviors: A comparison of methods for modeling longitudinal, categorical adolescent drinking data. *Developmental Psychology*, *45*(3), 652–676. https://doi.org/10.1037/a0014851.

Gerth, M. (2022). Does truancy make the delinquent? A situational and longitudinal analysis of the truancy–delinquency relationship. *European Journal of Criminology*, *19*(5), 1205–1224. https://doi.org/10.1177/1477370820952681.

Grimm, K. J., & Ram, N. (2012). Growth curve modeling from a structural equation modeling perspective. In B. Laursen, T. Little, & N. A. Card (Eds.), *Handbook of developmental research methods* (pp. 411–431). New York: The Guildford Press.

Hamaker, E. L., Asparouhov, T., Brose, A., Schmiedek, F., & Muthen, B. (2018). At the frontiers of modeling intensive longitudinal data: Dynamic structural equation models for the affective measurements from the COGITO study. *Multivariate Behavioral Research*, *53*(6), 820–841. https://doi.org/10.1080/00273171.2018.1446819.

Hamaker, E. L., Kuiper, R. M., & Grasman, R. P. (2015). A critique of the cross-lagged panel model. *Psychological Methods*, *20*(1), 102–116. https://doi.org/10.1037/a0038889.

Haynie, D. L., & Osgood, D. W. (2005). Reconsidering peers and delinquency: How do peers matter? *Social Forces*, *84*(2), 1109–1130. https://doi.org/10.1353/sof.2006.0018.

Herrenkohl, T. I., Huang, B., Kosterman, R., Hawkins, J. D., Catalano, R. F., & Smith, B. H. (2001). A comparison of social development processes leading to violent behavior in late adolescence for childhood initiators and adolescent initiators of violence. *Journal of Research in Crime and Delinquency*, *38*(1), 45–63. https://doi.org/10.1177/0022427801038001003.

Homel, R. J., & Thomsen, L. (2017). Developmental crime prevention. In N. Tilley & A. Sidebottom (Eds.), *Handbook of crime prevention and community safety* (pp. 57–86). New York: Routledge.

Jennings, W. G., & Reingle, J. M. (2012). On the number and shape of developmental/life-course violence, aggression, and delinquency trajectories: A state-of-the-art review. *Journal of Criminal Justice*, *40*(6), 472–489. https://doi.org/https://doi.org/10.1016/j.jcrimjus.2012.07.001

Laub, J. H., & Sampson, R. J. (2003). *Shared Beginnings, Divergent Lives: Delinquent Boys to Age, 70*. Harvard: Harvard University Press.

Mason, A. W., Hitch, J. E., Kosterman, R., McCarty, C. A., Herrenkohl, T. I., & David Hawkins, J. (2010). Growth in adolescent delinquency and alcohol use in relation to young adult crime, alcohol use disorders, and risky sex: A comparison of youth from low- versus middle-income backgrounds. *Journal of Child Psychology and Psychiatry*, *51*(12), 1377–1385. https://doi.org/10.1111/j.1469-7610.2010.02292.x.

Mercer, N., Crocetti, E., Branje, S., van Lier, P., & Meeus, W. (2017). Linking delinquency and personal identity formation across adolescence: Examining between- and within-person associations. *Developmental Psychology*, *53*(11), 2182–2194. https://doi.org/10.1037/dev0000351.

Modecki, K. L., Goldberg, R. E., Ehrenreich, S. E., Russell, M., & Bellmore, A. (2019). The practicalities and perils of ambulatory assessment's promise: Introduction to a special section. *Journal of Research on Adolescence*, *29*(3), 542–550. https://doi.org/10.1111/jora.12532.

Mulder, J. D., & Hamaker, E. L. (2020). Three extensions of the random intercept cross-lagged panel model. *Structural Equation Modeling: A Multidisciplinary Journal*, *28*(4), 638–648. https://doi.org/10.1080/10705511.2020.1784738.

Nagin, D. S. & Kand, K. C. (1993). Age, criminal careers and population heterogeneity: Specification and estimation of nonparametric, mixed poisson model. *Criminology*, 31: 327–362. https://doi.org/10.1111/j.1745-9125.1993.tb01133.x

Nguyen, H., & Loughran, T. A. (2018). On the measurement and identification of turning points in criminology. *Annual Review of Criminology*, *1*(1), 335–358. https://doi.org/10.1146/annurev-criminol.

Pauwels, L. J. R., Svensson, R., & Hirtenlehner, H. (2018). Testing situational action theory: A narrative review of studies published between 2006 and 2015. *European Journal of Criminology*, *15*(1), 32–55. https://doi.org/10.1177/1477370817732185.

Ruiter, S., & Bernasco, W. (2018). Is travel actually risky? A study of situational causes of victimization. *Crime Science*, 7(1), 10. https://doi.org/10.1186/s40163-018-0084-6.

Russell, M. A., & Odgers, C. L. (2016). Desistance and life-course persistence: Findings from longitudinal studies using group-based trajectory modeling of antisocial behavior. In *APA handbook of psychology and juvenile justice* (pp. 159–175). American Psychological Association. https://doi.org/10.1037/14643-008.

Sampson, R. J., & Laub, J. H. (1993). *Crime in the making: Pathways and turning points through life*. Cambridge, MA: Harvard University Press.

Shamsollahi, A., Zyphur, M. J., & Ozkok, O. (2022). Long-run effects in dynamic systems: New tools for cross-lagged panel models. *Organizational Research Methods*, *25*(3), 435–458. https://doi.org/10.1177/1094428121993228.

Sliwinski, M., Hoffman, L., & Hofer, S. (2010). Modeling retest and aging effects in a measurement burst design. In P. C. M. Molenaar & K. M. Newell (Eds.), *Individual pathways of change: Statistical models for analyzing learning and development* (pp. 37–50). American Psychological Association. https://doi.org/https://psycnet.apa.org/doi/10.1037/12140-003.

Sugie, N. F. (2018). Utilizing smartphones to study disadvantaged and hard-to-reach groups. *Sociological Methods and Research*, *47*(3), 458–491. https://doi.org/10.1177/0049124115626176.

Ttofi, M. M., Farrington, D. P., Piquero, A. R., & DeLisi, M. (2016). Protective factors against offending and violence: Results from prospective longitudinal studies. *Journal of Criminal Justice*, *45*, 1–3. https://doi.org/10.1016/j.jcrimjus.2016.02.001.

Wiesner, M., Capaldi, D. M., & Kim, H. K. (2007). Arrest trajectories across a 17-year span for young men: Relation to dual taxonomies and self-reported offense trajectories. *Criminology*, *45*(4), 835–863. https://doi.org/10.1111/j.1745-9125.2007.00099.x.

Wikström, P. O. H. (2006). Individuals, settings and acts of crime: Situational mechanisms and the explanation of crime. In P. O. H. Wikström & R. J. Sampson (Eds.), *The explanation of crime: Context, mechanisms and development* (pp. 61–107). Cambridge: Cambridge University Press.

Woodin, E. M., Sukhawathanakul, P., Caldeira, V., Homel, J., & Leadbeater, B. (2016). Pathways to romantic relational aggression through adolescent peer aggression and heavy episodic drinking. *Aggressive Behavior*, *42*(6), 563–576. https://doi.org/10.1002/ab.21651.

Chapter 5

How to Work with Visual Artists to Move Developmental and Life-Course Criminology Forward

David John Harris and Danielle Arlanda Harris

Introduction

Information graphics and data visualisation have become common and increasingly prominent in many communication and information environments including education, journalism, social media, and academic research and publishing. Although visual communication serves a variety of roles in culture, there has been comparatively little progress in the actual development of data visualisation among criminologists specifically (Francis & Pritchard, 1998; Harris & Harris, 2021). We consider this lacuna to be an exciting frontier that is ripe for exploration, and use this chapter to reflect on our shared experiences of: collaboration between art and science; connections between developmental and life-course criminology (DLC) and data visualisation; but even more so, applying creative arts approaches to problem-solving.

We adopt Wheeldon and Harris's (2015) definition of visual criminology as

> the use of any image (including, but not limited, to paintings, photographs, drawings, maps, diagrams, graphs, charts, and other visual/graphic approaches) to: collect information from participants; describe, present, and analyse data; and/or examine or interrogate the meaning(s) of those data.
>
> (p. 144)

Any sort of data visualisation is a step outside traditional criminology's comfort zone, where there is a heavy reliance on cross-sectional sampling methods and spreadsheet-based statistics. These data sources do not easily lend themselves to longitudinal analysis and certainly not to answering qualitative questions. Our visualisation techniques are a response to Maltz's (1998) appeal for the field to consider the benefits of representing criminological elements in graphical ways (see also Maltz, 2010). While progress in visualisation is occurring, it is also worth considering what additional opportunities arise when criminologists and creative artists collaborate.

DOI: 10.4324/9781003294740-5

DLC favours individual-level explanations of offending where the unit of analysis might be a person, an incident, or a location (rather than population level data). When the unit of analysis is a person, it becomes possible to focus on how events are sequenced over time, how those events interact with each other, and how the individual is affected by those variables differently over time (Maltz & Mullany, 2000). It thus becomes possible to ask questions about whether those events happen sequentially, or co-occur, for example.

We showcase two specific methodological innovations in this chapter that have been used to both visualise and better understand complex patterns of variables such as pathways to offending: the Life History Plot (LHP) and the Adverse Childhood Experiences (ACE) Matrix. Both are informed by a DLC approach and allow for a selection of variables (including criminal history, childhood adversity, and other life events) to be viewed in a temporal way, in a single image. We reflect on what happened when a criminologist and a science communicator/graphic designer/artist worked together to develop these visual innovations, hopefully inspiring other seemingly non-traditional collaborations. First, we provide a brief overview of the LHP, but direct interested readers to other sources where it has been described in more detail (Harris, 2013; Harris & Harris, 2021). We then introduce the second of our data visualisations, the ACE Matrix, and discuss its recent development (again, more detail can be found in Harris et al., 2022). Next, we consider the ways these tools have been received by the research and practitioner community. We have a decade of positive feedback on the clinical and research utility of the LHP and consider what opportunities lie ahead. The ACE Matrix launched in early 2022 and has already captured the attention of practitioners working in child safety and youth justice. Finally, we propose some fruitful directions for further interdisciplinary collaboration that have the potential to propel the DLC field forward.

The Life History Plot

The Life History Plot (LHP; Harris, 2013) visually depicts the temporal ordering of criminologically relevant life events. Users can plot the details of an individual's officially recorded offending (such as criminal charges, age of onset, and criminal career length) against other relevant life events including military service, marriage/s, parenthood, and employment. Each event can be observed in context and compared to other events that may have preceded, followed, or co-occurred with it.

An example LHP is shown in Figure 5.1 to give a sense of the visual output. It is designed to suit the "use cases" (the categories of uses with associated contexts) such as being easily printable for use in prison environments where portable technology might be excluded. The plots themselves encode significant quantities of information representing type, number, severity, and time of reported criminal behaviour along with key life events, and custody,

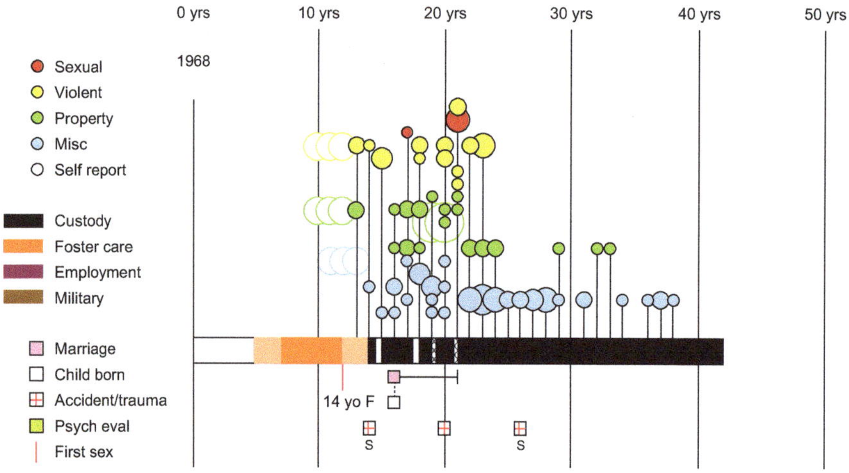

Figure 5.1 An example LHP for a 43-year-old man who was incarcerated for a sexually motivated homicide at age 21. In a single image we can see that he spent several years in alternative accommodation (including foster care), his adolescent onset of violent and versatile offending, his frequent stints in custody, and short marriage that produced one child, born when he was 16. It is also clear that although his adjustment to prison was initially marked by multiple infractions for violence and property crime, his antisocial behaviour de-escalated in seriousness, and he has not been written up (or received any disciplinary reports) for anything in five years.

caregiving, and employment circumstances. The plots are intended to be used as a shorthand for experts to gain a high-level summary of an offender's history, with some salient details, or as a tool for discussion between a clinician and client (or researcher and participant). This level of detail has proven warranted and fit-for-purpose.

The ACE Matrix

The ACE Matrix (Harris et al., 2022) is a new visualisation model that we developed to account for and describe the temporal ordering of ACEs. Developed by the CDC almost 25 years ago, the ACE checklist was a pioneering measure of childhood adversity and continues to be used widely across the world. It features a list of ten types of abuse, neglect, and other measures of household dysfunction and generates a single score out of ten that reflects the reported presence or absence of that experience – ever – prior to the individual's 18th birthday. The ACE Matrix extends our understanding of these adversities experienced during childhood by plotting the onset, duration, and temporal ordering of several early developmental experiences known to be empirically correlated with subsequent involvement in the justice system (discussed in Chapter 10, this volume). The ACE Matrix elucidates this information by zooming in at an individual level and plotting the ACEs over time, in one-year increments, until arrest.

Unlike the more organic conception of the LHP, the ACE Matrix was created very deliberately as an integrated application of graphic design and data visualisation principles and processes to the DLC-inspired research question: can we account for the nature and extent of ACEs over time? (Harris & Harris, 2021; Harris et al., 2022). Through the development of the ACE Matrix using well-tested principles of design processes, we not only developed an effective representational schema but were able to interrogate the data more deeply. This has led to a more nuanced understanding of the dataset, and the ACE checklist itself, in addition to providing a simpler means for drawing narrative conclusions from the data.

To build the Matrix we purposively selected 20 cases with the highest ACE scores (from a sample of more than 400 young men adjudicated for sexual offences). This approach was consistent with the foundations of DLC (Blumstein et al., 1986; LeBlanc & Frechette, 1989) and followed Patton's (2002) "extreme or deviant case" sampling strategy (p. 242). Participant files were coded to capture the known presence of each ACE at any time prior to the participant's referral.

As an example for reference, we present an ACE Matrix in Figure 5.2 with a key to the residential instability shading.

Interpretation of an Example ACE Matrix

Figure 5.2 presents the ACE Matrix. The 18 columns of the Matrix represent 12-month periods in the young person's life, with a solid circle appearing in rows corresponding to the reported presence of that ACE at that age.

The client represented in Figure 5.2 had an ACE checklist score of 9 (i.e., was reported to have been subject to at least one occurrence of each of the 9 ACEs by the age of 18 years). However, knowing a total ACE score reveals little about the history of the case and masks potentially important details such as the timing or frequency of these experiences across the life-course. Using this visualisation schema, we can see at once the nature and extent of adversity to which he was exposed and "zoom in" to examine the onset, duration, and temporal ordering of those adversities.

The column shading (residential instability) provides a tool for rapidly identifying his experience of co-occurring ACEs. This case illustrates the utility of the tool for instances in which a high ACE score by itself occludes any detailed understanding of the life-course. It also brings to the fore the temporality of ACEs and how they are strongly connected with changes in caregiving and residence.

Through the process of prototyping the ACE Matrix and classifying cases using existing variables, we revealed some shortcomings in the level of details

	0*	1	2	3	4	5	6	7	8	9	10	11	12	13	14	15	16	17
CG inco							●	●	●	●	●	●	●	●	●	●	●	●
Emo A							●											
Phys A							●					●		●		●		
Sex A						●												
Neglect	●	●	●	●	●	●	●			●	●							
DFV										●	●							
Subst	●	●	●	●	●	●	●								●	●		
MH	●	●	●	●	●	●	●											
Separ							●											
Incarc							●									●		

*age in years

	Living with at least one biological parent or kinship care
	Foster care
	Residential care, crisis accommodation, shelter, transient
	Custody
●	Presence of ACE in 12-month period

Figure 5.2 An example ACE Matrix with the shading key for residential instability. Note: Columns are labelled by the age (in years) at which the factor was reported to be present. Row labels in the Matrix indicate, in order: Caregiver Inconsistency (CG inco), Emotional Abuse (Emo A), Physical Abuse (Phys A), Sexual Abuse (Sex A), Neglect, Domestic, or Family Violence (DFV), Parental Substance Abuse (Subst), Parental Mental Health Diagnosis (MH), Parental Separation (Separ), Parental Incarceration (Incarc).

contained in the files. For example, based on the information available, we decided to collapse "emotional neglect" and "physical neglect" into a single item (Harris et al., 2022; Pammenter et al., 2022). Second, based on the depth of information available on family circumstances, out-of-home care, and caregiver continuity, we incorporated "caregiver inconsistency" and "residential instability" as additional important and potentially adverse life events that might also be highly relevant in the development of offending pathways. We discuss each one briefly.

Caregiver inconsistency was included as a variable and is represented in the top row of Figure 5.2. Caregiver inconsistency was coded dichotomously for each 12-month interval. Endorsing this item represented credible evidence of a transition in primary caregiver during that year. The measure was intended to create a visual impression of the number of different adults responsible for the primary care of the participants over their development and therefore does not capture the actual number of changes in caregiver in any given year.

Residential instability was also included as a variable and is represented by the progressively darker shading of cells across the entire matrix (Figure 5.2). Based on the literature on out-of-home care, and in consultation with several front line child safety officers, we arrived at four mutually exclusive response options representing progressive levels of seriousness: (1) living at home with at least one biological parent or in kinship care; (2) living in foster care; (3) living in residential care, crisis accommodation/shelter, or transient; and (4) custody/detention. We employed a hierarchical approach to their classification and note that although this scale is imperfect, we attempted to find a balance between a detailed description of the data and a visual presentation simple enough to be comprehended effectively.

The ACE Matrix itself was designed to be created using commonly available word processing or spreadsheet applications such as Microsoft Word or Excel. Although these might not easily provide the most visually appealing visualisations, they are effective from the perspectives of pragmatic interaction design (Cooper et al., 2014, p.171) and situated action (Suchman, 1987) as they are easily and rapidly created with tools that are likely to be available readily. They can easily be copied into other documents and styled to match the destination document in a straightforward way, obviating specialised graphic design skills. The visualisations can be reproduced in greyscale without any loss of information and are accessible to those with colour-vision deficiencies. In this example, darker shades indicate approximately escalating intensities of residential instability. Although the attention to accessibility, in both practical usage and human needs dimensions, might not seem particularly remarkable, it arises naturally as a fundamental value in human-centred design and is standard practice for designers, while typically is incorporated by those in the non-design research community only in a far more *ad hoc* manner.

Reflections

The use cases for the LHPs and ACE Matrixes are different although overlapping. Both tools' use cases include helping researchers achieve different understandings of a person's development and aiding clinicians to quickly gain an overview of a client's life-course, albeit in different circumstances. The LHPs additionally find use as a tool for clinicians when working with clients. It has reportedly been useful to present the plot to a client and use it as a visual aid to spark discussion, seek clarity on the timing and frequency of occasions, and to jog the client's memory on the temporal ordering of events. ACE Matrixes are similarly useful as an aid to communication and discussion among researchers, clinicians, and stakeholders, particularly in drawing out relevant life history events that would be hidden behind the oversimplicity of a dichotomous ACE checklist score.

The use of these tools for stakeholder engagement emerged as both a consequence and a driver of the design choices made during the iterative process of developing the ACE Matrix. The development of the tool revealed ways in which narratives could be discovered and then expressed effectively for different audiences. Critical for the usefulness of these tools is their positioning as data visualisations rather than infographics, to employ Cairo's (2016) formulation. Specifically, infographics primarily intend to communicate one or more specific messages, whereas data visualisations are displays of data designed to enable analysis, exploration, and discovery. Adopting this perspective during their development meant that these tools are suited for discovery and not only for communication.

Having a designer as part of this collaborative process allowed for an externalisation and conscious consideration of the criminologist's user experience when creating and employing the plots. Designers typically have expertise in usability, which in this case applies not only to the end users of the visualisations but also to criminologists as creators of them. In other words, usability considerations are applied in service of criminologists' translational work needs. The validation and affirmation by the designer of the importance of researcher-side usability provides a kind of permission for the researcher to arrive at and accept visualisation solutions that diverge from the norms of the research field.

Additionally, the separation of perspective and skills of the collaborators meant that the designer could continually ask questions of the criminologist that aided in turning the tools into drivers for a variety of applications through continued application of human-centred design principles. Sometimes this was as simple as repeatedly asking "what story do you want to tell?" and "who is your audience?", but also more deeply interrogative concerns such as "how will you obtain this data?" and "how can you extract that data in a form suitable for this kind of representation?" Although these are questions at the core of all research communication, they are inherent in the perspective and agenda of designers in a way that might not be the case for all researchers.

We have alluded to design frameworks, perspectives, and methods in a variety of ways in the discussion so far without specifying in detail many particularities. This is partly due to space constraints but also because design methods are not prescriptive. However, the central concern of the method is to iterate on possible solutions considering the needs of all stakeholders, including the researcher and designer, testing each iteration to inform the next.

In practice, designers tend to develop bespoke methodologies through experience, informed by a blending of well-established frameworks. A more detailed discussion of relevant design methodologies to this kind of work is included in Harris and Harris (2021). The core message arising from the history of interdisciplinary collaboration with design in general and our own experience is that the application of design methodologies is a developed skill that cannot be mastered only through a design thinking workshop or bootcamp. Although those processes are valuable in helping researchers understand how designers approach problem-solving from different perspectives, the brief engagements with process can leave the impression that design methodologies offer a prescription to "innovate your business in these seven easy steps," to crib from typical marketing materials for design thinking courses. It is precisely the nature of design that there are not linear steps, nor are they necessarily easy as they rely on the mindsets of iteration, empathy, making, creative confidence, learning from failure, optimism, and embracing ambiguity, to list those core to IDEO's approach to human-centred design (2015).

One of these mindsets is particularly worth calling out in the context of this work: Empathy. Empathy refers here to gaining an understanding that considers the experiences and needs of those being designed for and with. The stakeholders in this design process are quite varied including the criminologist collaborator, other researchers, clinicians, funders, policy makers, and of course clients with lived experience. As much as designers espouse their values of empathy, there also appears to be significant self-delusion in the field with failed design projects left in the wake of mistaken beliefs in their success at empathetic engagement. The extended two-way engagement of criminologist and designer is a valuable resource that is less easily replicated in a drop-in collaborative model, although designers have developed processes that aim to make the process efficient. In particular, the criminologist has invested significant time in explaining and contextualising the needs and experiences of all the relevant stakeholders to the designer, while the designer has applied their toolkit to propose and iterate on a vast number of potential approaches to specific problems in criminology. So, although the designer has not spent time with all the stakeholders themselves, there is an operational and effective "received empathy" available to the designer due to a well-developed trust and commitment to collaboration by both parties. However, there is importantly a continued check for coherence with needs and experience via the criminologist understanding the design perspective to avoid self-delusions of "empathy."

This collaboration has led to what is effectively an internalised social semiotic framework (Aiello, 2020) for data visualisation through the interplay of criminology and design perspectives. We do not wish to imply that the kind of work described here can only come from long-term collaboration, although increasing time spent in collaboration deepens possibilities and makes processes either more efficient or effective. But from this extended experience we can identify the features of collaboration that have been effective and can provide potential shortcuts for others.

We have found a useful framing of collaboration that suits our purposes within the typology of Harris (2022). The typology describes six key archetypes of collaboration between creative artists and scientists, based on a set of 18 descriptive dimensions of collaboration. Within that framework, our collaboration is of the "Labour Distribution" type, described as:

> *Collaborators find that they can achieve their individual aims effectively by working together. The kinds of work that the collaborators do might be quite disjoint on a day-to-day level, applying their own discipline knowledge to their components of the work, but which are conducted in cooperation and consultation with each other.*

Some of the defining dimensions of this archetype include the following: joint initiation of the project; different but compatible goals of the collaborators; the scientist has institutional funding/support; the attribution of outcomes is varied; and the individual project duration is best measured on a timescale of months.

Understanding the nature of the collaborative effort within Harris' (2022) typology can help guide us to consider what is effective in similar types of collaboration and what might be adopted and adapted in similar interdisciplinary collaborative efforts, even when involving disciplines other than design and criminology.

We do not wish to give the impression that visualisations can only be prepared via the collaboration of a researcher and a designer. As the collaborative effort has been concerned with an outcome that is usable by researchers by themselves, the particular tools of the Life History Plot and ACE Matrix can be used by the researcher alone but might be more efficient in some cases with the aid of a designer. The development or modification of the tools would certainly benefit from a collaboration such as the one recounted here.

Future Directions

In the decade since the LHPs were conceived, the range of visualisation tools available and their sophistication has increased markedly. A refreshing or redesign of the LHPs would make use of many new options although some of the core requirements of the originals remain. So far, we have not given in to the allure of interactive, screen-based visualisations, which is undeniable and can be of great value to researchers if well designed. Such an interactive version could feature options to select or hide various domains (such as to show only sexual offences, hide arrests that did not progress to prosecution, or show only formal marriages and hide co-habitation, and so on). This could also allow for the magnification of sections of the plot, "to inspect a sequence of closely-packed events" (Maltz & Mullany, 2000, p. 277). A prior design constraint has been the restriction in custodial facilities of electronic devices that might facilitate interactive visualisation. However, we note that the sharp uptick in lifting of that restriction during the COVID-19 global pandemic makes the use of these visualisations more relevant. These changing contexts and new potential use cases warrant a re-examination of the LHPs, but again relying on the subject matter expertise of both criminologist and interactive designer.

Similarly, the ACE Matrix could become an interactive visualisation in which individual circles in the Matrix could be clicked on or activated to show the relevant parts of case history documents to help the researcher dig deeper into the life history, for example. These kinds of interactive visualisations can be used for data interrogation and are well within technological capability but are still relatively labour intensive to construct. Whether the utility justifies the cost deserves careful consideration.

A more quotidian intermediate step to fully automated interrogation of the data is simply technologically assisted preparation of the visualisations. An easy-to-use interface would allow researchers to prepare these visualisations more easily with no explicit designer assistance. However, those tools are also time-consuming and challenging to make truly usable, in line with what we all observe in software that never quite does what we need, the way we need it to. At this point, the designer has created computer-assisted tools that make the production of these specific visualisations more efficient, but they still require a certain expertise to use effectively.

Making data collection and coding somewhat automated seems increasingly feasible due to advances in natural language processing (in which information would be extracted directly from narrative case reports and include semantic analysis and discourse analysis). These possibilities have been increasingly enabled by recent machine learning techniques such as by the Large Learning Model (LLM) and ChatGPT3 (OpenAI, 2023). In a more speculative direction, future machine learning/algorithmic/artificial intelligence techniques might be able to extract potentially unnoticed patterns from the raw case reports. Those discovered patterns might be best communicated via visualisations. Such techniques would need to be developed cautiously to avoid many of the known issues, such as obscured biases, non-transparent algorithms, and unethical use of data, that come with injudicious use of these emerging technologies. If such avenues were pursued, criminologists, designers, technologists, and technology ethicists would be essential collaborators. Given the nature of such work, appropriate design methodologies would need to be adopted, perhaps incorporating steps or methods that strongly centre values (human, societal, etc.) Nilsson and Jahnke's (2018) norm-critical and norm-creative design steps provide means to interrogate social norms, socially constructed mental models, outlooks, and values and then design to accommodate or counteract such norms in line with a value set.

If a creative artist in collaboration with a criminologist is given the agency and resources to think and experiment even more broadly about potentials for addressing the needs of DLC or other stakeholders, a vast variety of creative and technological tools become available. On the process approach, positioning the collaboration within the other archetypes of collaboration (Harris, 2022) could allow for the achievement of different types of goals, whether more communication- and outreach-oriented, more exploratory, and speculative problem-finding and problem-solving, or via a freer and more opportunistic wandering through possibility space to come upon approaches less constrained by immediate concrete goals. Regarding technologies and outputs, there is much potential for using interactive technologies, including immersive or location-, time-, and history-based experiences, extended realities (virtual reality/augmented reality), design futures, and speculative design. Although beyond the scope of this chapter to discuss, based on brief ideation exercises we can see all those technologies having reasonably immediate application to core issues in DLC.

As visual criminology progresses, and the expertise of creative artists beyond "pretty-making" is further incorporated, there is much potential for the collaboration of researchers and practitioners in these fields to generate novel, interesting, and useful tools, outputs, and outcomes that would not otherwise be possible.

References

Aiello, G. (2020). Visual semiotics: Key concepts and new directions. In L. Pauwels & D. Mannay (Eds.), *The SAGE handbook of visual research methods*. London: SAGE.

Blumstein, A., Cohen, J., Roth, J., & Visher, C. (1986). *Criminal careers and career criminals*. Washington, DC: National Academy Press.

Cairo, A. (2016). *The truthful art: Data, charts, and maps for communication*. San Francisco: New Riders.

Cooper, A. et al. (2014). *About face: The essentials of interaction design*. Indianapolis: Wiley.

Francis, B., & Pritchard, J. (1998). Bertin, lexis and the graphical representation of event histories. *Bull. Comite Francais de Cartographie*, *156*, 80–87.

Harris, D. A. (2013, January). Using Life History Plots to visualize criminal careers. *Criminal Justice Review*, *38*(1), 94–109. https://doi.org/10.1177/0734016812463729.

Harris, D. A., & Harris, D. J. (2021). Visualising criminology with the life history plot. In J. Wheeldon (Ed.), *Visualisation of criminological data* (pp. 118–138). New York: Routledge.

Harris, D. A., Ogilvie, J., Thomsen, L., Barton, J., Rynne, J., & O'Leary, P. (2022). *Exploring the onset, duration, and temporal ordering of adverse childhood experiences in young people adjudicated for sexual offences: A longitudinal qualitative study* (Research report, 07/2022). Australia's National Research Organisation for Women's Safety (ANROWS).

Harris, D. J. (2022). Collaborating with algae (and humans), SPECTRA 2022 conference, Melbourne.

IDEO.org. (2015). *The field guide to human-centered design: Design kit.* Retrieved from http://www.designkit.org//resources/1.

LeBlanc, M., & Frechette, M. (1989). *Male criminal activity from childhood through youth: Multilevel and developmental perspectives.* New York: Springer-Verlag.

Maltz, M. (1998). Visualizing homicide: A research note. *Journal of Quantitative Criminology*, *15*(4), 397–410.

Maltz, M. (2010). Look before you analyze: Visualizing data in criminal justice. In A. Piquero & D. Weisburd (Eds.), *Handbook of quantitative criminology* (pp. 25–52). New York: Springer Science.

Maltz, M., & Mullany, J. (2000). Visualizing lives: New pathways for analyzing life course trajectories. *Journal of Quantitative Criminology*, *16*(2), 255–281.

Nilsson, Å. W., & Jahnke, M. (2018). Tactics for norm-creative innovation. *She Ji: The Journal of Design, Economics, and Innovation*, *4*(4), 375–391. https://doi.org/10.1016/j.sheji.2018.11.002.

Open, A. I. (2023). ChatGPT. Retrieved March 12, 2023, from https://chat.openai.com.

Pammenter, A., Woodford, E., & Harris, D. A. (2022). Adverse childhood experiences in Australian youth adjudicated for sexual offences and non-sexual violent offences. *Child Abuse and Neglect, 129*, 105678.

Patton, M. Q. (2002). Qualitative research and evaluation methods (3rd ed.). Thousand Oaks, CA: Sage Publications.

Suchman, L. (1987). *Plans and situated actions: The problem of human-machine communication.* Cambridge MA: Cambridge University Press.

Wheeldon, J., & Harris, D. A. (2015). Expanding visual criminology: Definitions, data, and dissemination. *Current Issues in Criminal Justice*, *27*(2), 141–162.

Chapter 6

The Life Event Calendar Methodology

Challenges and Considerations for DLC Research

Li Eriksson, Susan Dennison, Chantelle Baguley, Krystal Lockwood, Paul Mazerolle, and Tara Renae McGee

Introduction

Prospective longitudinal studies are considered the gold standard for DLC scholars. However, some topics may not lend themselves well to a prospective longitudinal methodology, particularly those with relatively low incidence rates within the population. In addition, prospective longitudinal research designs are not always possible due to the significant cost and time associated with data collection. Further, longitudinal administrative data is often absent of sufficiently rich information to explore causal mechanisms. When facing the above constraints, an alternative method is the life event calendar approach, also referred to as life history calendars, event history calendars, and life chart interviews. This methodology has gained much traction in recent decades as a method of collecting life history information (DeHart, 2021; Horney et al., 1995; Roberts & Horney, 2010; Sutton, 2010) because it overcomes many of the practical challenges associated with prospective longitudinal designs.

While every study using life event calendars is unique in its implementation, we propose the approach as a useful, alternative method for collecting data to examine within-individual change across time, as well as between-group differences. In this chapter we discuss the application of the life event calendar approach to two important topics: lethal violence and maternal incarceration. Additionally, we demonstrate how the approach has been used by scholars to address DLC research questions. We draw on our own application of the calendar method as part of two projects conducted at Griffith University in Australia, namely with homicide offenders in the "Australian Homicide Project"[1] and with mothers in prison in the "Maternal Incarceration Project."[2] We discuss challenges and benefits associated with this methodology and identify potential strategies to help DLC researchers incorporating life event calendars into their own research methodology toolbox.

Life Event Calendars: Background and Benefits

DLC researchers increasingly use life event calendars to explore aspects of offending behaviour over time (Bellair et al., 2018; Caspi et al., 1996; Horney et al., 1995; Laub & Sampson, 2003; Simpson et al., 2016). The first appearance

DOI: 10.4324/9781003294740-6

of this methodology in criminology by Julie Horney, Wayne Osgood, and Ineke Marshall was based on their 1995 study of offending change and local life circumstances of over 650 male prisoners in the United States (Horney et al., 1995). This important study illuminated the value, flexibility, and practicality of employing life event history calendars to explore variability of offending and precursors of offending over time. Since then, life event calendars have been used in a variety of research settings and for a variety of important topics.

One of the most-cited rationales for using life event calendars is increased data collection accuracy. People who encounter the criminal justice system often have impaired cognitive capacities due to, for example, prolonged exposure to substances or experiences of traumatic life events. Further, their lives may be unstable, chaotic, and complex, with widespread experiences of homelessness and frequent contact with social service agencies. The calendar approach represents an ideal tool for use in research with people who encounter the criminal justice system, as it has been shown to improve memory retrieval (Axinn et al., 2020; Belli et al., 2001; Engel et al., 2001). As illustrated by Belli (1998), life event calendars tap into both the temporal and thematic aspects of memory. Temporally, such calendars evoke memories of specific events that occurred at specific times, and the timeline, or chronology, of events. Thematically, calendars allow respondents to recall events across different life domains that occurred around the same time.

Accuracy is further enhanced given the conversational and collaborative nature of the interview process, through which the interviewer can probe and clarify responses and resolve any potential discrepancies immediately (Morselli et al., 2016). The collaborative approach enhances rapport building which in turn fosters respondents' willingness to participate in the data collection process, which helps assure the production of meaningful and accurate data (Belli & Callegaro, 2009; Engel et al., 2001; Roberts & Horney, 2010; Sutton et al., 2011). The conversational and collaborative nature further appears to make it a relatively enjoyable experience for both interviewers and respondents compared with traditional question-answer interviews (Stafford & Belli, 2009).

However, life event calendars are not only used because they provide more accurate data or because they are "enjoyable." One of the most important reasons for using life event calendars is that the data produced can assist in answering research questions about offending trajectories, change or stability across time, and how life events and circumstances shape developmental risk. This is because such calendars allow researchers to retrospectively place events in temporal sequences across units of time. In this chapter, we discuss how we implemented the tool in our projects.

Applying the Life Event Calendar Approach

There are notable projects where this methodology has been used previously to answer DLC-related questions (see, e.g., Bellair et al., 2018; Simpson et al., 2016), but due to space constraints we cannot describe these here in any detail. We instead focus on two of our own projects where we implemented the calendar methodology. Both projects were grappling with how to measure change over time in individuals using retrospective data designs and decided to implement life event calendars to overcome these challenges. The implementation occurred at a time when the method was becoming increasingly prevalent within criminology. We were fortunate to have international colleagues with experience in using the method with whom we could consult. We hosted a series of visits from international scholars well-versed in using the approach, namely Julie Horney, Wayne Osgood, and Sally Simpson. We also collaborated with a number of DLC and corrections colleagues at the Netherlands Institute for the Study of Crime and Law Enforcement (NSCR) who had adopted calendars in their research. We were also guided by the growing body of scholarly literature, including two seminal reviews of the method (Roberts & Horney, 2010; Sutton, 2010).

In the Australian Homicide Project (AHP), calendars were implemented as part of face-to-face interviews with 302 men and women convicted of murder or manslaughter. With the aim of improving our understanding of the pathways to homicide, respondents were asked about their developmental backgrounds and the situational aspects of the homicide they committed (Eriksson et al., 2021; Mazerolle et al., 2015). Interviews lasted approximately 2–3 hours and were conducted within custodial (and some community) corrections. The Maternal Incarceration Project (MIP) focuses on children's exposure to risk prior to, and during, maternal incarceration. Though the project is ongoing, having been paused due to restricted access to correctional facilities during the COVID-19 pandemic, 65 face-to-face interviews were conducted with mothers in prison during 2019–2020. Each interview lasted approximately 2–2.5 hours. Below we detail some of the logistical, administrative, and design considerations for the implementation of life event calendars into the methodology of these projects.

Data Collection

Within both projects, data were collected in custodial facilities, and the security arrangements in place affected the data collection methods used. Importantly, both projects used paper-based, rather than computer-based, calendars, as the use of electronic equipment by researchers was not permitted. The MIP project, however, was allowed to audio-record the interviews, which aided in verification of interviewer notes. Further, seating arrangements were carefully considered. Given that side-by-side seating fosters a collaborative approach between interviewers and respondents (Martyn & Martin, 2003; Yoshihama & Bybee, 2011), MIP interviewers were seated perpendicular to the respondents, near the corner of a table. This meant respondents could view the full calendar and work together with the interviewer in filling it out, thus sharing a common goal. Such arrangements were not possible in the AHP, given the high-security restrictions for homicide offenders. Instead, AHP interviewers sat across from the respondents and provided a simplified version of the calendar to the interviewee to facilitate understanding of the timeline.

Administration of the Calendar

In both projects, the calendars were used as part of a longer interview. The MIP interviews started with a survey to collect background and demographic information. Given the focus on children's experiences of maternal incarceration, the interviewer also established the "focal" child. The calendar information was gathered across the life of the focal child. The first part of the interview in the MIP collected information about the primary caregiver of the focal child, income, financial stress, and welfare measures for the period immediately prior to incarceration and information about the current incarceration period. The remainder of the survey, with a focus on the current health and wellbeing of the focal child, was completed after the calendar. In the AHP, the calendar section was preceded by a series of demographic and relationship questions, as well as scales to measure attitudes, criminal involvement, drug and alcohol use, self-control, and more. The section immediately following the life event calendar consisted of open-ended questions about the situational aspects (e.g., what, how, why) of the homicide. Gathering contextual and background information prior to commencing the calendars aided the interviewer in both projects to tailor relevant prompts and likely created a better experience for participants. As such, it is recommended that researchers gather essential information (likely in a structured format) prior to completing calendars, particularly in relation to key timelines, key people, and key events relevant to the focus and objectives of the life events calendar.

Calendar Timeframe

The projects used varying timeframes for the calendar. The MIP focused on the time from the birth of the focal children (i.e., a child between 5 and 17 years who met the eligibility criteria and was next to have a birthday) to the time of the interview. Because the time period could be as long as 18 years an annual calendar was used. The AHP focused on the 12 months (monthly calendar) and 7 days (daily calendar) preceding the homicide. The placement of the time unit was the same for both projects, namely on the calendars' horizontal axis, while the domains were placed on the vertical axis. Both projects collected data on the prevalence, frequency, and duration of events located within specific life domains.

Our Experiences Using Life Event Calendars: Challenges and Benefits

Improved Accuracy

Though neither project specifically aimed to examine the reliability and/or validity of life event calendars, anecdotal evidence from the interviewers suggests that the accuracy of data collection was improved through the use of this method. The calendar structure (even the simplified calendar used in the AHP study) appeared to be especially useful, with interviewers noting that respondents would gesticulate (e.g., point) towards the calendar while establishing when events occurred along the timeline. The calendar was also particularly useful for retrieving memories of events located at the same timepoint but across domains (so-called "parallel memory retrieval"; see Belli, 1998). For example, when asked about living arrangements, one AHP respondent referred to his work situation and noted that he moved houses because he started a new job. In this way, the respondent moved across parallel domains (housing and work) that occurred around the same time.

Positive Interviewer Experiences

Many of the interviewers found it a relatively enjoyable method of collecting data. Across both projects, interviewers had undergone a series of training workshops to ensure proficiency in completing the calendar. Despite extensive training, several of the interviewers reported feeling nervous prior to entering the field. However, after some time in the field, many interviewers reported that the calendar allowed for a relatively conversational interview format, despite its seemingly inflexible and overwhelming appearance. Moreover, the conversational nature allowed for a gentler and less rigid style of interviewer probing across domains and across time, either as verification of previously recorded data or as a means of reconciling discrepancies in interviewer responses.

Positive Respondent Experiences

The calendar format helped overcome the impersonal and restrictive format often associated with surveys, which can be especially problematic when interviewing individuals about stressful life events. People who participated in our studies did so because they wanted to share their stories, and the calendar allowed for them to provide chronological accounts of their lives. The mothers who participated in the MIP provided accounts of pathways into prison that were often long and marred by trauma, victimisation, substance use, disadvantage, and ongoing challenges with mental health. Although the events leading up to incarceration were certainly different for the men and women who participated in AHP compared with the mothers, their accounts also contained descriptions of substance use, mental health challenges, and trauma. While it was challenging for some participants to see their complex lives mapped out in black and white, many found completing the calendar to be a positive experience. To illustrate, in one of the interviews, one mother said "[completing the calendar] actually made me feel like I'm not that bad of a parent. Because when you put it in a timeline it's only like the past like 3.5 years and there's major reason for that, so I see that before that, like [daughter] lived a very good life, probably doesn't help her now (laughs a little) but you know like I was a good mother right up until that point. And even with a few of the questions, like it did make me see that, yes, I am a good mother when I'm present, I'm just not present. So, yeah, it was good." Nevertheless, given the complex and difficult topics covered, it was important for the interviewer to monitor and be responsive to the participant's wellbeing throughout the interview.

Time Restrictions

One main challenge for interviewers, especially in the MIP with its partial focus on experiences of the mother's victimisation during the focal child's life, was how to move respondents along to the next question when they were in the midst of discussing significant trauma. While the flexible nature of the calendar facilitated a more conversational style of interviewing, it also meant longer interviews were necessary. However, given that our projects focused on respondents currently incarcerated, we were limited in terms of the time allocated to us.

Interviewer Attentiveness and Recollection

An additional challenge was the necessity for interviewers to remember significant amounts of information from the beginning of the interview to be used in the calendar section. For example, in the AHP study, information about the respondent's life circumstances at the time of committing the homicide was used to initiate the conversation about change over time (e.g., "you mentioned earlier that at the time of the homicide you were living in a rental property, for how long had you lived there?"). To assist interviewers, the AHP study used a "prompt" sheet, which interviewers filled out in addition to the interview schedule, to be used during the calendar section. In the MIP, administering the calendar required interviewers to be agile and to retain extensive information about time periods. For example, because the MIP covered an extensive time period, it was often necessary to pause and cross-check information across domains to ensure consistency when allocating events to years (e.g., experiences of domestic violence, hospitalisations, termination of relationships, custody of children, housing moves, and homelessness).

Memory Recall Challenges

Although the calendar method generally aids memory retrieval, both projects interviewed respondents with chaotic and complex lives, many of whom were largely unfamiliar with criminal justice system processes. In the MIP, several respondents reported difficulty with recall as a result of, for example, heavy drug use, or the frequency and intensity of events, such as victimisation and episodic homelessness. While memory recall appeared to be less of a challenge in the AHP study (possibly because of the shorter time period for recall, i.e., months versus years) (Morris & Slocum, 2010; Roberts et al., 2005), interviewers did report some difficulties working out the exact timing of events. This led to the implementation of a variable value to indicate that, although the event had occurred, the exact months could not be established. In these instances, a specified value was inserted across all months affected, with decisions about imputation made during the data analysis phase. Similarly, in the MIP, variation in the specificity of information provided about events that occurred each year posed challenges for data entry and analyses. Prompting for further information on the frequency and duration of events did not always provide additional clarity.

Challenges of Data Entry

With over thousands of individual data points, data entry was an enormous task across both projects. To minimise data entry time and effort, the AHP team created a syntax for those events which respondents reported as stable over time (or, alternatively, events that did not occur within the specified timeframe). To illustrate, for respondents reporting no job loss during the calendar timeframe, a syntax was run that automatically filled the 19 individual data points (12 months + 7 days) for that particular life event. Based on the experiences of the AHP and MIP, data entry and cleaning tasks require a senior research assistant with significant experience working with complex datasets and the capacity to attend to detail in documenting decision-making rules regarding the interpretation and recording of events that may span vague timeframes rather than specific months or years or that occurred with uncertain frequency.

Choosing Analytical Technique

Since life event calendars allow researchers to retrospectively place significant life events in temporal sequences across units of time, such data can be used to answer DLC-related questions about offending trajectories, change/stability across time, and developmental risks. The challenge here lies not so much in what can be done with the data, as options for methodological approaches are plenty, including (but not limited to) qualitative analyses (e.g., DeHart et al., 2014; Nelson, 2010), descriptive histograms (e.g., Mazerolle et al., 2015), survival analysis (e.g., DeHart et al., 2014), and hierarchical linear modelling (e.g., Horney et al., 1995; Slocum et al., 2005). Rather, the challenge lies in deciding the specific research questions and analytical approach prior to data collection, as the richness and seemingly endless possibilities of the data may distract from the established analytical path, especially for scholars with curious and inquisitive minds.

Normative Experiences and Western Concepts of Time

Beyond practical considerations, it is important for scholars to consider whether the calendar approach is an appropriate tool for the research questions of interest and the population surveyed. As Morselli et al. (2016) point out in their work on vulnerability across the life course, the grid-like style of life event calendars assumes that life has a linear trajectory, and the emphasis on some aspects of life as opposed to others further suggests that some events are normative (and thus key to human development) while others are not. In addition, as Lockwood and colleagues highlight in the next chapter in this book, an alternative to techniques that employ linear Western conceptions of time is to conduct a *life story interview* which while designed within an indigenist framework with the First Nations Peoples of Australia in mind may also have application with appropriate modification for others seeking to deal with the fluidity of memory and the interconnectedness of events in culturally appropriate ways.

Ways Forward: Challenges and Considerations for DLC Research

Life event calendars have clear benefits, especially for researchers interested in examining processes of stability and change over time. The approach enables the examination of dynamic and inter-related sequences over time. For DLC scholars interested in understanding change within individuals over time, life event history calendars provide a great deal of flexibility and practicality. Although the approach has its drawbacks, careful planning and implementation can strengthen the quality of data collected.

The calendar approach can also be adapted to capture cultural specificity across various measurement domains (see Lockwood et al., following chapter). While interviewers require comprehensive training in delivering this measurement approach while maintaining a conversational interaction with the respondent, they will also need to be sensitive to cultural issues in order to decide which mode of interview is most appropriate.

Computer-based life event calendars may simplify data entry (Roberts & Horney, 2010), and open-source software complete with step-by-step instructions is now available to scholars who wish to use such an approach (Wieczorek et al., 2020). However, consideration should be given as to whether responses are likely to neatly fit into pre-ordained categories during computerised administration, or whether flexibility is required during the interview process to account for challenges to event recall across complex lives.

One important challenge for those working in DLC is the need for a shift from the traditional dominance of between-individual data analyses to a better understanding of within-individual changes across the life course. Life event calendars allow for greater within-individual examination of change when using cross-sectional techniques, especially with respect to gauging risk across an individual's social ecology, including individual-, family-, community-, and institutional-level risks. Being able to overlay co-occurring risks and examine processes of offending frequency and duration will help inform theoretical development regarding causal mechanisms for offending persistence and desistance.

There has also been a move towards capturing a better understanding of the role of prosocial behaviours, strength-based approaches, protective factors, and resilience within DLC (e.g., Jolliffe et al., 2016). The focus on "risk," and the largely deficit approach taken in criminology to date, means that in many existing prospectively collected longitudinal data sets, individuals' strengths and protective factors are often not measured or when considered, are conceptualised as the "other end" of a risk variable. Rigorous retrospective data collection of life histories assists in bridging this gap for researchers who may be otherwise reliant on historical prospective longitudinal data or administrative data.

While there are many challenges, both with administration and data analysis, the life event calendar methodology is worthwhile. To ensure that the methodology is employed appropriately and reliably, transparency and information sharing around collection, data entry, and analysis in studies using life event calendars is key. Opportunities to share learnings and improve administration and analytic methodologies could include establishing virtual learning communities or roundtables and workshops at discipline conferences and should be pursued to develop the field.

Notes

1 ARC Discovery Project (DP0878364) Developmental pathways to intimate partner homicide: Understanding individual and situational dimensions. CIs: Mazerolle, P., Wortley, R., & Johnson, H.

2 ARC Discovery Project (DP170100649) *Maternal incarceration: Mechanisms of risk and resilience in children.* CIs: Dennison, S.M., Broidy, L., & Bijleveld, C.C.H.

References

Axinn, W. G., Chardoul, S., Gatny, H., Ghimire, D. J., Smoller, J. W., Zhang, Y., & Scott, K. M. (2020). Using life history calendars to improve measurement of lifetime experience with mental disorders. *Psychological Medicine*, *50*(3), 515–522. https://doi.org/10.1017/S0033291719000394.

Bellair, P. E., Vuolo, M., & LaPlant, E. G. (2018). Frequent drug use and negative employment outcomes among the criminally active. *Substance Use and Misuse*, *53*(5), 828–836. https://doi.org/10.1080/10826084.2017.1388260.

Belli, R. F. (1998). The structure of autobiographical memory and the event history calendar: Potential improvements in the quality of retrospective reports in surveys. *Memory*, 6(4), 383–406. Retrieved from http://www.informaworld.com/10.1080/741942610.

Belli, R. F., & Callegaro, M. (2009). The emergence of calendar interviewing: A theoretical and empirical rationale. In R. F. Belli, F. P. Stafford, & D. F. Alwin (Eds.), *Calendar and time diary*. SAGE Publications, Inc. https://doi.org/10.4135/9781412990295.

Belli, R. F., Shay, W. L., & Stafford, F. P. (2001). Event history calendars and question list surveys. *Public Opinion Quarterly*, *65*(1), 45–74. Retrieved from http://libraryproxy.griffith.edu.au/login?url=http://search.ebscohost.com/login.aspx?direct=true&db=buh&AN=4431870&site=ehost-live&scope=site.

Caspi, A., Moffitt, T. E., Thornton, A., Freedman, D., Amell, J. W., Harrington, H., … Silva, P. A. (1996). The life-history calendar: A research and clinical assessment method for collecting retrospective event-history data. *International Journal of Methods in Psychiatric Research*, 6(2), 101–114.

DeHart, D. (2021). Life history calendar method. In *The encyclopedia of research methods in criminology and criminal justice* (pp. 68–71). https://doi.org/10.1002/9781119111931.ch14.

DeHart, D., Lynch, S., Belknap, J., Dass-Brailsford, P., & Green, B. (2014). Life history models of female offending: The roles of serious mental illness and trauma in women's pathways to jail. *Psychology of Women Quarterly*, *38*(1), 138–151. https://doi.org/10.1177/0361684313494357.

Engel, L. S., Keifer, M. C., & Zahm, S. H. (2001). Comparison of a traditional questionnaire with an icon/calendar-based questionnaire to assess occupational history†. *American Journal of Industrial Medicine*, *40*(5), 502–511. https://doi.org/10.1002/ajim.1118.

Eriksson, L., Bryant, S., McPhedran, S., Mazerolle, P., & Wortley, R. (2021). Alcohol and drug problems among Australian homicide offenders. *Addiction*, *116*(3), 618–631. https://doi.org/10.1111/add.15169.

Horney, J., Osgood, D. W., & Marshall, I. H. (1995). Criminal careers in the short-term: Intra-individual variability in crime and its relation to local life circumstances. *American Sociological Review*, *60*(5), 655–673. Retrieved from http://www.jstor.org/stable/2096316.

Jolliffe, D., Farrington, D. P., Loeber, R., & Pardini, D. (2016). Protective factors for violence: Results from the Pittsburgh Youth Study. *Journal of Criminal Justice*, *45*, 32–40. https://doi.org/10.1016/j.jcrimjus.2016.02.007.

Laub, J. H., & Sampson, R. J. (2003). *Shared beginnings, divergent lives: Delinquent boys to age 70*. Cambridge, MA: Harvard University Press.

Martyn, K. K., & Martin, R. (2003). Adolescent sexual risk assessment. *The Journal of Midwifery and Women's Health*, *48*(3), 213–219. https://doi.org/10.1016/S1526-9523(03)00064-3.

Mazerolle, P., Eriksson, L., Wortley, R., & Johnson, H. (2015). Understanding homicide in Australia: Exploring perpetrator accounts. In A. Day & E. Fernandez (Eds.), *Preventing violence in Australia: Policy, practice and solutions* (pp. 25–44). Annandale: The Federation Press.

Morris, N. A., & Slocum, L. A. (2010). The validity of self-reported prevalence, frequency, and timing of arrest: An evaluation of data collected using a life event calendar. *Journal of Research in Crime and Delinquency*, *47*(2), 210–240. https://doi.org/10.1177/0022427809357719.

Morselli, D., Dasoki, N., Gabriel, R., Gauthier, J.-A., Henke, J., & Le Goff, J.-M. (2016). Using life history calendars to survey vulnerability. In M. Oris, C. Roberts, D. Joye, & M. E. Stähli (Eds.), *Surveying human vulnerabilities across the life course* (pp. 179–201). Berlin: Springer.

Nelson, I. (2010). From quantitative to qualitative: Adapting the life history calendar method. *Field Methods*, *22*(4), 413–428.

Roberts, J. J., & Horney, J. (2010). The life event calendar method in criminological research. In A. Piquero & D. Weisburd (Eds.), *Handbook of quantitative criminology* (pp. 289–312). Berlin: Springer.

Roberts, J., Mulvey, E. P., Horney, J., Lewis, J., & Arter, M. L. (2005). A test of two methods of recall for violent events. *Journal of Quantitative Criminology*, *21*(2), 175–193. Retrieved from http://libraryproxy.griffith.edu.au/login?url=http://proquest.umi.com/pqdweb?did=945098561&Fmt=7&clientId=13713&RQT=309&VName=PQD.

Simpson, S. S., Alper, M., Dugan, L., Horney, J., Kruttschnitt, C., & Gartner, R. (2016). Age-graded pathways into crime: Evidence from a multi-site retrospective study of incarcerated women [journal article]. *Journal of Developmental and Life-Course Criminology*, 1–25. https://doi.org/10.1007/s40865-016-0042-5.

Slocum, L. A., Simpson, S. S., & Smith, D. A. (2005). Strained lives and crime: Examining intra-individual variation in strain and offending in a sample of incarcerated women. *Criminology*, *43*(4), 1067–1110. http://doi.org/10.1111/j.1745-9125.2005.00033.x.

Stafford, F. P., & Belli, R. F. (2009). Future directions in calendar and time diary methods. In R. F. Belli, F. P. Stafford, & D. F. Alwin (Eds.), *Calendar and time diary*. SAGE Publications, Inc. https://doi.org/10.4135/9781412990295.

Sutton, J. E. (2010). A review of the life-events calendar method for criminological research. *Journal of Criminal Justice*, *38*(5), 1038–1044. Retrieved from http://www.sciencedirect.com/science/article/B6V75-50RMPJ0-2/2/4b75b66b7d80e1eedb3c4166a60b6f1c.

Sutton, J. E., Bellair, P. E., Kowalski, B. R., Light, R., & Hutcherson, D. T. (2011). Reliability and validity of prisoner self-reports gathered using the life event calendar method. *Journal of Quantitative Criminology*, *27*(2), 151–173.

Wieczorek, L. L., Tata, C. S., Penke, L., & Gerlach, T. M. (2020). Online implementation of an event history calendar with formr: A tutorial. *Personal Relationships*, *27*(1), 176–208. https://doi.org/10.1111/pere.12305.

Yoshihama, M., & Bybee, D. (2011). The life history calendar method and multilevel modeling: Application to research on intimate partner violence. *Violence Against Women*, *17*(3), 295–308. https://doi.org/10.1177/1077801211398229.

Chapter 7

"Life History Research" with Aboriginal and Torres Strait Islander Peoples

How Indigenous Methodologies Inform Culturally Appropriate Research

Krystal Lockwood, Li Eriksson, Tara Renae McGee, and Sjharn Leeson

Introduction

Racial, ethnic, and cultural minority populations across the world continue to have disproportionally high contact throughout criminal justice systems compared to majority populations (Killias, 2011; Nielsen & Robyn, 2003). These disparities are attributed to colonial and settler-colonial practices, individual and systemic biases, and the impact these practices have on behaviour (Agozino, 2019; Cunneen & Tauri, 2016). Criminal justice inequalities are commonly known, yet race and ethnicity continue to be the "least understood and underexplored correlates of offending" (Piquero, 2015, p.21) in Developmental and Life-Course Criminology (DLC). This is concerning, considering the detrimental impact that criminal justice system interventions have across the life-course, particularly in exacerbating the impacts of intergenerational trauma.

Racial, ethnic, and cultural minority populations have also had challenging and exploitative experiences in research practices (Smith, 2021), particularly criminological research (Cunneen & Tauri, 2016; Yusef & Yusef, 2017). Culturally appropriate methodologies have been used to reframe research to benefit populations that have been exploited by research and gather data in ways that are conducive to the population with whom researchers are engaging (Smith, 2021). Consequently, DLC researchers could develop meaningful outcomes for minority populations by embedding appropriate methodologies. This chapter provides an example of how DLC can apply Indigenous methodologies of First Peoples[1] of Australia. First, we briefly outline who First Peoples are and note research within the scope of DLC, including the role of systemic racism and intergenerational trauma in shaping Indigenous developmental models and offending trajectories. Then we build on Chapter 6 in this volume to critique the use of one specific methodological approach that has been employed by DLC researchers to study offending pathways: life event calendars. We identify the compatibilities and barriers of using life event calendars with Indigenous methodologies and, in so doing, propose

DOI: 10.4324/9781003294740-7

significant amendments to this method to ensure cultural appropriateness when studying the life experiences of First Peoples and how these influence offending trajectories. Importantly, we note the inherent problems with using the term "life event calendar" and propose an alternative term and methodology: "life story interviews." Overall, we demonstrate how DLC researchers can embed culturally appropriate methodologies to more accurately represent how life experiences influence criminal justice system pathways for minority groups in DLC but, more importantly, inform opportunities to address ongoing social justice challenges.

First Peoples of Australia

First Peoples are a distinct population who make up approximately 3.2% of the Australian population (approx. 800,000 people) (Australian Bureau of Statistics, 2022). First Peoples' culture is diverse with people belonging to over 250 different language groups with "numerous groupings, languages, kinships and tribes, as well as ways of living" (Dudgeon et al., 2014, p. xxiv). Although First Peoples have diverse views and values, there has been significant work to build and inform developmental models that reflect the ontologies, epistemologies, and axiologies of First Peoples. Culturally specific determinants of social and emotional wellbeing have been identified and embedded into culturally appropriate service delivery. For example, in Figure 7.1, Gee and colleagues (2014) depict the domains for positive developmental wellbeing for First Peoples. Here, holistic wellbeing is grounded in connections to: body, mind, and emotions; family, Kinships, and community; and spirituality, Land, and culture. These connections are impacted by social determinants (e.g., housing, racial discrimination, education), cultural determinants (e.g., cultural continuity, self-determination), and political determinants (e.g., individual and collective rights of Indigenous peoples). This foundational understanding of context outlines domains for positive development of First Peoples across the life-course and has informed culturally appropriate programmes for different stages of the life-course from the first 1000 days to youth, to adults, to older First Peoples and Elders, and intergenerationally (Dobia & Roffey, 2017; Gibson et al., 2020; Ritte et al., 2016).

There has been limited overlap between DLC and Indigenous worldviews (such as in Gee et al., 2014), yet there has been significant research on First Peoples criminal justice system contact. For example, like other indigenous peoples of settler-colonial countries, First Peoples are over-represented throughout the criminal justice system and are the most incarcerated people in the world (Uluru Statement from the Heart, 2017). First Peoples have significantly different offending trajectories than non-Indigenous people in Australia (Broidy et al., 2015; Ogilvie et al., 2021). Divergent trajectories result from First Peoples' higher exposure to adverse life events and life stressors (Stevens & Paradies, 2014), as well as compounding and

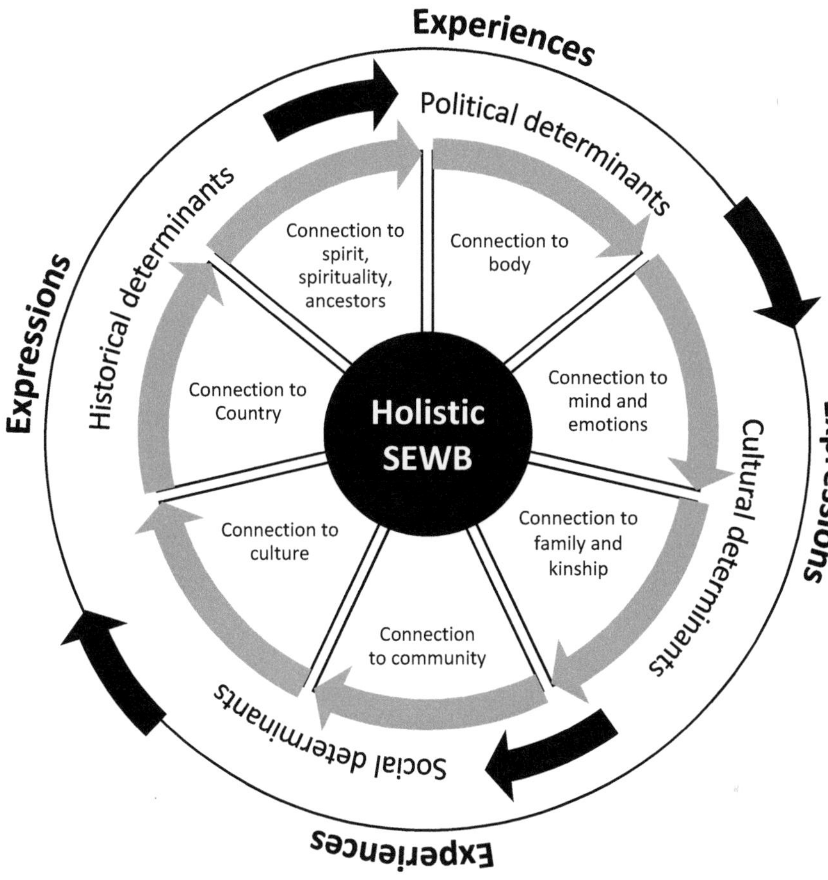

Figure 7.1 Social and emotional wellbeing: Social, cultural, political, and historical contexts (adapted from Gee et al., 2014)

intergenerational entrenchment within the criminal justice system itself, including higher rates of parental incarceration, contact with the system at an earlier age, and longer contact over the life course (Ogilvie et al., 2021; Roettger et al., 2019).

Although there has been a significant volume of work examining First Peoples within a DLC context, a notable and significant limitation is the reliance on administrative data. The primary intent of administrative data is to inform bureaucratic goals, a process that is far removed from Indigenous worldviews. This has resulted in datasets that have been collected "about" First Peoples and set within a deficit-discourse. Walter (2018) has dubbed these "5D Data": data that focus on Difference, Disparity, Disadvantage,

Dysfunction, and Deprivation. Because of the nature of the datasets, there is a lack of strengths-based variables (such as cultural determinants which are protective factors), and limited recognition of Indigenous worldviews.

Embedding First Peoples' social and emotional wellbeing frameworks (such as Figure 7.1) into DLC would have significant research and practical benefits, leading to culturally appropriate practices ranging from understanding offending pathways and how they may be influenced by life experiences and developmental-related factors, to embedding Indigenous social systems and networks into re-integration programmes (Williams, 2015), to embedding cultural factors within risk assessments (Shepard & Lewis-Fernandez, 2016). In the next section, we demonstrate how DLC can bridge this gap by embedding culturally relevant methodologies, using the example of the life story interview. In Chapter 6, Eriksson and colleagues explained and critically evaluated the method of life event calendars. We build from this analysis to demonstrate how this approach can be reimagined using Indigenous methodologies that can inform DLC work and ultimately inform social justice issues.

Questioning the Appropriateness of the Use of Life Event Calendars with Culturally Diverse Groups

Life event calendars (or life history calendars, event history calendars, and life chart interviews) have been used across multiple disciplines to retrospectively collect data about participants' lives. Data is collected using a standardised instrument where the researcher makes key time markers on a calendar. Other retrospective techniques suffer from poor recall; however, life event calendars address this by using significant life events and visual and mental cues (see Chapter 6 for further details).

The life event calendar method has strong evidence of reliability and validity for completeness of recall, consistency (test-retest), and timing of events (such as arrest) (Sutton et al., 2011). However, Sutton and colleagues identified that the impact of racial differences on the reliability and validity of life event calendars remained an unresolved and central issue (Thornberry & Krohn, 2000). From a US sample of persons of African American (43%), Caucasian (55%), and multiracial or Hispanic (2%) descent, Sutton and colleagues found that the test-retest reliability of the data was not impacted by race (nor age, education, legal income, or illegal income). They also argued that there were no differences in comparing the life event calendar's self-reported offending with official offending data, demonstrating strong validity.

However, race is not synonymous with culture. As Smith (2021) notes in her discussion of methodological approaches to research with indigenous peoples, the worldview and cultural context of African American peoples differ substantially from indigenous populations. Moreover, historically similar experiences (Wilkins, 2005) are not sufficient to confer similarity in worldview, as worldview is instead vested in "sets of beliefs and assumptions that describe reality" (Koltko-Rivera, 2004, p. 3). Race, in the way the word is used by Sutton and colleagues (2011), represents membership in a group, as opposed to considerations of participants' cultural context. The latter requires going beyond considerations of validity and reliability in the positivist tradition to include considerations of the cultural appropriateness of the tools, processes, and data to be able to accurately understand the phenomena being investigated (Leung, 2015).

There is limited consideration of life event methodologies in Indigenous research across any discipline. Cooke's (2013) use of a life-course framework with First Nations peoples in Canada explored the effect of early childbearing on the life course and considers the intersection of life-course methodologies and indigeneity (see also Cooke & McWhirter, 2011). After consultation with Elders, Cooke (2013, p.7) developed a "tree" instrument instead of a standard life event calendar. Trees are consistent with Canadian First Nations peoples' views of the life trajectory, where individuals grow in different directions at different times, but their lives are rooted in family and community. The tree contained unique themes centred around health and spirituality, work and education, and family and community, and interviews were mostly conducted by Canadian First Nations peoples. Results suggested that specially designed measures, such as the tree, may be appropriate in completing life-course research with indigenous and minority-status populations.

Although Cooke's (2013) work was promising, there are significant ontological, epistemological, and axiological differences among indigenous communities. If ignored, these can perpetuate deep colonisation and oppression by ignoring the diversity of indigenous peoples' views and values (Rose, 1996). Therefore, the generalisability of Cooke's success should be considered, as we consider this approach for First Peoples in Australia.

First Peoples and Life Event Calendars

In Australia, Human Research Ethics boards ensure research impacting First Peoples considers *cultural safety*, *reciprocity*, *respect*, *equality*, *responsibility*, *survival and protection*, *and spirit and integrity* from project development through to dissemination (National Health and Medical Research Council, 2018). These procedures are founded on principles of Indigenist and Indigenous research (Martin & Mirraboopa, 2003; Moreton-Robinson, 2013; Rigney, 1999; Smith, 2021) which exposed how Western academic scholarship lacked cultural relevance, suppressed indigenous perspectives, and exploited indigenous communities. Indigenist research privileges the goal for self-determination and First Peoples ways of knowing, being, and doing, which disrupts the continued colonisation of knowledge. In this section, we consider four points of consideration when using life event calendars within Indigenist research. To note, our analysis follows principles of "wise practice," which prioritises "locally-appropriate actions, tools, principles or decisions that contribute significantly to the development of sustainable and equitable social conditions" (Wesley-Esquimaux & Calliou, 2010, p.19). In doing so, we acknowledge diverse First Peoples perspectives and that, consequently, meeting Indigenist research principles will differ among projects.

Reframing Research Using Indigenist Approaches

Indigenist approaches reframe research and promote culturally appropriate and non-exploitative processes. In overtly prioritising self-determination, the acquisition of knowledge is *decolonised* where "those who have suffered a long history of oppression and [marginalisation] are given space to communicate from their frames of reference" (Chilisa, 2012, p. 14). This leads to "research at the interface," that "aims to harness the energy from two systems of understanding in order to create new knowledge that can be used to advance understanding in two worlds" (Durie, 2005, p.306). This brings together Western academic scholarship and First Peoples epistemologies, ontologies, and axiologies (Leeson et al., 2016). Here, First Peoples' values and protocols are not just a tool, but valued knowledge systems.

This is a broad but essential step to research that should not only be applied for the use of life event calendars but research in general. In collaboration with First Peoples, researchers should first identify what the community goals of the research are and, importantly, determine whether life event calendars are an appropriate method to achieve these goals. As discussed below, researchers should adapt life event calendars to the participants' worldviews and ensure the data collected represents the participants' lived experiences rather than impose foreign theories and perspectives. Reframed research should do no harm and be meaningful, relevant, practical, and long-term in ways that align with communities' priorities. Research should be led by First Peoples and the focus should be working *with* First Peoples and, rather than objectifying First Peoples, position participants as *knowers* of knowledge. Such practices have been shown to increase First Peoples' wellbeing (Martin & Mirraboopa, 2003; Moreton-Robinson, 2013; Rigney, 1999; Smith, 2021).

First Peoples' Worldview: Perceptions of Time

Researchers must consider whether their methods prioritise Westernised worldviews whilst invalidating different worldviews. For example, perceptions of time can differ between Western and Indigenous cultures. Western Anglophone populations tend to perceive time as linear, structured according to the past, present, and future. First Peoples by contrast are more likely to perceive time as cyclical, rhythmic, and within relational networks and collectivist values (Bohn & Bundgaard-Nielsen, 2021; Janca & Bullen, 2003;

Postill, 2002; Yeo, 2003). First Peoples understand linear concepts of time; however, family and community commitments are valued over scheduled events, at times at the expense of individual commitments (e.g., missing parole appointments to fulfil cultural obligations). These social and cultural differences – especially relational roles – have also been shown to impact autobiographical memory (Bohn & Bundgaard-Nielsen, 2021). A prevailing belief prioritises not *when* things happen, but *that* they happen (Janca & Bullen, 2003). This impacts retrospective accounts of life events which are placed in time according to their relative importance to the individual and their community. More important events are perceived to have occurred more closely in time; irrelevant events occupy a peripheral space in time, although they may have occurred more recently, if subscribing to a linear understanding (Janca & Bullen, 2003).

Differing temporal perceptions may lead to difficulties when using life event calendars which privilege a Westernised linear way of cataloguing events. In the Western imagination events are countable, measurable, and singular rather than interconnected (as depicted in Figure 1). Researchers should engage methods that accord primacy to First Peoples' worldviews, experiences, and recollections. For example, researchers can journey with participants through story and narrative to places associated with the purpose of the research (Bessarab & Ng'andu, 2010; Dean, 2010), deprioritising the Western conception of linear time, to instead focus on lived experience and memory. This mode of communication is supported by the plethora of storied autobiographical narratives by First Peoples in "life writings" (which encompasses diverse mediums of personal narratives) (Griffiths, 2013). Consequently, this reframes both "calendars" and "events" in life event calendars. Therefore, we propose that when working with First Peoples to better understand their lives, a more appropriate mode of engaging is via what we call a "life story interview." A life story interview prioritises narrative accounts which allow First Peoples to provide their own account of events without forcing these accounts into a constricting linear timeline.

Ways of Doing: Yarning

Researchers need to consider whether their ways of interacting with participants are culturally appropriate. Life event calendar research to date has predominantly involved question-answer formats delivered within one sitting over a relatively short period of time (e.g., 1–3 hours). However, such Western modes of scholarship (particularly positivist quantitative research) tend to demand objectivity–research devoid of emotion (Smith, 2021), which invalidates relational values of First Peoples communities and objectifies participants. The Indigenous approach of yarning "reflects a formal process of sharing knowledge that is reliant upon relationships, expected outcomes, responsibility and accountability between the [contributors], country and culture" (Dean, 2010, p. 6). Yarning can be broadly understood as a form of First Peoples cultural conversation that has been adapted to research to create a culturally appropriate environment to gather and collect data (Bessarab & Ng'andu, 2010; Dean, 2010). Conversation shifts through four modalities: (i) *social yarning* builds rapport and trust; (ii) *research topic yarning* is purposeful conversations related to the topic; (iii) *collaborative yarning* provides a space to discuss, validate, and build on research findings; and finally (iv) *therapeutic yarns* may occur where the researcher becomes the listener to emotional stories.

For the life story interview method (in lieu of life event calendar method) to be valid, culturally sensitive, and able to collect valid data that can be used to effect social change, it would need to adhere to cultural expectations of communication. In research development, yarning can guide engagement with First Peoples in developing tools to collect life history information (as done by Cooke, 2013) which allows First Peoples to infuse cultural knowledge within the research (Bessarab & Ng'andu, 2010; Dean, 2010). This instils ownership, provides participants with power over what information is disclosed, and contributes to the generation of knowledge in a culturally appropriate way. As a data collection tool, yarning provides a way to appropriately share and transfer knowledge between participant and researcher (Bessarab & Ng'andu, 2010; Dean, 2010). Researchers are positioned as the *learners* of knowledge and First Peoples as the authority concerning their knowledge. This can assist researchers journey through stories and time as a way to collect data in a culturally appropriate way.

Variables Grounded in Ontologies, Epistemologies, and Axiologies

Finally, researchers need to consider whether the data they are gathering reflect the participant's ontologies, epistemologies, and axiologies. Criticisms of criminological research for First Peoples include the perpetuated deficit-discourse, the use of theories and perspectives that are detached from First Peoples worldview, and the focus of positivist research methodologies that dismiss cultural risk and protective factors (Agozino, 2019; Cunneen & Tauri, 2016; Shepard & Lewis-Fernandez, 2016). This is prevalent in DLC and can be perpetuated with longitudinal secondary data that were not conceptualised or operationalised to consider the lived experiences of First Peoples in a settler-colonial country.

The variables and events included in life story interviews need to be justified. Unlike secondary data analysis, researchers using life story interviews to collect primary data within an iterative framework have the opportunity to identify relevant variables at the outset and identify emerging themes. Therefore, coding books can include culturally relevant domains, such as those in Figure 1 (Gee et al., 2014). To date, life event calendar research predominantly collects person-centric variables, with some projects recording information about children or parents. From a First Peoples perspective, this excludes significant kinship relationships, connection to culture and Country, and how these are interconnected with the individual's wellbeing (Gee et al., 2014). We assert that this can be overcome in our proposed life story interview method, particularly through ways of doing research (e.g., yarning methods) and adapting methods to participants' worldviews (e.g., by considering different concepts of time). There can also be topics participants may, culturally, not be inclined to disclose, such as discussing men's or women's business (roles specific to gender), or someone who has passed away (Glynn-McDonald, n.d). Familiarity with cultural protocols and events would be essential during data collection, where researchers know what to discuss, and can also relate to cultural events to assist in building a participant's life history. These steps would produce more accurate data that would more likely lead to relevant and constructive outcomes.

Conclusion

Racial, ethnic, and cultural minority populations continue to have high contact with criminal justice systems. Although this is well known, DLC (among other areas of criminology) still misunderstands and misrepresents the experiences of minority populations and offending behaviour. In this chapter we provided a worked example of how DLC researchers can improve this research agenda. Focusing on First Peoples in Australia, we outlined steps to adopt life history research within an Indigenist framework. Building on Chapter 6, we demonstrated why and how reconceptualising life event calendars to life story interviews would strengthen outcomes. The Indigenist framework sets priorities from every stage of the research process. Research agendas should be driven by First Peoples, and methods of interacting and data collection should be conducive to the community with whom the researcher is working. Notably, ontologies, epistemologies, and axiologies differ for minority populations around the world (and between First Peoples), so our observations are suggested within a framework of "wise practice." Wise practice allows us to acknowledge that although there are similar issues (e.g., disproportionate contact with the criminal justice system), solutions should be derived from locally appropriate approaches that can empower and give agency to communities. With this in mind, Indigenist research has made considerable impact in reframing research to benefit First Peoples, a minority population that has had an extensive history of being exploited by research practices. DLC can also apply Indigenist frameworks which could not only benefit First Peoples but also lead to more considered research within the field that has the potential to inform effective ways of reducing over-representation in the justice system. Overall, reframing research for racial, ethnic, and cultural minority populations and using culturally appropriate methodologies would greatly improve the relevance and accuracy of DLC research and would also help to address ongoing and significant social justice issues.

Note

1 We respectfully use "First Peoples" to refer to Aboriginal and Torres Strait Islander people – the Indigenous peoples of Australia who belong to over 250 language groups.

References

Agozino, B. (2019). Humanifesto of the decolonization of criminology and justice. *Decolonization of Criminology and Justice*, *1*(1), 5–28. https://doi.org/10.24135/dcj.v1i1.5.

Australian Bureau of Statistics. (2022). Aboriginal and Torres Strait Islander people: Census. *Information on Aboriginal and Torres Strait Islander peoples including language and ancestry*. Retrieved from https://www.abs.gov.au/statistics/people/aboriginal-and-torres-strait-islander-peoples/aboriginal-and-torres-strait-islander-people-census/2021.

Bessarab, D., & Ng'andu, B. (2010). Yarning about yarning as a legitimate method of indigenous research. *International Journal of Critical Indigenous Studies*, *3*(1), 37–50. https://doi.org/10.5204/ijcis.v3i1.57.

Bohn, A., & Bundgaard-Nielsen, R. L. (2021). Not "weird" but truly different: Cultural life scripts and autobiographical memory in indigenous Australia. *Journal of Applied Research in Memory and Cognition*, *10*(1), 85–94. https://doi.org/10.1016/j.jarmac.2020.09.006.

Broidy, L. M., Stewart, A. L., Thompson, C. M., Chrzanowski, A., Allard, T., & Dennison, S. M. (2015). Life course offending pathways across gender and race/ethnicity. *Journal of Developmental and Life-Course Criminology*, *1*(2), 118–149. https://doi.org/10.1007/s40865-015-0008-z.

Chilisa, B. (2012). *Indigenous research methodologies*. California, USA, SAGE.

Cooke, M. (2013). "And then I got pregnant": Early childbearing and the first nations life course. *The International Indigenous Policy Journal*, *4*(1), 1–17. https://doi.org/10.18584/iipj.2013.4.1.6.

Cooke, M., & McWhirter, J. (2011). Public policy and Aboriginal peoples in Canada: Take a life-course perspective. *Canadian Public Policy*, *37*(S1), 15–31.

Cunneen, C., & Tauri, J. (2016). *Indigenous criminology*. Bristol, United Kingdom, Policy Press.

Dean, C. (2010). A yarning place in narrative histories. *History of Education Review*, *39*(2), 6–13. https://doi.org/10.1108/08198691201000005.

Dobia, B., & Roffey, S. (2017). Respect for culture—Social and emotional learning with Aboriginal and Torres Strait Islander youth. In *Social and emotional learning in Australia and the Asia-Pacific* (pp. 313–334). Springer. https://doi.org/10.1007/978-981-10-3394-0_17.

Dudgeon, P., Milroy, H., & Walker, R. (2014). *Working together: Aboriginal and Torres Strait Islander health and wellbeing principles and practice* (2nd ed.).

Australian Council for Education Research and Telethon Institute for Child Health Research, Office for Aboriginal and Torres Strait Islander Health, Department of Health and Ageing.

Durie, M. (2005). Indigenous knowledge within a global knowledge system. *Higher Education Policy*, *18*(3), 301–312. https://doi.org/10.1057/palgrave.hep.8300092.

Gee, G., Dudgeon, P., Schultz, C., Hart, A., & Kelley, K. (2014). Understanding social and emotional wellbeing and mental health from an Aboriginal and Torres Strait Islander perspective. In P. Dudgeon, H. Milroy & R. Walker (Eds.), *Working together: Aboriginal and Torres Strait Islander health and wellbeing principles and practice* (2nd Edition, pp. 55–68). Australian Council for Education Research and Telethon Institute for Child Health Research, Office for Aboriginal and Torres Strait Islander Health, Department of Health and Ageing.

Gibson, C., Crockett, J., Dudgeon, P., Bernoth, M., & Lincoln, M. (2020). Sharing and valuing older Aboriginal people's voices about social and emotional wellbeing services: A strength-based approach for service providers. *Aging and Mental Health*, *24*(3), 481–488.

Glynn-McDonald, R. (n.d.). *Death and sorry business*. Common Ground. Retrieved from https://www.commonground.org.au/learn/death-and-sorry-business.

Griffiths, M. R. (2013). Indigenous life writing: Rethinking poetics and practice. *A companion to Australian Aboriginal literature*, 2, 15.

Janca, A., & Bullen, C. (2003). The Aboriginal concept of time and its mental health implications. *Australasian Psychiatry*, *11*(Suppl.), S40–S44. https://doi.org/10.1046/j.1038-5282.2003.02009.x.

Killias, M. (2011). *Immigration and crime: The European experience* (EU-US Immigration Systems 2011/19). Robert Schuman Centre for Advanced Studies. European University Institute. https://cadmus.eui.eu/handle/1814/18960.

Koltko-Rivera, M. E. (2004). The psychology of worldviews. *Review of General Psychology*, *8*(1), 3–58. https://doi.org/10.1037/1089-2680.8.1.3.

Leeson, S., Smith, C., & Rynne, J. (2016). Yarning and appreciative inquiry: The use of culturally appropriate and respectful research methods when working with Aboriginal and Torres Strait Islander women in Australian prisons. *Methodological Innovations*, *9*, 1–17. https://doi.org/10.1177/2059799116630660.

Leung, L. (2015). Validity, reliability, and generalizability in qualitative research. *Journal of Family Medicine and Primary Care*, *4*(3), 324–327. https://doi.org/10.4103/2249-4863.161306.

Martin, K. L., & Mirraboopa, B. (2003). Ways of knowing, being and doing: A theoretical framework and methods for indigenous and indigenist re-search. *Journal of Australian Studies*, *27*(76), 203–214. https://doi.org/10.1080/14443050309387838.

Moreton-Robinson, A. (2013). Towards and Australian Indigenous women's standpoint theory. *Australian Feminist Studies*, *28*(78), 331–347. https://doi.org/10.1080/08164649.2013.876664.

National Health and Medical Research Council. (2018). *Ethical conduct in research with Aboriginal and Torres Strait Islander Peoples and communities: Guidelines for researchers and stakeholders*. Canberra: Commonwealth of Australia.

Nielsen, M. O., & Robyn, L. (2003). Colonialism and criminal justice for Indigenous peoples in Australia, Canada, New Zealand and the United States of America.

Indigenous Nations Studies Journal, *4*(1). Retrieved from https://kuscholarworks.ku.edu/handle/1808/5791.

Ogilvie, J. M., Allard, T., Thompson, C., Dennison, S., Little, S. B., Lockwood, K., ... Stewart, A. (2021). Psychiatric disorders and offending in an Australian birth cohort: Overrepresentation in the health and criminal justice systems for Indigenous Australians. *Australian and New Zealand Journal of Psychiatry*. https://doi.org/10.1177/00048674211063814.

Piquero, A. R. (2015). Understanding race/ethnicity differences in offending across the life course: Gaps and opportunities. *Journal of Developmental and Life-Course Criminology*, *1*(1), 21–32. https://doi.org/10.1007/s40865-015-0004-3.

Postill, J. (2002). Clock and calendar time: A missing anthropological problem. *Time and Society*, *11*(2–3), 251–270. https://doi.org/10.1177/0961463X02011002005.

Rigney, L. I. (1999). Internationalisation of an Indigenous anti-colonial cultural critique of research methodologies: A guide to Indigenist research methodology and its principles. *Wicazo Sa Review*, *14*(2), 109–212. https://doi.org/10.2307/1409555.

Ritte, R., Panozzo, S., Johnston, L., Agerholm, J., Kvernmo, S. E., Rowley, K., & Arabena, K. (2016). An Australian model of the First 1000 days: An Indigenous-led process to turn an international initiative into an early-life strategy benefiting indigenous families. *Global Health, Epidemiology and Genomics*, *1*, E11. https://doi.org/10.1017/gheg.2016.7.

Roettger, M., Lockwood, K., & Dennison, S. (2019). Indigenous people in Australia and New Zealand and the intergenerational effects of incarceration. *Indigenous justice clearinghouse*, Attorney General's Department of NSW. Retrieved from https://www.indigenousjustice.gov.au/wp-content/uploads/mp/files/publications/files/intergenerational-effects-of-incarceration-fa.pdf.

Rose, D. (1996). Land rights and deep colonising: The erasure of women. *Aboriginal Law Bulletin*, *3*(85), 6–13. Retrieved from https://search.informit.com.au/browseJournalTitle;res=IELAPA;issn=0728-5671.

Shepherd, S. M., & Lewis-Fernandez, R. (2016). Forensic risk assessment and cultural diversity: Contemporary challenges and future directions. *Psychology, Public Policy, and Law*, *22*(4), 427. https://doi.org/10.1037/law0000102.

Smith, L. T. (2021). *Decolonizing methodologies: Research and Indigenous peoples* (3rd ed.). London, United Kingdom Zed Books.

Stevens, M., & Paradies, Y. (2014). Changes in exposure to 'life stressors' in the Aboriginal and Torres Strait Islander population, 2002 to 2008. *BMC Public Health*, *14*(1), 144. https://doi.org/10.1186/1471-2458-14-144.

Sutton, J., Bellair, P. E., Kowalski, R. L., Light, R., & Hutcherson, D. T. (2011). Reliability and validity of prisoner self-reports gathered using the life event calendar method. *Journal of Quantitative Criminology*, *27*(2), 151–171. https://doi.org/10.1007/s10940-010-9101-y.

Thornberry, T. P., & Krohn, M. (2000). The self-report method for measuring delinquency and crime. In D. Duffee (Ed.), *Measurement and analysis of crime and justice* Vol. 4 (pp.33–83). Washington, DC: National Institute of Justice.

Uluru Statement from the Heart (2017). *Uluru statement from the heart*, National Constitutional Convention, 26 May 2017. https://ulurustatement.org/.

Walter, M. (2018). The voice of Indigenous data: Beyond the markers of disadvantage. *Griffith Review*, *60*, 256–263.

Wesley-Esquimaux, C., & Calliou, B. (2010). *Best practices in Aboriginal community development: A literature review and wise practices approach*. The Banff Centre.

Wilkins, D. E. (2005). African Americans and Aboriginal peoples: Similarities and differences in historical experiences. *Cornell Law Review*, *90*, 515–530. Retrieved from http://www.lawschool.cornell.edu/research/cornell-law-review/.

Williams, M. (2015). Connective services: Post-prison release support in an urban Aboriginal population [Doctoral dissertation, University of New South Wales]. University of New South Wales Library. Retrieved from https://www.unsworks.unsw.edu.au/permalink/f/a5fmj0/unsworks_35269.

Yeo, S. S. (2003). Bonding and attachment of Australian Aboriginal children. *Child Abuse Review*, *12*(5), 292–304. https://doi.org/10.1002/car.817.

Yusef, K. W., & Yusef, T. (2017). Criminalizing race, racializing crime. In *The handbook of the history and philosophy of criminology* (pp. 272–288). John Wiley & Sons, Ltd. https://doi.org/10.1002/9781119011385.ch16.

Chapter 8

Rumbles Quest

A Digital Game-Based Assessment of Social and Emotional Wellbeing in Middle Childhood

Kate Freiberg and Ross Homel

Introduction

Online technology is an integral part of everyday life, particularly for children. Its ubiquitous role in the lives of our so-called digital natives has opened new opportunities to promote young people's social-emotional skills, mental health, and wellbeing using tools like social media, online help forums, telehealth platforms, and electronic games (e.g., Burns, 2017; Beaumont, 2015; March, Spence, Donovan, & Kenardy, 2018). To date, the use of digital technology to deliver supportive services and programmes has not been matched by exploration of its potential to innovate assessment. This chapter describes the application of digital technology to the measurement of child wellbeing using a game-based assessment system called Rumble's Quest.

The measure was initially conceived, and a prototype developed and tested during the Pathways to Prevention Project (Freiberg, Homel, Batchelor et al., 2005). Ongoing advancement then continued through the Creating Pathways to Child Wellbeing Project (Homel, Freiberg, & Branch, 2015) during which time the game was rebuilt and integrated with a comprehensive user management platform and support system.

From start to finish, the work to develop the wellbeing assessment took place under the umbrella of a multi-phase research-to-action project. The overriding goal of the project was to create a pathway to wellbeing for children as they transition through successive life phases. The Pathways approach took root in the empirical understanding that many factors interact to influence both the course of individual development and the emergence and persistence of wide-scale social problems such as delinquency and disengagement from education. The implication of muti-causality is that complex social problems can only be addressed effectively through collective multi-sectoral efforts. The Pathways approach therefore sought to strengthen networks of support for children's positive development. The goal was to improve the way the developmental system works.

The project was funded in stages by a series of competitive and philanthropic grants and was led by a university-based research group. The goal

DOI: 10.4324/9781003294740-8

that underpinned this long-running body of work was to bring science to the forefront of developmental service systems (see Chapter 14 for further discussion of how the infrastructure to address this goal was created). The research team operationalised their mission to translate research to practice by working cooperatively with two distinct types of service providers. On the one hand, we worked with practice partners (i.e., schools, education jurisdictions, and non-profit community service organisations). On the other hand, we also worked with a technology partner (i.e., a multi-media production firm). The research, practitioner, and technology partners all shared a common goal to promote positive development and wellbeing outcomes for children. At their heart, these partnerships focused on supporting access to and efficient use of evidence and data. The aim was to guide continuous cycles of decision-making, action planning, programme implementation, and review to achieve better outcomes for children in communities that experience social and economic adversity.

Identifying the Need for a New Wellbeing Measure for Use in Community-Based Practice

We identified the need for a practical measure of wellbeing for use in routine community service settings, such as primary schools and helping agencies, during the Pathways to Prevention project. The fundamental goal to promote children's social and emotional wellbeing was one of the common threads that tied together the project's diverse range of programme activities and participation styles. We therefore needed an appropriate way to measure what impact the project's complex offering of family support and school-based initiatives was having on the wellbeing of children in the community.

In the context of a community-based initiative, an appropriate measure of child wellbeing needs to meet several important requirements. To begin, it must be practical: it should be efficient with respect to the amount of time and staff resourcing it requires to implement and should not be too disruptive of daily routine at the sites where it is used. Next, it should lend itself to use at scale: with all children of the target age in the community (e.g., at all primary schools across the community), and within recurrent data collection schedules that serve as a consistent source of timely data to guide programme decisions and review their effects. Of course, it also must be trustworthy or scientifically sound: valid and reliable. Furthermore, it should capture the multidimensional nature of child wellbeing in a way that is suited to the developmental stage of the children it is used with: its content and presentation format should be age-appropriate and invite children's perspectives on issues that are meaningful and relevant to them, in a way they can understand and relate to.

Developing the Measure

With these requirements in mind, the Pathways project team considered an extensive range of measures that were available at the time and were guided by published systematic reviews of empirical literature on child wellbeing (e.g., Pollard & Lee, 2003). This search did not prove fruitful, so we set about the task of devising a means to measure children's social and emotional wellbeing in a way that met the needs expressed by stakeholders in the project community.

Our work to develop this measure proceeded in four steps.

Step 1: Framing the Measure for Content Development

The first step was to establish conceptual clarity around what would be assessed. Although this may seem obvious, the question of what wellbeing means defies an easy answer. The consensus regarding the importance of wellbeing to children's current and future lives (e.g., Domitrovitch et al., 2017) is not reflected in the ways the construct is defined and understood (e.g., Sloan & Gowing, 2022). Wellbeing is a broad domain: and a wide range of often discipline-specific dimensions and indicators have been put forward to frame it.

The conceptual frame that we formulated as a guide to understanding children's social-emotional wellbeing drew on a range of empirical viewpoints. These included: positive psychology (Seligman & Csikszentmihalyi, 2000), social development models (Catalano et al., 2021), psychosocial development (Erikson, 1968), social-emotional learning perspectives (e.g., Domitrovich et al., 2017), ecological theory (Bronfenbrenner, 1979), and developmental assets-based approaches (Theokas & Lerner, 2006). As we analysed these empirically based perspectives, four inter-related themes came to prominence in our thinking. These themes helped us focus on the picture of wellbeing during the stage of middle childhood that we wanted to capture in our new measure. We used them to develop its content and shape its format.

The first theme that guided construction of the measure is that the changes that occur as children progress through successive developmental stages are the backdrop to children's wellbeing. The cognitive and neurological advances of middle childhood facilitate a growing sense of competence, self-awareness, social awareness, and self-regulation. These internal developmental assets serve as important indicators of wellbeing at this stage.

Second, children's wellbeing is embedded in context and reflects what is going on in their lives. The contexts that are of major importance to children during middle childhood are home, school, and peer group. The conditions of these contexts are external developmental assets that also serve as critical indicators of wellbeing.

Third, healthy connections flourish in contexts attuned to children's needs. Developmental contexts are most conducive to wellbeing when they are places of warmth, encouragement, support, reliable structure, and safety. Wellbeing is indicated by secure and positive relationships with caring adults who provide rewarding and developmentally appropriate learning experiences.

Fourth, wellbeing is a positive and protective state. It represents more than merely the absence of ill-being. While indicators of factors that undermine wellbeing can help data users intervene to mitigate risk, the effective measurement of wellbeing must do more than focus on deficit. To be of practical use, a measure must also indicate factors that uphold current wellbeing and promote future wellbeing outcomes. These indicators direct attention to opportunities to foster protective factors. They facilitate strengths-based practices.

We applied these themes to formulate a set of questions that explore children's perception of their own wellbeing. Items address wellbeing assets within the domains of education (attachment to school and commitment to learning); contexts of care (supportive relationships and experiences in family and community settings); social interaction (peer relationships, social confidence, social awareness); and emotional intelligence (self-regulation and self-awareness). Children's social awareness fosters adherence to prosocial norms and promotes empathy for others. It therefore underpins caring, behavioural conformity, and the ability to resolve interpersonal conflicts. Self-awareness facilitates children's ability to recognise and manage their emotions, and to develop a sense of competence and self-worth, thus helping to promote a positive state of mind and mental health.

The questions were previewed in focus groups where children shared opinions on language, comprehensibility, relevance, and interest in providing information for their school to use when making decisions that affect them: exercising an entitlement outlined in Article 12 of the UN Convention on the Rights of the Child (United Nations, 1989). Their feedback was used to make minor refinements to the question set.

Step 2: Building a Game Prototype as a Delivery Platform for the Measure

Once the task of creating developmentally appropriate content had been completed, we turned our focus to the issue of how to make the delivery format developmentally appropriate. Our goal was to present the measure in a way that would support young children's capacity to make sense of what they are being asked. We believed that using a computer game as a measurement methodology would give children the power to participate confidently in the process of providing information. The game-based format offers a fairer option than conventional assessment formats that often fail to engage young children in a meaningful way or to help them understand what they are being asked. It affords children the opportunity to respond within the context of their own experience rather than in the abstract. As such, it aligns with their level of cognitive maturity.

Work to develop a prototype game began when the researcher set out a basic storyboard, script, and game scenario then worked with a student programmer to build a simple 2-D animated game using Macromedia Flash software. The game was set out as a day at the circus. We called it *Clowning Around*. It was played on desktop PCs. The cheerful cartoon imagery was very appealing with bright colourful artwork. Lively sound effects and jokes were used along with visual gags to carry the action through a series of circus scenes where questions were presented with clear voiceovers. We also enlisted the help of colleagues at the university's office of information services to ensure the interactive web application would communicate with a secure university-based server to host data posted from the game.

Once the game was ready for use, the research team downloaded Clowning Around onto devices at Pathways project schools and supported its implementation at each site. Data were collected at these schools over four consecutive years. Schools collected their wellbeing data with the consent of parents, and the analysis of data by the project research team was approved by university and education department ethics committees. The project team prepared annual reports for each school principal based on their own student data.

The use of Clowning Around as an outcome measure in the latter stages of the Pathways Project demonstrated its usefulness as a tool for evaluating the effects of interventions, and for assessing the impact of adverse events on child wellbeing. At the same time, Clowning Around was also used in several schools located beyond the Pathways community in areas that represented a wide cross-section of the socio-economic demographic. This parallel work established the validity and reliability of the measure (Freiberg, Homel, Branch et al., 2023).

Clowning Around provided proof of concept: it showed that it is feasible and fitting to use a computer game to assess the social-emotional wellbeing of primary school aged children. It also demonstrated the practicality and value of using a game to collect reliable data at scale in routine service settings. Furthermore, its use in the Pathways project generated interest and we began to receive requests to use it from other groups. Among these groups was a major non-government organisation that had been looking for a way to measure wellbeing as an outcome of some of their externally funded child service programmes. That organisation approached us with an offer of some funding they had secured from one of their philanthropic supporters to help us kick-start a major enhancement of the game technology.

Step 3: Game Enhancement – Rumble's Quest

Not long before this funding opportunity arose, we had been introduced to the managing director of a multi-media production firm (InVision Pty Ltd). This company's members combined talent in the development of digital platforms, video production, and game design. After extensive briefing and brainstorming the game designer pitched a story scenario. Then the researcher worked with the whole team to integrate the measure into a video game that uses an archetypal quest format. The game script is built around the items, and 57 questions are presented in a sequence that guides an engaging narrative structure. The central motif of the quest focuses on relationships. The central character, Rumble, combines vulnerability with mischievousness. The idea was to make the game fun but meaningful. During Rumble's Quest the hero and other characters face and overcome obstacles. The story unfolds with warmth and quirky comedy and resolves with an optimistic message.

At the game starts the player adopts an avatar and becomes part of the mythical story world. This immersive engagement helps children experience the story firsthand. Their direct involvement provides a genuine context for the questions, which form part of a meaningful conversation. This promotes deeper understanding and supports children's capacity to respond in a way that reliably reflects their feelings. The graphic style of the artwork is matched to the target age group. Music was specially composed, and actors matched voiceovers to their characters. Great care was taken to make the story flow. The mechanics of the game guide play intuitively, so as not to detract from user experience. This allows children freedom to play spontaneously without need for didactic instruction.

The game, which came to be called *Rumble's Quest*, was built as a 3-D animation on the cross-platform Unity game engine so it could be deployed on iPads as well as on desktop devices. When the first release version reached the beta phase, the team tested its performance in real-world settings. We reached out to schools located in suburbs that represented distinctly different demographic characteristics. Children at these schools played Rumbles Quest on devices that reflected equipment resourcing disparities across different socio-economic contexts: some used adequate but dated PCs with rudimentary handheld pointing devices while others used newer touchscreen devices.

Audience perspective during the testing was uniformly positive, with the game creating a genuine sense of excitement among the children. The beta testing initiated some bug fixing, particularly in relation to the experience of slow scene transitions on older devices.

Step 4: More Than a Game – Building an Assessment System

Once Rumble's Quest was launched for full release, we turned our attention to the task of constructing a user management platform to make it possible for schools and community services to collect and use their own data. This stage of the research translation project worked to embed the research product into the practice of local data-guided decision-making. This was achieved by constructing a web-based infrastructure to support wide-scale deployment of the measure in everyday service settings.

This step was initiated after a game launch event when we were approached by wellbeing leaders from several education jurisdictions. Each expressed interest in trialling Rumble's Quest at schools in their precincts. To facilitate initial dissemination, the researcher worked closely with the digital platform designer to set up a user interface for online system management. After running orientation workshops to prepare schools to use the platform to administer Rumble's Quest at their sites, we conducted a closely managed implementation pilot that rolled out Rumble's Quest across 20 schools.

Working with schools during the pilot provided firsthand understanding of the type of support users need to use the system. This live learning lab was invaluable as a guide when developing the user guides and training modules which were ultimately included in the user dashboard. Consultations to help schools review their pilot data triggered a deep dive into the question of how to present results in ways that foster sound interpretation and robust data use routines. They helped us refine the report generation features and functions to ensure data are presented clearly and in ways that serve user needs.

Reports present results at both group and child levels. The system generates results as a profile across the core domains of supportive relationships, educational, social, emotional, and behavioural wellbeing.

The assessment tool is linked to a secure data server housed in accordance with strict ethical and privacy rules. Authorised users generate reports based on the data they have collected for groups of children in their care. They access only those data associated with their account.

Reflections on the Reward and Challenge of Innovation

The implementation stories communicated to us by user organisations uphold the tangible value of the data as a guide to positive action and confirm that enthusiasm is based on more than the novelty of a game. Some of the themes that emerged in feedback from user experience are presented in Table 8.1.

The opportunity to undertake this creative work was rewarding – but the obstacles were real. Our most substantial challenge was how to reconcile the disparity between several divergent realities: technology is expensive; research budgets and timeframes are limited; innovation and partnerships are time consuming, resource intensive, and require long-haul commitment.

Our university-based team was well versed in action research and had developed protocols for working in partnership with community partitioner groups, schools, and service providers during the Pathways projects. As we began to work with InVision, however, it was important to establish new structures and processes for working with a commercial partner to ensure our involvement in product development went beyond the passive contracting of a service to render a product. Rather, this partnership needed to take an active, hands-on form to ensure product development remained firmly anchored in live research.

Consequently, the research team member who had developed the measure worked with the technology firm in a way that resembled an embedded

Table 8.1 Themes emerging in feedback from school leaders, practitioners, and children

Theme	*Children's responses*	*User organisation responses*
Engagement	*"this made my day" "it was fun" "it felt like magic" "I like Rumble – he was funny"; "it made me feel like I had a new friend"*	*"We've had great buy-in" "We found it a more reliable representation of student wellbeing – in other surveys we had noticed children would click any response without really reading the questions"*
Value	*"I get to share my troubles about not being safe at school"; "I shared my life with the little dog, and it was a good experience for me"; "It felt good to help Rumble grow"*	*"Having our Rumbles data has been worth its weight in gold"; "it gave us direction"; "now we have data to drive our wellbeing plans"; "We felt we could trust the integrity of the data"*
Insight	*"it helped me think about what kind of problems I have, and I think it's good to talk to someone when you need them"; "it helped me think about the way I feel"*	*"It helped us deal with an issue we might otherwise have missed"*
Mechanism for Change	*"it made me start to be nice to other people"*	*"The evidence was what we needed to decide where to reinvest"; "Great data that let us go forward with confidence to restructure our student support program"; "We saw we'd made a real difference"*

partnership model. The company director actively facilitated the process. The researcher became part of their extended team. The group brought together a diverse but complementary set of knowledge and specialised talent to create a product that would not have been possible without this unique blend of perspectives and breadth of skills. The group worked together at all stages of planning, development, testing, and refinement. The partnership operated over a long period during which we established regular routines for weekly formal meetings with interim contact to keep things moving during intense periods of activity. As a generous and trusting partner, InVision was also willing to facilitate our progress over a continuum during which our research funding waxed and waned.

Development of the game, user dashboard, and support resources proceeded as an iterative process within which the researcher formed a bridge connecting the worlds of product use (at schools) and product development (at InVision). Through the active involvement of our practitioner and technical partners, Rumble's Quest technology has grown beyond the game software into a comprehensive platform where the game app is integrated into an assessment system that users operate via a secure administration dashboard.

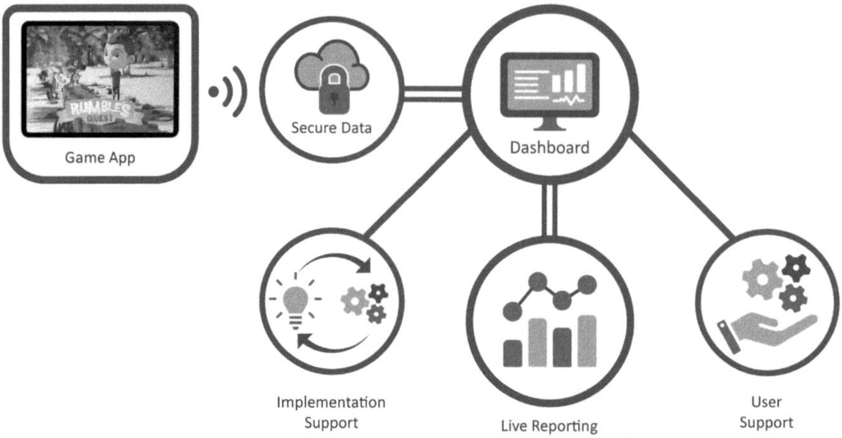

Figure 8.1 Pictorial summary of components of the child wellbeing assessment and user support system of which the Rumble's Quest game forms a part

The platform provides a suite of training guides and resources that streamline the way schools and helping agencies collect, consume, and act on their data to support children's needs. Some of the components of the online system are outlined in Figure 8.1.

Our commitment to the long and onerous process that was required to develop the electronic child wellbeing assessment system and to support its dissemination to end users in frontline services was a choice we made at the expense of vigorously pursuing more traditional academic goals like high-volume publishing. That choice, and the risk we took to fund it in waves by competing for uncertain project funding, is ultimately what afforded us a rare freedom to dedicate the substantial time and effort needed to lead innovation in translational research by engaging creatively with practice and technical partners. However, it is precisely because of this choice that valuable population-level data now ensues to advance the science of child wellbeing.

Conclusion

The critical interplay between research and practice remains live as the use of the game-based measure continues to grow in scale. Our long journey to convert research into real-world practice by constructing a utilitarian assessment system has reached a critical juncture. An enterprise called RealWell (https://www.realwell.org.au/) has been established to make the system available to help schools and service providers gather information to establish a clear vision of wellbeing issues currently relevant to children in their community. These data offer a sound basis for planning appropriate action to effect meaningful change. They help frontline professionals apply logical decision-making processes when implementing strategies designed to achieve positive child wellbeing outcomes.

References

Beaumont, R. (2015). The secret agent society social-emotional skills training program for children with autism spectrum disorders. *The Australian Clinical Psychologist*, *1*(2), 27–29.

Bronfenbrenner, U. (1979). *The ecology of human development: Experiments by nature and design*. Cambridge, MA: Harvard University Press.

Burns, J. (2017). *Take Action Now – Strengthening children and young people's mental health and wellbeing through technology and social media. Report of the 2016–17 thinker in residence, commissioner for children and young people.* Western Australia ccyp.wa.gov.au ISBN: 978-0-9925925-2-3.

Catalano, R. F., Hawkins, J. D., Kosterman, R., Bailey, J. A., Oesterle, S., Cambron, C., & Farrington, D. P. (2021). Applying the social development model in middle childhood to promote healthy development: Effects from primary school through the 30s and across generations. *Journal of Developmental and Life-Course Criminology*, *7*(1), 66–86. https://doi.org/10.1007/s40865-020-00152-6.

Domitrovich, C., Durlak, J., Staley, K., & Weissberg, R. (2017). Social-emotional competence: An essential factor for promoting positive adjustment and reducing risk in school children. *Child Development*, *88*(2), 408–416. https://doi.org/10.1111/cdev.12739.

Erikson, E. H. (1968). *Identity: Youth and crisis*. New York: Norton.

Freiberg, K., Homel, R., Batchelor, S., Carr, A., Hay, I., & Elias, G. (2005). Creating pathways to participation: A community-based developmental prevention project in Australia. *Children and Society*, *19*(2), 144–157. https://doi.org/10.1002/chi.867.

Freiberg, K., Homel, R., Branch, S., Allen, J., McGee, T. R., Vasco, D., & Haskard, K. (2023). The development and psychometric properties of a scalable digital measure of social and emotional wellbeing for middle childhood. *Applied Developmental Science*. https://doi.org/10.1080/10888691.2023.2208753.

Homel, R., Freiberg, K., & Branch, S. (2015). CREATE-ing capacity to take developmental crime prevention to scale: A community-based approach within a national framework. *Australian and New Zealand Journal of Criminology*, *48*(3), 367–385. https://doi.org/10.1177/0004865815589826.

March, S., Spence, S., Donovan, C., & Kenardy, J. (2018). Large-scale dissemination of Internet-based cognitive behavioral therapy for youth anxiety: Feasibility and acceptability study. *Journal of Medical Internet Research*, *20*(7), e234. Published online 2018 July 4. https://doi.org/10.2196/jmir.9211.

Pollard, E., & Lee, P. (2003). Child well-being: A systematic review of the literature. *Social Indicators Research*, *61*(1), 59–78. https://doi.org/1.1023/A:1021284215801.

Seligman, M., & Csikszentmihalyi, M. (2000). Positive psychology. *American Psychologist*, *55*(1), 5–14. https://doi.org/10.1037/0003-066X.55.1.5

Sloane, R., & Gowing, A. (2022). Schools will now be required to support well-being, but the standards aren't clear on what that means. *The Conversation*, June, 30.

Theokas, C., & Lerner, R. M. (2006). Observed ecological assets in families, schools, and neighborhoods: Conceptualization, measurement, and relations with positive and negative developmental outcomes. *Applied Developmental Science*, *10*(2), 61–74.

United Nations. (1989). *Convention on the Rights of the Child*. New York: Office of the High Commissioner. Retrieved from https://www.ohchr.org/en/professionalinterest/pages/crc.aspx.

Chapter 9

Knowledge Brokers as Agents for Change

The Role of Lived Experience and Translational Research in Breaking Intergenerational Cycles of Offending

Corrie Williams, Susan Dennison, Tara Renae McGee, and Janet Ransley

Introduction

Transforming Corrections to Transform Lives (TCTL) is a project led by university researchers in partnership with philanthropy and state government and supported in varying ways by non-government agencies. The key aim of the project was to co-create a new model of service provision for imprisoned mothers and their children, during custody and after release, to create conditions for families to thrive through a holistic system of practice that supports wellbeing and social inclusion. The project is heavily informed by the extensive DLC research that has established the risk factors for and patterns of recidivism and intergenerational transmission for incarcerated mothers and their children (e.g., Auty et al., 2017; Besemer et al., 2016; Giordano et al., 2019). We build on this body of knowledge to establish a model of service provision to overcome these risk factors. Our co-creation approach drew on the systemic design approach of the Design Council of the UK (2021), working through the explore, reframe, and create steps in collaboration with mothers in prison and stakeholders whose services connect with incarcerated mothers and/or their children (i.e., government and non-government sectors). The initial consultation with the mothers during the *explore* step of the co-creation process is the focus of this chapter, conducted via focus group sessions held in women's correctional centres in Queensland, Australia. We focus on how knowledge brokering became an important characteristic of the approach and outcomes of this initiative.

There were three contextual characteristics that supported the success of the co-creation approach. First, the project timing coincided with State Government interest in policy changes in relation to women's incarceration. Second, our project benefited from strong relationships between project leads and relevant government and non-government partners. Third, philanthropic funding and university support ensured we had access to resources that

DOI: 10.4324/9781003294740-9

allowed for an intensive but rapid period of engagement. We discuss each of these characteristics in turn.

Prior to TCTL's commencement, the correctional agency had signalled its intention to engage in change processes relating to the management of imprisoned women. This came in the context of rapidly rising rates of female imprisonment (Australian Bureau of Statistics, 2021) and a recognition that facilities and programmes designed for men did not meet the needs of female prison populations characterised by high levels of poverty, homelessness, violence and victimisation, substance use, and mental health problems (Burch, 2017; Frye & Dawe, 2008). Two initiatives signalled this appetite for change: (1) a project to establish a more gender-responsive and trauma-informed approach for women and (2) the implementation and trial of an end-to-end case management framework for all prisoners. The broader aims of the TCTL project complemented these initiatives and paved the way for a mutually beneficial relationship with correctional agency executives. The correctional agency facilitated access to mothers in prison through advertising the project, organising for mothers to come together for focus groups, and facilitating access by the research team to women's correctional facilities. Most importantly for the knowledge brokering activities described in this chapter, the correctional agency executives were open and willing to listen to the views of the mothers in prison presented through the project. This was facilitated through the longstanding partnership between the correctional agency and the researchers and the executives' understanding that the research team could better elicit the mothers' views and experiences than the correctional agency itself, due to the power imbalance between mothers and the State.

Although the timing of the project allowed for mutually beneficial relationships among those involved in the project, it would not have been possible without pre-existing relationships, trust, and the deep knowledge of the landscape built by the project director through 20 years of research in the field. This knowledge, along with the experience of the research team, allowed access to a wide range of service providers who interact with incarcerated mothers and their children, in both the government and non-government sectors. This included decision-makers in government who could recommend changes to policy or practice concerning incarcerated mothers and their children. A network of trust was built, where the project leaders could share the mothers' views on improvements knowing that suggestions would be genuinely considered. Further, the project leaders had opportunities to learn more about the nuances of the system that are specific to the experiences of the mothers in a particular jurisdiction at a specific time but that may have wider relevance to mothers in other jurisdictions.

Philanthropic funding for the first phase of the project also contributed to the success of the co-creation process with the mothers. This funding allowed the project leaders to overcome three common issues related to research in prison settings and the challenges of conducting research more generally. First, as this phase of the project was fully funded by philanthropy, the partnership with the correctional agency and not-for-profit sector was uncomplicated by pre-determined government contract guidelines or competition across the sector for scarce resources. Second, the funding allowed the project leads to hire a team of full-time researchers who were able to efficiently collect, code, and analyse the knowledge that was collated during the explore step of co-creation. Finally, the funding released the project director from other university commitments to engage fully with the project. In terms of the consultation with the mothers, overcoming these issues allowed for a more efficient and deeper process ensuring that many of the mothers were able to be involved in the subsequent feedback and validation of the model developed. In sum, the project benefited greatly from optimal timing, strong relationships, and access to resources. The next section details our co-creation approach by positioning it within the participatory research paradigm and describes how knowledge brokering became an important aspect of our work. We start with a description of the participatory research paradigm and consider how knowledge brokering fits within that paradigm.

Knowledge Brokering in the TCTL Project

We contend that the co-creation approach taken by TCTL has all the hallmarks of a good participatory research paradigm and its "nothing about us without us" philosophy (Bell & Pahl, 2018). A key characteristic of participatory research and an aim of the co-creation method are to support the translation of new and existing knowledge to programmes and services so that they are more able to withstand real-world pressures (Greenhalgh et al., 2016). However, challenges often arise in the sharing of knowledge due to power imbalances or other practical limitations – for example, where all parties are unable to access the same space. In this case, knowledge brokering may be used to ensure that shared knowledge can successfully move across boundaries (McCloughlin et al., 2020). Traditionally, knowledge brokering refers to how information is disseminated and integrated within organisations to facilitate service improvement. However, researchers often contribute to this process by sharing knowledge with service providers and policy makers, who then apply it to their own contexts (Reid et al., 2017). Thus, the flow of knowledge is generally a top-down process. However, utilising participatory approaches enables the voices of mothers to be privileged, ensuring that in our project knowledge brokering could also be a bottom-up process.

Two kinds of knowledge brokering occurred through the focus groups with the mothers in prison. First, the TCTL team became knowledge brokers between mothers and those that work within the systems in which they are embedded, for example, the correctional agency and child protection. This was possible due to the lead researcher's extensive engagement of top-level decision-makers within government systems and a willingness by the correctional agency to listen to the mothers' views and learn from workshop findings. Second, the mothers became knowledge brokers for their children, families, and other mothers experiencing incarceration. The mothers came to the focus groups' sessions armed not only with their own knowledge but with knowledge gathered through their experiences and direct conversations with their peers who were unable to attend the sessions. We discuss these two kinds of knowledge brokering in the following sections.

The TCTL Team as Knowledge Brokers

We commenced the TCTL project to co-create a new model of support for incarcerated mothers and their children. We did not intend to become knowledge brokers, yet we found that this is not uncommon among researchers undertaking participatory research in prisons (e.g., Fine, 2013; Sherwood & Kendall, 2013; Wilson et al., 2014), though the literature is somewhat sparse. Fine and Torre (2006) detail one example of this in their work on the intimate details of participatory action research in women's prisons, where they became privy to knowledge that they were entrusted to communicate on behalf of the women: "We write here, explicitly without our collaborators' names, although with their review, permission, and blessing, because we speak some truths they dare not say" (p. 225). The aim of Fine and Torre's research was to co-design an employment programme for the women, yet they were compelled to broker the knowledge that women provided them with (and some which they observed) through a research commentary on violence that imprisoned women experience.

The participatory approach taken by our TCTL research team allowed for an open and flexible dialogue between all parties, specifically designed to encourage the exchange and co-production of knowledge. Hence, in retrospect it was not surprising that the mothers provided the research team with new knowledge so that they could have their concerns addressed. Many of these concerns related to local conditions or processes that the mothers did not feel comfortable raising themselves directly with correctional staff. This was often due to power imbalances between themselves and correctional staff, or the perception that their concerns would not traverse the levels of a large correctional agency to achieve real change. For example, during the focus sessions, mothers discussed the consequences of speaking out in an emotional way to correctional staff, including confinement to a secure unit for perceived suicide threat or loss of privileges, and expressed scepticism over whether their feedback would achieve change. Despite this, the mothers took the opportunity to safely raise issues with the TCTL team, trusting us to be the knowledge brokers between them and decision-makers within the correctional system. The project leaders separated issues around mothers' needs and ideas for support into those that could be addressed in a new model of support, and those that were more closely the remit of the correctional agency and could be either addressed quickly (low effort, high impact such as modification to resources provided to mothers) versus those that may need further consideration, planning, and funding (high effort, high impact such as broader changes to policies and procedures). In presenting this information to the correctional agency it became apparent that while many of these issues were deeply concerning for the mothers, some were previously unknown to decision-makers. The agency responded quickly to improve particular conditions for the mothers (and where relevant, children who were residing in custody with their mothers), allowing the project team to focus on developing a model to address more complex system-wide concerns.

The Mothers as Knowledge Brokers for Their Children and Others

The mothers were also knowledge brokers for their children who were not directly included in the consultations at this phase of the project and the other mothers in prison who were unable to attend the workshops. One powerful example is where a mother surveyed other mothers who could not attend the focus groups and brought their responses to our sessions. Mothers also told their own stories, where there was a generative purpose to doing so, despite experiencing an emotional toll from this. For example, many mothers discussed experiences of complex child protection processes, sharing with others that they were not alone in their experiences, providing advice on completing different processes, and advocating for their children.

The active engagement of the mothers, including their willingness to support one another and share their lived experiences, provides a valuable example of how knowledge brokering can facilitate generative actions within a correctional setting. Previous DLC research has shown that generative pursuits, or actions that contribute to the wellbeing of others, are crucial for maintaining a sense of self and providing meaning to one's experiences, particularly for mothers in prison (Heidemann et al., 2016; Maruna et al., 2004). Additionally, these pursuits have been found to be a significant predictor of desistance from criminal behaviour and a protective factor against intergenerational cycles of incarceration (Cullen, 1994; Maruna et al., 2004). Therefore, by using knowledge brokering, DLC researchers can gain a deeper understanding of the role of generativity in the desistance of offending among mothers in prison, while also providing opportunities for mothers to engage in generative actions.

Importantly, mothers' roles as knowledge brokers provided the research team with knowledge that could not have been gained from other sources. The lived experience of mothers was critical in: generating new knowledge about the daily challenges of navigating government systems within and outside of prison; providing richer knowledge of system barriers to information exchange and the way in which imprisonment diminishes availability of support and retraumatises women; deepening our understanding of the complexity of family contact, relationships and needs for holistic support; and highlighting the importance of correctional staff communicating in ways that support the dignity of women. Examples of the disempowerment of mothers and the barriers to transformation prompted deeper questioning about the ability of a programme to support desistance and the breaking of intergenerational cycles of offending in the absence of systems and cultural change. The participatory approach allowed mothers in prison to be knowledge brokers, to advocate for their peers and their children, to claim their identities as mothers, and to be part of the solution. In the next section we discuss why and how knowledge brokering worked in our project.

Knowledge to Meaningful Action

The TCTL approach and subsequent knowledge brokering supported a process of knowledge generation leading to meaningful action, providing a blueprint for developmental and life-course criminology researchers with consonant aims. Reflecting on why the process became more than the co-creation of a new model, we identified four conditions that bridged power imbalances: reciprocity of approach, collaborative inquiry, a visible process of change, and sufficient resources.

First, there was reciprocity in our approach. Mothers saw value in participating even when it was made clear that it was unlikely that there would be direct benefits to them. They imagined they were helping other mothers who were much like them and were hopeful that such mothers would encounter more support in the future. Reciprocity is an important feature of research with vulnerable participants, who may experience fatigue from participating in research, especially where direct benefits to them are unclear (Pittaway et al., 2010; Trainor & Bouchard, 2013). Mothers in prison are rarely asked about what is needed to support them. Rather, developmental and life-course criminology research tends to focus on their offending pathways and the effects of incarceration on their children. By including the mothers in the *explore* stage of the project and encouraging them to provide feedback on the draft model during the *create* stage, the project demonstrated to the mothers they were heard, and their knowledge valued.

Second, the approach contributed to a legacy of collaborative inquiry. The co-creation and knowledge brokering approach provided the opportunity for all parties – the State, the mothers, the research team, and other partners – to continually question and explore what could be done better and more effectively. These opportunities for collaborative inquiry emerged because we, the research team, were committed to communicating clearly throughout the entirety of the first phase of the project. We returned to the prison and delivered feedback sessions with the mothers and in doing so we communicated and tested our understanding of the mothers' needs and the types of support they identified would benefit them. We presented posters and talked through the findings with mothers, seeking their feedback and further validating findings, before leaving posters to be placed around the correctional centres. We communicated face-to-face with senior executives in government to discuss opportunities for change identified by the mothers. By communicating face-to-face, rather than through reports, we ensured that the voices of mothers were amplified. These meetings provided an opportunity for all parties to challenge each other, the researchers based on their academic knowledge and data gathered through focus groups, and the senior executives based on their legislative and operational knowledge.

Third, collaborative inquiry contributed to a visible process of change. In our commitment to amplifying mothers' voices, we were bold in our feedback and suggestions to senior executives. The opportunity to do this was supported by strong relationships established before and during the project. Areas for change were presented both as opportunities for quick wins and as longer-term challenges. It was because the senior executives followed through on these quick wins that the mothers were able to see the process of change. However, it was not always clear to mothers that the impetus for change was due to the TCTL project, and their contribution to it. There are opportunities to develop better communication around the change process. When we were able to create visibility of our role in changes, such as through our follow-up workshops, mothers felt encouraged to contribute further.

Finally, the collective contributions of all co-creators demonstrated where resources were required to enact both rapid- and long-term change. Quick wins included identifying how existing resources could be deployed differently to overcome some of the challenges experienced by mothers and their children, or identifying low-cost changes (i.e., improving information sharing with mothers). Further, the project team were able to demonstrate to philanthropic partners the direct benefits of providing resources to honour commitments to the mothers for their comprehensive engagement and input and to receive feedback on progress. This was reinforced by the knowledge brokering which ensured that resources were focused on addressing needs, as described by the mothers themselves.

Limitations and Future Challenges

The processes described so far benefited from and encouraged knowledge brokering. However, there are potential challenges that may limit the capacity of knowledge brokering to effect more long-term change for mothers in prison and their children. Here, we discuss the challenge of recruiting a representative sample of mothers and the potential challenge in maintaining the strong relationships formed with government during the first phase of this project.

Ensuring a representative sample of mothers in the focus groups was particularly challenging due to the nature of research within prisons, the timeframe required under funding arrangements, and the impact of the COVID-19 pandemic during which correctional centres were repeatedly closed to researchers and visitors for extended periods. Participation by the mothers was ensured by the strong relationships with the correctional agency so that focus groups took place between lockdowns. There were, however, still restrictions around which mothers were approved to attend the workshops. That is, relevant correctional staff determined whether mothers were able to participate in a focus group setting, taking into consideration mental health, cognitive functioning, substance withdrawal, or other security issues. Therefore, the mothers in focus groups may not be representative of all mothers in prison. Further, the timeframe of the first stage restricted opportunities to build rapport with the mothers, which may have limited the representation of Aboriginal and Torres Strait Islander mothers (noting though that 28% of mothers in our explore workshops were First Nations women, representative of the number of First Nations women in prison in Southeast Queensland but likely under-representative of First Nations women in prison in North Queensland (Townsville)). This has possible implications for the success of the model's implementation. Nevertheless, the model has been designed to be individually tailored to mothers' needs, is underpinned by a process of rapid evaluation and iteration, and by a focus on continuing engagement with Aboriginal and Torres Strait Islander-led services to support the empowerment and self-determination of mothers and their families.

The strong relationship with government formed during the first phase of the TCTL project enabled the TCTL team to be effective knowledge brokers on behalf of the mothers. However, the shifting nature of government that accompanies election cycles and changes in legislation and policy may impact the ability to maintain this culture of knowledge brokering. In this rapidly changing environment, it can be difficult to maintain buy-in from politicians, because intrapersonal change is incremental, and unlikely to bring immediate benefits to current agendas. To date, however, there is continuing acceptance by key agencies of the role of the TCTL team as knowledge brokers which includes their commitment to support TCTL in the implementation of the project.

Methodological Innovation and Social Benefit

The approach presented in this chapter provides one example of how developmental and life-course criminologists may move beyond traditional approaches to methodological innovation to achieve social benefit. This is by no means a criticism of the extensive DLC knowledge on risk factors for offending and the intergenerational transmission of offending (Auty et al., 2017; Besemer et al., 2016; Giordano et al., 2019) that has been gained from multi-generational prospective longitudinal studies. Rather, we leverage this established body of knowledge to gain the perspectives of those who are grappling with these challenges, to advance ideas on mitigating risk and reducing intergenerational transmission.

Privileging the voices of the mothers in prison was a key driver of the success of the first phase of this project. It enabled a culture of knowledge brokering, cutting through barriers related to prison power structures and avoiding women's disempowerment, as can be the case in standard research participation. Mothers were given genuine roles as co-creators and assessors. We suggest that valuing the expertise of those whose lives are most closely affected by incarceration is good research practice, regardless of the context, size, or aims of the research. Furthermore, for researchers, knowledge brokering is a privileged role and should be treated as such. This requires a commitment that partnerships between researchers and those with lived experience are not one-sided. Promises to provide feedback and updates on progress are honoured and suggestions for improvements are fully considered.

The co-creation process also helped develop legitimacy in the ultimate design of the model. It is important to be able to demonstrate to a philanthropic funder that those whom the new model is designed to support, but who are typically the most marginalised, have been an integral part of the design process. It demonstrates the team's ability to elicit trusting, respectful relationships with the population of interest, build confidence that they will opt into the programme, and that the programme will likely meet their needs.

Current service delivery systems are not meeting the needs of mothers in prison or their children. The co-creation process, and its consequent knowledge brokering, helped create a shift in understanding of the needs of mothers and children and of the barriers to support among correctional and other government and non-government agencies. This, we contend, is an important first step in the process of creating social impact through transformative individual and system change and should be the focus of further research.

Acknowledgements

The research was funded by the Paul Ramsay Foundation (grant number: 5090). Any opinions, findings, or conclusions expressed in this report are those of the authors and do not necessarily reflect the views of the Foundation.

This work was carried out as part of the *Transforming Corrections to Transform Lives* project (www.transformingcorrections.com.au). The authors thank the Paul Ramsay Foundation for funding this project and the Griffith Criminology Institute and School of Criminology and Criminal Justice at Griffith University for their additional support. This project was carried out in close consultation with Queensland Corrective Services, and we are grateful for their support. The authors also acknowledge that this project work was carried out by research team members, past and present. The project draws on expert insights from a number of stakeholders and their time and contributions are greatly valued. This project would not have been possible without the enthusiastic and detailed contributions of incarcerated women who shared personal accounts of their lives and suggestions for correctional system change.

References

Australian Bureau of Statistics. (2021). *Corrective services Australia, march quarter 2021* (Report no. 45120DO001_202103). Australian Government.

Auty, K. M., Farrington, D. P., & Coid, J. W. (2017). The intergenerational transmission of criminal offending: Exploring gender-specific mechanisms. *The British Journal of Criminology*, *57*(1), 215–237. https://doi.org/10.1093/bjc/azv115.

Bell, D. M., & Pahl, K. (2018). Co-production: Towards a utopian approach. *International Journal of Social Research Methodology*, *21*(1), 105–117. https://doi.org/10.1080/13645579.2017.1348581.

Besemer, S., Axelsson, J., & Sarnecki, J. (2016). Intergenerational transmission of trajectories of offending over three generations. *Journal of Developmental and Life-Course Criminology*, *2*(4), 417–441. https://doi.org/10.1007/s40865-016-0037-2.

Burch, M. (2017). (Re)entry from the bottom up: Case study of a critical approach to assisting women coming home from prison. *Critical Criminology*, *25*(3), 357–374. https://doi-org/10.1007/s10612-016-9346-3.

Cullen, F. T. (1994). Social support as an organizing concept for criminology: Presidential address to the academy of criminal justice sciences. *Justice Quarterly*, *11*(4), 527–559. https://doi.org/10.1080/07418829400092421.

Design Council UK. (2021). *Beyond Net Zero*. Retrieved from https://www.designcouncil.org.uk.

Fine, M. (2013). Echoes of Bedford: A 20-year social psychology memoir on participatory action research hatched behind bars. *American Psychologist*, *68*(8), 687–698. https://doi.org/10.1037/a0034359.

Fine, M., & Torre, M. E. (2006). Intimate details: Participatory action research in prison. *Action Research*, *4*(3), 253–269. https://doi.org/10.1177/1476750306066801.

Frye, S., & Dawe, S. (2008). Interventions for women prisoners and their children in the post-release period. *Clinical Psychologist*, *12*(3), 99–108.

Giordano, P. C., Copp, J. E., Manning, W. D., & Longmore, M. A. (2019). Linking parental incarceration and family dynamics associated with intergenerational transmission: A life-course perspective. *Criminology*, *57*(3), 395–423.

Greenhalgh, T., Jackson, C., Shaw, S., & Janamian, T. (2016). Achieving research impact through co-creation in community-based health services: Literature review and case study. *The Milbank Quarterly*, *94*(2), 392–429. https://doi.org/10.1111/1468-0009.12197.

Heidemann, G., Cederbaum, J. A., Martinez, S., & LeBel, T. P. (2016). Wounded healers: How formerly incarcerated women help themselves by helping others. *Punishment and Society*, *18*(1), 3–26. https://doi.org/10.1177/1462474515623101.

Maruna, S., LeBel, T. P., & Lanier, C. S. (2004). Generativity behind bars: Some 'redemptive truth' about prison society. In E. de St. Aubin, D. P. McAdams, & T. C. Kim (Eds.), *The generative society: Caring for future generations* (pp. 131–151). American Psychological Association. https://doi.org/10.1037/10622-009.

McLoughlin, I., Burns, P., Looi, E., Sohal, A., & Teede, H. (2020). Brokering knowledge into the public sector: Understanding improvement facilitators' priorities in the redesign of hospital care. *Public Management Review*, *22*(6), 836–856. https://doi.org/10.1080/14719037.2019.1604795.

Pittaway, E., Bartolomei, L., & Hugman, R. (2010). 'Stop stealing our stories': The ethics of research with vulnerable groups. *Journal of Human Rights Practice*, *2*(2), 229–251. https://doi.org/10.1093/jhuman/huq004.

Reid, G., Connolly, J., Halliday, W., Love, A.-M., Higgins, M., & MacGregor, A. (2017). Minding the gap: The barriers and facilitators of getting evidence into policy when using a knowledge-brokering approach. *Evidence and Policy: A Journal of Research, Debate and Practice*, *13*(1), 29–38. https://doi.org/10.1332/174426416X14526131924179.

Sherwood, J., & Kendall, S. (2013). Reframing spaces by building relationships: Community collaborative participatory action research with Aboriginal mothers in prison. *Contemporary Nurse*, *46*(1), 83–94. https://doi.org/10.5172/conu.2013.46.1.83.

Trainor, A., & Bouchard, K. A. (2013). Exploring and developing reciprocity in research design. *International Journal of Qualitative Studies in Education*, *26*(8), 986–1003. https://doi.org/10.1080/09518398.2012.724467.

Wilson, M., Jones, J., & Gilles, M. (2014). The Aboriginal mothers in prison project: An example of how consultation can inform research practice. *Australian Aboriginal Studies*. Retrieved from http://search.informit.org/doi/abs/10.3316/ielapa.794482444647336.

Chapter 10

The Implications of Adverse Childhood Experiences (ACEs) Research in the Treatment and Prevention of Offending Behaviour

Hype or Hope?

Catia Malvaso, Danielle Harris, Tara Renae McGee, and Jessica Craig

One of the purposes of this volume of *Criminology at the Edge* is to explore ways in which developmental and life-course criminologists can help to bridge the gap between science and service by engaging with the designers, deliverers, and consumers of "interventions" – that is, with policymakers and practitioners working in government and non-government agencies, and with communities alike. One topic that has polarised researchers yet captivated policymakers and practitioners working across a range of disciplines is the role of Adverse Childhood Experiences or "ACEs"[1] on health and psychological and criminological outcomes later in life. Ascertained through a simple checklist of ten life events that may occur before age 18, research on ACEs has engaged policymakers and practitioners in a way that more complicated theories of social inequalities and crime have not. The simplicity of the ACEs inventory appeals to governments and policymakers searching for simple solutions to some of our most intractable societal problems. Yet, it has become a source of frustration for scholars who have raised numerous concerns about the assumptions made about the utility – or lack thereof – of this inventory in both predicting and explaining why some people experience poor health or engage in criminal behaviour while others do not (Anda et al., 2020; Batty & Kivimaki, 2021; Finkelhor, 2018; Lacey & Minnis, 2020; Underwood, 2020). For developmental and life-course criminologists in particular, ACEs may simply represent a set of arguably incomplete risk factors that sit within a much broader and complex matrix of both risk and protective factors that accumulate to increase (or reduce) risk for offending behaviour (Sutton, 2022).

In this chapter, we consider the unintended consequences of some assumptions made about the ACEs inventory and the implications for criminal justice system policy and practice. We discuss three contestable assumptions that: (1) the ACEs inventory can be used as a screening tool for assessing individual risk and directing treatment; (2) measuring experiences after they

DOI: 10.4324/9781003294740-10

have already occurred in adulthood can inform prevention and early intervention; and (3) ACEs can explain why people experience poor outcomes later in life.

We preface our discussion of the consequences of assumptions made about ACEs with the acknowledgement that the framework was never designed as an explanatory model of the impacts of developmental adversity. Therefore, to question the uses made by others of the framework is not to criticise the work of Felitti, his colleagues, or other ACEs researchers. The attention garnered by ACEs is a timely reminder that too little attention has been paid to the role of developmental adversity in offending pathways. This is particularly important given increased policy interest in the impact of ACEs on youth crime in particular, which has resulted in more pressure being placed on youth justice systems to manage the trauma-related and developmental needs of young people under their supervision (Children and Young People's Centre for Justice, 2022; Commission for Children and Young People, 2021; Logan-Greene et al., 2016; Modrowski et al., 2022; Royal Commission and Board of Inquiry into the Protection and Detention of Children in the Northern Territory, 2017).

From a DLC perspective, ACEs may be considered insufficient on their own in either predicting or explaining offending behaviour. However, their prevalence in justice-involved populations encourages us to think more deeply about how exposure to ACEs interacts with other criminogenic risk factors that underlie offending pathways. This is critical to the advancement of DLC which, although well-regarded as the premier approach for studying and identifying the abundance of risk and protective factors that influence criminal pathways, must do more to translate findings from empirical studies into evidence that can be used to meaningfully inform prevention and intervention efforts (France & Homel, 2014). With its strong theoretical and empirical foundations, DLC is well-positioned to generate and translate high-quality evidence about the association between ACEs and offending behaviour that is needed to inform treatment, early investment, and prevention efforts.

Why Do Adverse Childhood Experiences (ACEs) Matter?

Early life is regarded as a crucial period of neurobiological, physical, social, and emotional development. Health researchers and psychologists have been studying how adversity during childhood impacts development across the life course for decades (Cicchetti & Lynch, 1993; Finkelhor & Kendall-Tackett, 1997; Kempe et al., 1962). There is ample evidence demonstrating that experiences of adversity during childhood are associated with interrupted peri- and post-natal growth (Perry et al., 1996), as well as physical and mental ill-health and behavioural problems later in adolescence and adulthood (Manly et al., 2001; Moffitt, 1993; van der Kolk, 1994). We also know that adversities during childhood do not occur in isolation but tend to cluster (Dong et al., 2004). ACEs were born of the idea that the cumulative impact of multiple adversities, not just one or two isolated events, leads to poorer outcomes (Dube et al., 2006; Felitti et al., 1998). Felitti and colleagues' landmark 1998 study has received an overwhelming amount of attention from researchers, policymakers, and practitioners alike. Google Scholar metrics indicate that the landmark study has now been cited more than 17,000 times. Over the last two decades in particular, there has been a proliferation of studies on ACEs across many disciplines. In fact, a Scopus analysis suggests that the number of documents citing the term "adverse childhood experiences" in their titles or abstracts has increased sixfold from ~200 documents per year in 2015 to ~1,200 documents per year in 2021. Many of these studies have documented correlations between exposure to ACEs and a range of poor life outcomes, including chronic diseases (Anda et al., 2006; Anda et al., 2010); smoking and substance abuse (Dube et al., 2006; Ford et al., 2011); mental health problems (Chapman et al., 2004; Chapman & Ford, 2008); and engagement in criminal behaviour (Craig et al., 2017; DeLisi & Beauregard, 2018; Fox et al., 2015; Malvaso et al., 2018).

The increased attention ACEs have garnered has been a particular boon for DLC, which for decades has had a strong focus on identifying developmental risk factors associated with offending behaviour. The reinvigorated focus on childhood adversity has triggered further investigation into the developmental causes of crime, which also resonates strongly with policymakers and practitioners, and has led to increased calls for more compassionate and "trauma-informed" responses to offending behaviour (Willmot & Jones, 2022). However, ACEs research has also been fuelled by a number of assumptions about the utility of an inventory in screening for individual risk and directing treatment, as well as in informing the development of prevention and early investment initiatives. The implications of these assumptions for policy and practice development have prompted concern from a number of researchers and triggered considerable debate (Underwood, 2020).

Implications of Contestable Assumptions Made About the ACEs Inventory

Rather than providing a lengthy account of the limitations already detailed in the broader ACEs literature, such as the number and type of ACEs selected for inclusion (see Lacey & Minnis, 2020, for a comprehensive review), we focus on three critical assumptions that are commonly made about the ACEs inventory that we suggested at the beginning of this chapter warrant further discussion. Below we examine these contestable assumptions in more detail, discussing their unintended consequences and offering some reflections on what is needed to deal with these consequences and to translate evidence about ACEs into practical policy and practice initiatives.

Assumption 1: The ACEs Inventory Is a Screening Tool That Can Be Used to Assess Individual Risk and Guide Treatment

One of the most consequential assumptions made about the ACEs inventory is that it can be used to screen individuals and assign risk for poor outcomes, including offending behaviour and recidivism. Numerous papers include statements about the need to screen for ACEs, including in criminal justice populations (e.g., Baglivio et al., 2014). However, as recently explicated by one of the original authors, "the ACE score is not suitable for screening individuals and assigning risk for use in decision making about need for services or treatment" (Anda et al., 2020, p. 2). Anda and colleagues assert that the ACEs inventory has been misappropriated as a diagnostic tool to guide individual treatment based on population-based risk from epidemiological research. They confirm that the inventory was designed for research, not for predicting individual-level risk, and that no cut-off score should be used to inform decision-making about risk or the need for treatment. So, how did an inventory designed for population research become so popular as a tool for screening individuals for treatment?

As noted by Felitti (2019), the government policy interest in screening has largely been because of the potential economic implications for reducing health and social care expenses. But, as articulated by Finkelhor (2018), there are consequences of rushing into screening for ACEs without considering potential pitfalls as well as putative benefits. There are two related goals of screening: (1) to identify individuals who are at increased risk of developing an outcome of interest and (2) to direct those identified as "at-risk" to appropriate and effective treatment. Indeed, there is evidence from health and medical fields that effective screening can assist in the early identification of problems that, if attended to, can prevent or mitigate undesired outcomes, but there have also been notable failures (as explained in Finkelhor, 2018). Nonetheless, the health and medical literature has made it explicit that screening regimes are only justified, and ethical, when there are appropriate treatment options in place that can effectively remedy or prevent the outcome of concern. But, Finkelhor (2018) observes even if we had highly skilled assessors who were able to identify and refer at-risk individuals to treatment, the ACEs literature provides little guidance on types of services required because it provides minimal insight into the explanatory mechanisms linking exposure to ACEs to poor life outcomes. One potential explanation is that ACEs lead to trauma symptoms (and indeed the terms ACEs and trauma are terms often used synonymously), but Finkelhor argues that even if the assumption is that exposure to ACEs leads to the experience of trauma symptomatology, it does not necessarily follow that all individuals with "high" ACE scores will display clinical-level trauma symptoms. In any case trauma is not necessarily the cause of all poor outcomes, further complicating the question of what treatment should be prescribed.

We reflected on Finkelhor's (2018) observations in our own systematic review which attempted to disentangle associations between exposure ACEs, the experience of trauma symptoms, and engagement in offending behaviour in adolescence (Malvaso et al., 2021). Just as Finkelhor asserted that not all individuals with high ACE scores will be traumatised, it also does not follow that all individuals with ACEs and/or trauma symptoms will go on to offend. In our systematic review of 124 studies, despite evidence that ACEs were associated with increased odds of criminal justice system involvement, we found minimal evidence that a higher ACEs score predicted trauma symptoms, nor that trauma symptoms mediated the association between ACEs and offending behaviour (Malvaso et al., 2021). We concluded that, based on the current literature, it is unclear whether ACEs are simply correlates or coinciding vulnerabilities in a high-risk population rather than explanatory factors that can differentiate young people who will go on to offend from those who will not. This distinction is critical – if the ACEs inventory cannot be used to predict or explain risk of later outcomes, nor tell us about the type of treatment required to mitigate the consequences of ACEs, then its use as a screening tool will likely be ineffective. This conclusion is consistent with those made in the other fields. As both Finkelhor (2018) and Batty and Kivimaki (2021) have pointed out, the ACEs research is still a long way from typical effective screening regimes employed, and scrutinised empirically, in the medical field (consider for example the pharmacological control of blood pressure proven in randomised controlled trials to reduce cardiovascular disease incidence).

It is also important to note that the idea of screening for risk continues to be a central but controversial focus of criminology and forensic psychology. There is a whole body of literature devoted to the issues associated with actuarial risk assessments (for a recent discussion about violence risk assessment, for example, see Desmarais & Zottola, 2020). However, even if ACE scores could be used to predict future offending behaviour, using this inventory would be considered only a first-generation risk assessment tool as there is no link to case management. It is possible that ACEs may be used as one domain assessed in a broader risk/needs tool that also measures dynamic risk. For example, the Youth Level of Service/Case Management Inventory measures both static and dynamic risk; however, there are questions about the validity of such tools in subgroups of young people in which recidivism scores are inflated due to socioeconomic disadvantage and maltreatment (Sheed et al., 2022). This raises questions about how well factors like ACEs can differentiate those who will recidivate from those who will not. Another issue is that when measured after they have occurred, all of the ACE items are static rather than dynamic in nature; therefore, it is unclear what programmes should target to reduce risk. There is a need for further inquiry into the ways in which trauma might influence dynamic risk, and what can be done to prevent ACEs-exposed individuals from becoming further entrenched in the justice system (Baglivio et al., 2014).

Assumption 2: Measuring Experiences After They Have Already Occurred in Adulthood Can Inform Prevention and Early Intervention

Systematic reviews in both health inequalities and criminology have both concluded that the current body of work on ACEs is based on methodologically weak study designs for testing causal associations between ACEs and outcomes (Batty & Kivimaki, 2021; Malvaso et al., 2021). That is, all of the studies were based on cross-sectional investigations that predominantly relied on retrospective self-reports of ACEs later in adolescence or in adulthood. We contend that when you know about ACEs – either as they happen early in life or after they have occurred in adulthood – has important implications for the development of treatment and prevention initiatives. While cross-sectional studies based on criminal justice system samples have documented the high prevalence of ACEs among young people and adults in the justice system, they are unable to provide the evidence needed to design preventive interventions that can either reduce the occurrence of ACEs or mitigate their sequelae. To inform efforts to prevent ACEs from occurring in the first instance, as well as early investment initiatives that are able to effectively reduce the sequelae of these experiences, research utilising prospective and longitudinal data is needed. Studies utilising these data are needed to elucidate potential causal mechanisms linking exposure to ACEs (as well as their different dimensions, such as type, timing, frequency, and chronicity) and increased risk of offending or re-offending. In other words, the extent to which ACEs are implicated in causal pathways responsible for increased risk for engagement in offending behaviour, or whether they are simply correlates or coinciding vulnerabilities in high-risk populations, is critical to the development of evidence-informed criminal justice policy and practice.

Prospective longitudinal studies are a hallmark of DLC research, and therefore, DLC researchers are well-positioned to design methodologically rigorous studies that can elucidate when, how, and for whom exposure to ACEs may lead to criminal justice system contact. Two logical questions that need to be answered in order to inform the development of effective prevention and treatment strategies are: (1) Can ACEs differentiate between individuals who do and do not offend later in life? and (2) Will we find different associations with the outcome using prospective versus retrospective measurements of ACEs? Indeed, Baldwin and colleagues (2021) showed that prospective longitudinal studies can be used to answer such questions, albeit for a different outcome: poor health in adulthood. In two population-based longitudinal cohort studies – the Dunedin Longitudinal Study in New Zealand and the E-Risk Longitudinal Study in England – these researchers explored whether prospective measures of ACEs could predict later health outcomes. They found that for every additional ACE experienced, there was between a 9 and 14% increased risk of mental and physical health problems at age

18 for individuals in the E-Risk Study, and between a 4 and 17% increased risk of physical and mental health problems at age 45 for individuals in the Dunedin Study. They also demonstrated that ACEs were still associated with poor health after accounting for other clinically relevant information typically available to health professionals (e.g., sex, socioeconomic disadvantage, and previous health problems). However, when they assessed whether ACEs can be used to predict which individuals will develop health problems and which ones will not, they found that high ACE scores predicted outcomes at a level between 7 and 10% above chance. They went on to complete a sensitivity analysis with a retrospective measure of ACEs – that is, they tested whether the predictive ability of ACEs improved using a retrospective measure of ACEs (reported at age 38 in the Dunedin Study). However, predictive validity remained poor. The conclusion from this study was that even though both prospective and retrospective measures of ACEs were associated with mental and physical health problems, screening for ACEs – either in childhood or adulthood – had limited utility for informing individual-level prediction of poor health outcomes. While this conclusion is consistent with our conclusions about why the ACEs inventory could not be used as a risk prediction tool, they also suggest that ACEs may simply be risk factors for poor outcomes rather than causes.

However, even if ACEs are not a direct cause of crime, they may still be implicated in causal pathways. For example, there is extensive evidence that exposure to child maltreatment (which makes up 5 out of the 10 ACEs) is associated with increased risk of criminal justice system contact in adolescence and adulthood (see Braga et al., 2017, and Malvaso et al., 2016, for reviews). Despite this, the reasons for this increased risk remain unclear, and few studies have provided insight into the potential factors that might mediate or moderate maltreatment-offending associations. Yet, Font and Kennedy's (2022) paper published in the *Annual Review of Criminology* serves as a timely reminder of the "centrality of child maltreatment to criminology." Thoughtful, systematic, and rigorous research is needed to better understand potential associations between different types, combinations, and severity of ACEs with offending behaviour, and we contend that developmental and life-course criminologists have the empirical and theoretical skills to generate the high-quality evidence needed to better inform prevention and early investment initiatives.

Now more than ever there is a clear opportunity for DLC researchers to conduct investigations utilising prospective longitudinal studies that focus on how ACEs might be associated with offending behaviour, or how they might strengthen associations with known causes of crime. One of the potential barriers to this is that many of the prospective cohort studies used to study offending pathways predate the inception of ACEs as they are commonly conceptualised today, and therefore do not always include the requisite information to investigate the role of ACEs in the development of offending behaviour. Nevertheless, attempts have been made to re-construct the ACEs inventory using data included in these cohort studies (Craig et al., 2021; Craig et al., 2017; Fagan & Novak, 2017). While these studies have similarly documented associations between ACEs and offending behaviour over the life course, further research is needed to understand the potential causal mechanisms underlying these associations.

As new cohort studies are being designed and developed, we recommend the inclusion of detailed information on ACEs that can be used in subsequent explorations of how they influence developmental pathways and outcomes. The inherent difficulties in capturing and disentangling the effects of ACEs on later life outcomes should not be underestimated. An additional concern is that we know that the vast majority of child protection reports of alleged maltreatment are first made about children before age five (Pilkington et al., 2017). It is clearly not possible to ask children and infants about these experiences at this age, and caregivers may be unwilling to disclose this information for a variety of reasons. Building in consent to access administrative data records for those participating in cohort studies may help address these limitations and provide another view of exposure to ACEs in early life (see Thompson et al., this edition). This is especially important in light of evidence that retrospective and prospective measures of ACEs largely identify different groups of individuals. A recent systematic review and meta-analysis found that 52% of adults with prospective observations of maltreatment did not retrospectively report these experiences, and 56% of those who retrospectively reported maltreatment did not have prospective observations (Baldwin et al., 2019). Including both prospective and retrospective data on ACEs will enable investigations of differences in outcomes utilising different exposure measures.

Assumption 3: ACEs Can Explain Why People Experience Poor Outcomes Later in Life

Our final but likely the most important reflection on the ACEs framework is that it was neither designed as a criminological theory nor could it be considered a very robust or complete framework for explaining engagement in crime. As demonstrated by Sutton (2022), ACEs may simply be another set of arguably incomplete risk factors that can be added to a long list of other known risk factors for offending. A history of ACEs is likely insufficient as an explanation of engagement in crime, especially given we know that the vast majority of individuals exposed to ACEs (particularly child maltreatment) never have contact with the justice system (Malvaso et al., 2020). For this reason, criticising the inadequacy of the framework in guiding the articulation or testing of explanatory mechanisms linking ACEs to criminal behaviour is unjustified. We also know that simple trauma hypotheses may not be supported (i.e., that ACEs lead to trauma symptoms which lead to offending), with currently limited evidence to suggest that trauma symptoms mediate the ACEs-offending association among adolescents (Malvaso et al., 2021). However, it is important to note that in our review we did not identify any longitudinal studies that have explicitly tested this theory about trauma symptoms mediating the association between ACEs and offending. Clearly there is an opportunity to advance knowledge in this area by articulating hypotheses about the potential causal mechanisms and testing these in prospective longitudinal data.

DLC researchers are well-positioned to make contributions in this area given the strong theoretical and empirical foundations of this perspective. Examining how particular ACEs items fit with more developed DLC theories, such as Farrington's Integrated Cognitive Antisocial Potential (ICAP) theory or Thornberry's Interactional Theory of Delinquency, may help us better understand which ACEs are theoretically and empirically meaningful in influencing or facilitating crime pathways. While DLC research has provided extensive insight into the array of factors that may increase (and also buffer) risk for offending, it has also highlighted the difficulty and complexity in identifying causal mechanisms. While there is some evidence to suggest that programmes targeting a range of risk factors at different developmental stages may reduce risk of engaging in offending behaviour, research that further elucidates the potential causal mechanisms underlying risk and resilience would undoubtedly lead to the design and implementation of more effective intervention. For example, to enable deeper understanding of how exposure to ACEs may be associated with dynamic risk factors for offending, measuring and analysing the biopsychosocial responses to adverse events and the personal meaning attached to these may provide new insight into intervention opportunities. While it is acknowledged that the nature and impact of each exposure to an adverse event will be unique, Willmot (2022) suggests that it may be possible to identify those which are particularly consequential for engagement in later offending behaviour, including neuropsychological impact, disrupted attachment, cognitive and attitudinal impact, social learning of abusive behaviour, and post-traumatic stress symptoms.

Conclusion

Assumptions made about the utility of a simple ACEs inventory in directing treatment and informing policy initiatives designed to prevent ACEs from occurring or to reduce their sequelae in both health and criminology are not supported by the current evidence. Despite this, it is well-established that the majority of individuals who come into contact with the justice system have experienced ACEs and present with a constellation of problems that pose challenges for efforts to support returns to more prosocial pathways. ACEs research continues to shine a light or, rather, expose the stark reality that justice-involved individuals have often experienced multiple adverse experiences throughout their childhoods. This body of literature has led to important social and political questions about whether we are criminalising childhood adversity and trauma especially in youth justice systems and provides a strong rationale for more compassionate and trauma-informed justice system practices.

While such responses are consistent with human rights treaties on which most Western countries are signatories, further theoretical and empirical work is needed to understand the role of adversity in the onset, continuation of, and desistance from offending behaviour so that evidence-informed interventions to promote prosocial pathways can be developed and evaluated. The association between exposure to cumulative, repeated, and chronic adverse events and offending is not simple or straightforward and is likely mediated by a wide range of individual, social, and environmental risk factors, as well as the unique personal meaning that individuals ascribe to these events. The investigation of these associations is a challenge well suited to developmental and life-course criminologists.

Note

1 In this chapter, we refer to ACEs as those originally conceptualised and published by Felitti and colleagues (1998) who identified ten distinct life events that can occur before age 18 that were hypothesised to influence health and wellbeing in later life. These included: physical abuse; sexual abuse; emotional abuse; physical neglect; emotional neglect; witnessing family violence; parental separation or divorce; household mental illness; household substance abuse; and, living with a household member who has been incarcerated.

References

Anda, R. F., Felitti, V. J., Bremner, J. D., Walker, J. D., Whitfield, C., Perry, B. D., ... Giles, W. H. (2006). The enduring effects of abuse and related adverse experiences in childhood. A convergence of evidence from neurobiology and epidemiology. *European Archives of Psychiatry and Clinical Neuroscience*, *256*(3), 174–186. https://doi.org/10.1007/s00406-005-0624-4.

Anda, R. F., Porter, L. E., & Brown, D. W. (2020). Inside the adverse childhood experience score: Strengths, limitations, and misapplications. *American Journal of Preventive Medicine*, 1–3. https://doi.org/10.1016/j.amepre.2020.01.009.

Anda, R. F., Tietjen, G., Schulman, E., Felitti, V., & Croft, J. (2010). Adverse childhood experiences and frequent headaches in adults. *Headache*, *50*(9), 1473–1481. https://doi.org/10.1111/j.1526-4610.2010.01756.x.

Baglivio, M. T., Epps, N., Swartz, K., Huq, M. S., Sheer, A., & Hardt, N. S. (2014). The prevalence of adverse childhood experiences (ACE) in the lives of juvenile offenders. *Journal of Juvenile Justice*, *3*(2). Retrieved from http://www.journalofjuvjustice.org/JOJJ0302/article01.htm.

Baldwin, J. R., Caspi, A., Meehan, A. J., Ambler, A., Arseneault, L., Fisher, H. L., ... Danese, A. (2021). Population vs individual prediction of poor health from results of adverse childhood experiences screening. *JAMA Pediatrics*, *175*(4), 385–393. https://doi.org/10.1001/jamapediatrics.2020.5602.

Baldwin, J. R., Reuben, A., Newbury, J. B., & Danese, A. (2019). Agreement between prospective and retrospective measures of childhood maltreatment: A systematic review and meta-analysis. *JAMA Psychiatry*, *76*(6), 584–593. https://doi.org/10.1001/jamapsychiatry.2019.0097.

Batty, G. D., & Kivimaki, M. (2021). Adverse childhood experiences and adult health: The need for stronger study designs to evaluate impact. *Journal of Epidemiology and Community Health*, *75*(6), 485–488.

Braga, T., Gonçalves, L. C., Basto-Pereira, M., & Maia, Â. (2017). Unraveling the link between maltreatment and juvenile antisocial behavior: A meta-analysis of prospective longitudinal studies. *Aggression and Violent Behavior*, *33*, 37–50. https://doi.org/10.1016/j.avb.2017.01.006

Chapman, D. P., Whitfield, C. L., Felitti, V. J., Dube, S. R., Edwards, V. J., & Anda, R. F. (2004). Adverse childhood experiences and the risk of depressive disorders in adulthood. *Journal of Affective Disorders*, *82*(2), 217–225. https://doi.org/10.1016/j.jad.2003.12.013.

Chapman, J. F., & Ford, J. D. (2008). Relationships between suicide risk, traumatic experiences, and substance use among juvenile detainees. *Archive of Suicide Research*, *12*(1), 50–61. https://doi.org/10.1080/13811110701800830.

Cicchetti, D., & Lynch, M. (1993). Toward an ecological/transactional model of community violence and child maltreatment: Consequences for children's development. *Psychiatry: Interpersonal and Biological Processes*, *56*(1), 96–117. https://doi.org/10.1521/00332747.1993.11024624.

Craig, J. M., Malvaso, C., & Farrington, D. P. (2021). All in the family? Exploring the intergenerational transmission of exposure to adverse childhood experiences and their effect on offending behavior. *Youth Violence and Juvenile Justice*, *19*(3), 292–307. https://doi.org/10.1177/15412040211003648.

Craig, J. M., Piquero, A. R., Farrington, D. P., & Ttofi, M. M. (2017). A little early risk goes a long bad way: Adverse childhood experiences and life-course offending in the Cambridge study. *Journal of Criminal Justice*, *53*, 34–45. https://doi.org/10.1016/j.jcrimjus.2017.09.005.

DeLisi, M., & Beauregard, E. (2018). Adverse childhood experiences and criminal extremity: New evidence for sexual homicide. *Journal of Forensic Sciences*, *63*(2), 484–489. https://doi.org/10.1111/1556-4029.13584.

Desmarais, S. L., & Zottola, S. A. (2020). Violence risk assessment: Current status and contemporary issues. *Marquette Law Review*, *103*(3), 793–818.

Dong, M., Anda, R. F., Felitti, V. J., Dube, S. R., Williamson, D. F., Thompson, T. J., ... Giles, W. H. (2004). The interrelatedness of multiple forms of childhood abuse, neglect, and household dysfunction. *Child Abuse and Neglect*, *28*(7), 771–784. https://doi.org/10.1016/j.chiabu.2004.01.008.

Dube, S. R., Miller, J. W., Brown, D. W., Giles, W. H., Felitti, V. J., Dong, M., & Anda, R. F. (2006). Adverse childhood experiences and the association with ever using alcohol and initiating alcohol use during adolescence. *Journal of Adolescent Health*, *38*(4), 444–454. https://doi.org/10.1016/j.jadohealth.2005.06.006.

Fagan, A. A., & Novak, A. (2017). Adverse childhood experiences and adolescent delinquency in a high-risk sample. *Youth Violence and Juvenile Justice*, *16*(4), 395–417. https://doi.org/10.1177/1541204017735568.

Felitti, V. (2019). Origins of the ACE Study. *American Journal of Preventative Medicine*, *56*(6), 787–789. https://doi.org/10.1016/j.amepre.2019.02.011

Felitti, V., Anda, R., Nordenberg, D., Williamson, D., Spitz, A. M., Edwards, V., … Marks, J. (1998). Relationship of childhood abuse and household dysfunction to many of the leading causes of death in adults. *American Journal of Preventive Medicine*, *14*(4), 245–258.

Font, S. A., & Kennedy, R. (2022). The centrality of child maltreatment to criminology. *Annual Review of Criminology*, *5*, 371–396.

Royal Commission and Board of Inquiry into the Protection and Detention of Children in the Northern Territory (2017). *Findings and recommendations*. Online ref: https://www.royalcommission.gov.au/system/files/2020-09/findings-and-recommendations.pdf

Finkelhor, D. (2018). Screening for adverse childhood experiences (ACEs): Cautions and suggestions. *Child Abuse and Neglect*, *85*, 174–179. https://doi.org/10.1016/j.chiabu.2017.07.016.

Finkelhor, D., & Kendall-Tackett, K. (1997). A developmental perspective on the childhood impact of crime, abuse, and violent victimization. In D. Cicchetti & S. L. Toth (Eds.), *Developmental perspectives on trauma: Theory, research and intervention* (pp. 1–32). Rochester: University of Rochester Press.

Ford, E. S., Anda, R. F., Edwards, V. J., Perry, G. S., Zhao, G., Li, C., & Croft, J. B. (2011). Adverse childhood experiences and smoking status in five states. *Preventive Medicine*, *53*(3), 188–193. https://doi.org/10.1016/j.ypmed.2011.06.015.

Fox, B. H., Perez, N., Cass, E., Baglivio, M. T., & Epps, N. (2015). Trauma changes everything: Examining the relationship between adverse childhood experiences and serious, violent and chronic juvenile offenders. *Child Abuse and Neglect*, *46*, 163–173. https://doi.org/10.1016/j.chiabu.2015.01.011.

France, A., & Homel, R. (2014). *Pathways and crime prevention: Theory, policy and practice*. Routledge.

Jones, L. (2022). Trauma-informed risk assessment and intervention: Understanding the role of triggering contexts and offence-related altered states of consciousness. In P. Willmot & L. Jones (Eds.), *Trauma-informed forensic practice*, 15–31. Oxon: Routledge.

Kempe, C. H., Silverman, F. N., Steele, B. F., Droegemueller, W., & Silver, H. K. (1962). The battered-child syndrome. *JAMA*, *181*(1), 17–24.

Lacey, R. E., & Minnis, H. (2020). Practitioner review: Twenty years of research with adverse childhood experience scores – Advantages, disadvantages and applications to practice. *Journal of Child Psychology and Psychiatry*, *61*(2), 116–130. https://doi.org/10.1111/jcpp.13135.

Logan-Greene, P., Kim, B. E. K., & Nurius, P. S. (2016). Childhood adversity among court-involved youth: Heterogeneous needs for prevention and treatment. *Journal of Juvenile Justice*, *5*(2), 68–85.

Malvaso, C. G., Delfabbro, P., & Day, A. (2016). Risk factors that influence the maltreatment-offending association: A systematic review of prospective and longitudinal studies. *Aggression & Violent Behavior*, 1–15. https://doi.org/10.1016/j.avb.2016.06.006

Malvaso, C. G., Cale, J., Whitten, T., Day, A., Singh, S., Hackett, L., Delfabbro, P. H., & Ross, S. (2021). Associations Between Adverse Childhood Experiences and Trauma Among Young People Who Offend: A Systematic Literature

Review. *Trauma, Violence, & Abuse*. https://doi.org/10.1177/15248380211013132

Malvaso, C. G., Delfabbro, P., & Day, A. (2018). Adverse childhood experiences in a South Australian sample of young people in detention. *Australian and New Zealand Journal of Criminology*, 1–21. https://doi.org/10.1177/0004865818810069.

Malvaso, C. G., Santiago, P., Pilkington, R., Montgomerie, A., Delfabbro, P. H., Day, A., & Lynch, J. (2020). *The intersection between the Child Protection and Youth Justice systems in South Australia*. Adelaide: BetterStart Child Health and Development Group, The University of Adelaide

Manly, J. T., Kim, J. E., Rogosch, F., & Cicchetti, D. (2001). Dimensions of child maltreatment and children's adjustment: Contributions of developmental timing and subtype. *Development and Psychopathology*, *13*(4), 759–782.

Modrowski, C. A., Chaplo, S. D., & Kerig, P. K. (2022). Advancing our understanding of the risk factors associated with crossover youth in the child welfare and juvenile justice systems: A trauma-informed research agenda. *Clinical Child and Family Psychology Review*, *25*(2), 283–299. https://doi.org/10.1007/s10567-021-00370-4.

Moffitt, T. (1993). Adolescence-limited and life-course-persistent antisocial behavior: A developmental taxonomy. *Psychological Review*, *100*(4), 674–701.

Perry, B. D., Pollard, R. A., Blakely, T. L., Baker, W. L., & Vigilante, D. (1996). Childhood trauma the neurobiology of adaptation and "use-dependent" development of the brain: How "states" become "traits". *Infant Mental Health Journal*, *16*(4), 271–291.

Pilkington, R., Grant, J., Chittleborough, C., Gialamas, A., Montgomerie, A., & Lynch, J. (2017). *Child protection in South Australia*. BetterStart Child Health and Development: The University of Adelaide.

Sheed, A., Papalia, N., Spivak, B., McEwan, T., & Luebbers, S. (2022). Exploring the utility of the YLS/CMI for Australian youth in custody according to child protection history. *Psychology, Public Policy, and Law*. https://doi.org/10.1037/law0000362.

Sutton, C. (2022). Adverse childhood experiences are important but not the only risk to child development: Revisiting a full risk/resilience matrix. *Criminal Behaviour and Mental Health*, *32*(2), 67–74. https://doi.org/10.1002/cbm.2238.

Underwood, E. (2020). Screen for childhood trauma triggers debate. *Science*, *367*(6477), 498. https://doi.org/10.1126/science.367.6477.498.

van der Kolk, B. (1994). The body keeps the score: Memory and evolving psychobiology of posttraumatic stress. *Harvard Review of Psychiatry*, *1*(5), 252–265.

Willmot, P., & Jones, L. (2022). *Trauma-informed forensic practice*. Oxon: Routledge.

Willmot, P. (2022). Childhood maltreatment and its links to offending. In P. Willmot & L. Jones (Eds.), *Trauma-informed forensic practice*. Routledge.

Chapter 11

Trauma-Informed Sentencing of Adults Who Are Life-Course Persistent Offenders

Katherine McLachlan

Introduction

Developmental and life-course criminology (DLC) investigates the risk and protective factors that predict the onset, persistence, and desistance of offending (McGee & Farrington, 2019). Experiences in childhood and adolescence can play a significant role in subsequent criminality. Many adults who offend have childhoods characterised by adverse childhood experiences (ACEs), including maltreatment and disadvantage (Chapter 10, this volume; Willmot & Jones, 2022). Longitudinal studies have demonstrated that ACEs are prevalent in the lives of adults who offend and are a predictor of both youth and adult offending (Craig et al., 2017; Sampson & Laub, 2003; Malvaso et al., 2022). "C," a woman convicted of assault, is an example of someone with ACEs as well as life-course adversity. In sentencing her, the judge acknowledged:

> *You have had a very difficult life thus far. You were raised by your mother in the same household as your six half siblings and have no memories of your father. Your mother has struggled with a drug addiction for most of her life and was involved in a number of short term relationships with violent and abusive men. You never felt safe in her care as a child.*
>
> *When you were 14 you were sexually abused over a three-month period and fell pregnant, subsequently terminating the pregnancy. The offender has only recently been apprehended for that offending, meaning you are now reliving the trauma of that abuse.*
>
> *Shortly after your abortion your mother was gaoled for 12 months leaving your oldest brother in charge of you and your siblings. Within a few weeks you were evicted from the house you were renting and you became separated from your siblings. You then spent time living with your boyfriend in a relationship perpetuated by domestic violence and mutual drug use. When you left that relationship you were homeless for some time, couch surfing, sleeping in cars and in women's shelters. Your*

DOI: 10.4324/9781003294740-11

> *former partner committed suicide shortly thereafter, causing you much grief and distress and you still blame yourself for his death.*[1]

Many life-course persistent offenders (i.e., people who continue criminal and antisocial behaviour throughout childhood into adulthood: Moffitt, 1993) experience the compounding effect of chronic adversity. For Aboriginal and Torres Strait Islander peoples, the impact of intergenerational and collective trauma may compound the impact of directly experienced adversity (ALRC, 2017). As emphasised by Craig and colleagues (2017), "[w]hile it is evident that ACEs are associated with an increased likelihood of offending, what is less known is what can be done to buffer this impact" (p. 40). This chapter articulates four trauma-informed sentencing strategies that may assist in promoting desistance for life-course persistent offenders.

What Is Trauma-Informed Sentencing?

To understand trauma-informed sentencing, it is necessary to first understand developmental trauma and sentencing.

Developmental Trauma

There is no universally accepted definition or understanding of "trauma" (Willmot & Jones, 2022). Substance Abuse and Mental Health Services Administration (SAMHSA, 2014) states that:

> *Individual trauma results from an event, series of events, or set of circumstances that is experienced by an individual as physically or emotionally harmful or life threatening and that has lasting adverse effects on the individual's functioning and mental, physical, social, emotional, or spiritual well-being. (p. 7)*

Developmental trauma refers to the impact of exposure to chronic adversity (e.g., ACEs) in childhood. Developmental trauma may manifest as impaired neurological development and functioning, poor emotional regulation, antisocial attitudes and behaviours, and unstable attachment (Griffin & Sallen, 2013). Intergenerational trauma specifically relates to trauma "across familial generations" (Menzies, 2019, p. 2), such that "unacknowledged or unresolved trauma in previous generations [is] linked to dysfunction within an extended family in later generations" (Atkinson et al, 2014, p. 294). Intergenerational trauma has been identified as an important construct in the Australian context, particularly in relation to Aboriginal and Torres Strait Islander peoples who have layered experiences of chronic and cumulative trauma, from the time of colonisation and continuing today (Anthony, 2013).

The Sentencing Calculus

Sentencing is the process of determining an appropriate sanction in response to proven criminal behaviour. The sentencing calculus is the "system of... reasoning by which a sentence is devised" (Bagaric et al., 2021, p. 5) and comprises sentencing purposes, principles, individual factors, and non-legal considerations. Judges apply the sentencing calculus to reach individualised, fair, and consistent decisions. Eight sentencing purposes (or objectives) are common to legislation across Australian jurisdictions: punishment, accountability, denunciation, community safety, harm recognition, general and personal deterrence, and rehabilitation (Warner et al., 2017). Judicial discretion allows judges to take their own approach when determining which purposes are most relevant when sentencing specific individuals.

Often young people are diverted from the criminal justice system before reaching the courts (Productivity Commission, 2021). Youth and Children's Courts' sanctions generally promote treatment and other evidence-informed intervention with the hope that the young people will desist from crime. Not surprisingly, once young people continue their criminal behaviour into adulthood, court sympathy for developmental trauma may begin to wane. Adult defendants' personal trauma histories may increase the severity of sentences if judges perceive trauma to be associated with a poor likelihood of rehabilitation and increased risk to community safety (Griffin & Sallen, 2013).

Judges also consider sentencing principles of proportionality, parity, parsimony, and totality. Parity is consistency of sentencing between defendants, totality relates to a fair overall aggregate sanction, and parsimony is the principle of imprisonment as last resort. Proportionality is a commonly cited principle that effectively sets the upper limit of an appropriate sentence, based on the objective seriousness of criminal behaviour. Moral culpability (which relates to intent, motive, and the circumstances of the offending) may then reduce the sentence but cannot increase the sentence beyond what would be perceived as proportionate (Bagaric et al., 2021). For life-course persistent offenders judges may recognise in some cases that moral culpability is influenced by the presence of developmental trauma.

Finally, individualised justice also involves the consideration of factors that are specific to the defendant and the offending behaviour, including trauma (i.e., as childhood and background factors as well as mental health conditions).

Trauma-Informed Sentencing

The concept of "trauma-informed" emerged in 2001 (Harris & Fallot, 2001). Trauma-informed practice aims to "recognize, understand and minimize" the long-term impact of trauma (Kubiak, Covington, & Hillier, 2017, p. 92).

SAMHSA (2014, p. 9f) articulated trauma-informed practice as four steps ("the 4Rs"), to:

- First **realise** what trauma is and the potential impacts of adversity
- **Recognise** trauma symptoms experienced by the individual accessing the service
- **Respond** appropriately to the individual's unique trauma, while also
- **Resist** re-traumatisation by avoiding insensitive or inappropriate responses

If this framework is applied to sentencing (e.g., Griffin & Sallen, 2013; SAMHSA, 2013), a judge must:

- **Realise** trauma may be present, e.g., acknowledge how adversity may result in trauma such as impacted brain function, emotional regulation, and social ability
- **Recognise** when specific adversity in a defendant's life may result in trauma impacting the defendant's functioning and criminal behaviour
- **Respond** by applying trauma-informed principles of practice to the sentencing process (i.e., safety, trust, collaboration, choice, and empowerment) and imposing sanctions likely to promote community safety
- **Resist re-traumatisation** for the defendant and others by working to avoid traumatic triggers throughout the process and when imposing the sanction

Trauma-informed sentencing may be considered as a form of therapeutic jurisprudence (McLachlan, 2021b). Taking a therapeutic jurisprudence approach (Wexler, 2000) arguably judges should strive to promote a therapeutic outcome and process (for the person who has offended and for others).

Four Trauma-Informed Sentencing Strategies to Promote Desistance from Crime for Life-Course Persistent Offenders

Because both trauma and the application of the sentencing calculus are complex, it is understandable that even when judges identify the presence of defendant trauma, there is no obvious effective sentencing response. Given the purposes of sentencing, sanctions should work to promote desistance from crime. In examining how to achieve desistance for life-course persistent offenders, Peggy Giordano and colleagues focus on "hooks for change." These turning points or change agents are "prosocial features of the environment" which individuals may leverage to make significant life changes (Giordano et al., 2002, p. 1000) and "self-reform" (Maruna et al., 2004, p. 132). In terms of sentencing, the following four evidence- and trauma-informed strategies provide opportunities for judges to create hooks to promote desistance for adults who are life-course persistent offenders.

1. Recognise developmental trauma as a sentencing factor related to moral culpability (trauma reports)
2. Recognise individual sentencing factors applicable to Aboriginal and Torres Strait Islander peoples (cultural reports)
3. Respond to exceptional, complex, and repeated trauma (exceptional circumstances)
4. Resist re-traumatisation of defendants' children, to actively prevent the next generation of youth offenders (promote generativity)

Trauma Reports: Recognise When ACEs Result in Developmental Trauma and the Relevance of Developmental Trauma to Criminality and Risk of Recidivism

Developmental trauma may be a sentencing factor related to proportionality (in terms of moral culpability). Judges require targeted education as well as expert evidence to determine when ACEs have resulted in persistent trauma symptoms that impact on a defendant's offending behaviour. Judges are already aware of the presence of ACEs in the lives of some adults who offend. Within a sample of 448 South Australian (SA) sentencing remarks, judges identified that ACEs were present in the lives of 204 defendants, including the example of "C" above (45.5%; McLachlan, 2021a). However, judges tended to identify extreme examples of ACEs, such as:

- Chronic and repeated child abuse and neglect, *often resulting in homelessness and/or out of home care* (e.g., "your mother and stepfather abused you in just about every way imaginable")[2]
- Household substance abuse, *often compounded by other dysfunction such as domestic abuse and family hardships* (e.g., KJB was introduced to "the intravenous use of methamphetamines" by his mother)[3]
- Household mental illness, *including parental and sibling suicidality* (e.g., "your mother, who suffered from mental illness was removed from the family environment when she stabbed you when you were just two")[4]
- Domestic abuse, *which often involved serial exposure to personal and maternal victimisation* (e.g., "you witnessed [your father] being physically violent towards your mother and siblings")[5]
- Incarcerated household members and parental separation/divorce *were less commonly referred to than parental absence due to abandonment or death* (e.g., "At age nine you witnessed your father's suicide. It was particularly gruesome, occurring directly in front of you.")[6]

South Australian judges were unlikely to explicitly identify how ACEs led to trauma and criminal behaviour. Longitudinal studies show that developmental trauma is a risk factor for crime (Baglivio et al., 2015; see also the narrative review of Fritzon et al., 2021). While some expert reports refer to trauma and trauma-informed strategies to address criminogenic needs, if all expert reports were to focus on factors associated with criminogenic risks rather than diagnostic information, they could better assist judges to impose sentencing responses likely to reduce recidivism and promote community safety.

Cultural Reports: Recognise When Intergenerational Trauma Is Relevant in Sentencing and Respond

Courts should recognise that Aboriginal and Torres Strait Islander peoples are over-represented in the child protection, youth justice, and adult criminal justice systems (Anthony, 2013; Malvaso et al., 2017) and respond by "consider[ing] unique systemic and background factors affecting Aboriginal and Torres Strait Islander peoples" (ALRC, 2017, p. 204). The relevance and prevalence of intergenerational trauma experienced by Australian Aboriginal and Torres Strait Islander peoples should be better understood by the judiciary so that it may be incorporated into sentencing decisions. Education for judges and legal practitioners as well as judicial policies and practices could enable (and indeed encourage) judges to request culture and trauma reports where it is apparent that a defendant has experienced intergenerational trauma. Such reports could articulate whether trauma is a relevant sentencing factor and how best to respond to achieve community safety. This approach reflects the Canadian model where all Aboriginal defendants have "Gladue" rights, i.e., the right to have specialist reports prepared before sentencing to advise the judge of circumstances relevant to the Aboriginal defendant, focusing on rehabilitation (refer: *R v Gladue*; Legal Services Society, 2011).

Exceptional Circumstances: Respond to Traumatised Defendants by Seeking to Establish When Trauma Is Exceptional

Courts could respond by recognising that, while trauma is not exceptional (Willmot & Jones, 2022), people who offend are often exposed to exceptional, complex, and repeated trauma. Exceptional circumstances are "special or uncommon" mitigating factors (*R v Constant*, para 57) which allow the judge to impose less significant penalties for serious offences by "outweigh[ing] the paramount consideration of protecting the safety of the community (whether as individuals or in general) and personal and general deterrence" (e.g., ss 51(2), 54(2) of the Sentencing Act 2017 (SA)). While developmental trauma from ACEs may be recognised by the courts as equating to "exceptional circumstances," in the SA sample, judges rarely accepted defendants' submissions of exceptional circumstances. When they did, it was often due to compounded adversity. For example, exceptional circumstances were found to exist for JA. The judge said:

> *I am satisfied that your personal circumstances involving as they do a history of brutal sexual assaults upon you as a very young child, your longstanding untreated mental illness as a result of that sexual abuse, your bashing at the hands of the two men and subsequent kidnapping, the accompanying threats on your life which led you to hold genuine fears that you would be killed, your relative youth, your new stable personal relationship and your secure employment in combination are truly extraordinary and are so exceptional that they do outweigh the considerations of protection of the safety of the community and deterrence.*[7]

Many defendants' life experiences which might be regarded as tragic or extraordinary by the public were treated by judges as mundane, or common. This was partly due to the prevalence of trauma in defendants' lives: judges compared individual defendant's life experiences with other defendants rather than the general public. This meant that adversity was sometimes regarded as commonplace rather than exceptional. Convincing a judge that exceptional circumstances exist due to developmental trauma often depends on a skilled defence lawyer and a persuasive expert report, but even then the threshold is high.

Promote Generativity: Resist Re-Traumatising the Children of Defendants

When sentencing parents, judges could impose sanctions intended to reduce the risk of defendants' children becoming the next generation of youth offenders. In some SA cases, judges acknowledged that a lengthy prison sentence would lead to traumatic impacts on the defendant or defendant's children. Judges in the SA sample indicated the prevention of intergenerational trauma on defendants' children was more a compelling reason to avoid sentences of incarceration than re-traumatisation of defendants themselves. Vincent Felitti and colleagues (1998) identified parental incarceration as a significant ACE. Parental absence can lead to additional adversity, including contact with the child protection system and the youth justice system, and increasing a child's risk of abuse and neglect (Walsh & Douglas, 2016). In the sentencing remarks of 32 defendants (17 women and 15 men), judges focused on how incarceration would traumatise defendants' children or family members. Given the significant traumatic impact of parental absence and intergenerational trauma experienced by adult defendants, sentencing judges have a responsibility to minimise further traumatisation of defendants' children.

In the sentencing remarks of "M," the judge referred to the defendant as "a responsible and loving father."[8] Maruna and colleagues (2004) emphasise the significance of generativity (i.e., accepting the responsibility of parenting) as a hook to desistance. They argue that "the development, encouragement, and facilitation of generativity should be at the center of the correctional enterprise" (p. 133). Thus, while sentencing to resist the re-traumatisation of defendants' children may avoid inflicting further intergenerational trauma (Walsh & Douglas, 2016), it is also a powerful opportunity to enable defendants to identify redemptive opportunities to desist from crime.

Conclusion

Children exposed to ACEs with resulting developmental trauma and antisocial behaviour may become life-course persistent offenders, offending into adulthood. When sentencing life-course persistent adults with developmental trauma, judges have opportunities within the current sentencing calculus to respond in a way that is likely to maximise desistance from crime by identifying and implementing hooks for change. An SA case study found there is a judicial appetite to implement trauma-informed sentencing. Trauma-informed sentencing is designed to realise the presence of trauma, recognise its relevance to criminality, respond in a way that acknowledged the trauma-crime association, and resist re-traumatisation of defendants and their children. This chapter has articulated four strategies to enhance trauma- and evidence-informed sentencing for life-course persistent offenders. These strategies could create hooks for change to promote desistance for adults who are life-course persistent offenders.

Notes

1 *R v CJT*
2 *R v DLH*
3 *R v KJB*
4 *R v CC*
5 *R v SDL*
6 *R v KRB*
7 *R v JA*
8 *R v MPC*

References

Anthony, T. (2013). *Indigenous people, crime and punishment*. Oxford: Routledge.

Atkinson, J., Nelson, J., Brooks, R., Atkinson, C., & Ryan, K. (2014). Addressing individual and community transgenerational trauma. In P. Dudgeon, H. Milroy, & R. Walker (Eds.), *Working together: Aboriginal and Torres Strait Islander mental health and wellbeing principles and practice* (2nd ed., pp. 289–305). Commonwealth of Australia. Perth.

Australian Law Reform Commission. (2017). *Pathways to justice—An inquiry into the incarceration rate of Aboriginal and Torres Strait Islander peoples: Final report, report no. 133*. Commonwealth of Australia. Sydney

Bagaric, M., Alexander, T., & Edney, R. (2021). *Sentencing in Australia* (8th ed.). Thomson: Reuters. Sydney.

Baglivio, M. T., Wolff, K. T., Piquero, A. R., & Epps, N. (2015). The relationship between adverse childhood experiences (ACE) and juvenile offending trajectories in a juvenile offender sample. *Journal of Criminal Justice*, *43*(3), 229–241.

Craig, J. M., Piquero, A. R., Farrington, D. P., & Ttofi, M. M. (2017). A little early risk goes a long bad way: Adverse childhood experiences and life-course offending in the Cambridge study. *Journal of Criminal Justice*, *53*, 34–45. https://doi.org/10.1016/j.jcrimjus.2017.09.005.

Felitti, V. J., Anda, R. F., Nordenberg, D., Williamson, D. F., Spitz, A. M., Edwards, V., ... Marks, J. S. (1998). Relationship of childhood abuse and household dysfunction to many of the leading causes of death in adults: The adverse childhood experiences (ACE) study. *American Journal of Preventative Medicine*, *14*(4), 245–258. https://doi.org/10.1016/s0749-3797(98)00017-8.

Fritzon, K., Miller, S., Bargh, D., Hollows, K., Osborne, A., & Howlett, A. (2021). Understanding the relationships between trauma and criminogenic risk using the risk-need-responsivity model. *Journal of Aggression, Maltreatment and Trauma*, *30*(3), 294–323.

Giordano, P. C., Cernkovich, S. A., & Rudolph, J. L. (2002). Gender, crime, and desistance: Toward a theory of cognitive transformation. *American Journal of Sociology*, *107*(4), 990–1064.

Griffin, G., & Sallen, S. (2013). Considering child trauma issues in juvenile court sentencing. *Children's Legal Rights Journal*, *34*(1), 1–22.

Kubiak, S. P., Covington, S. S., & Hillier, C. (2017). Trauma-informed corrections. In D. Springer & A. Robert (Eds.), *Social work in juvenile and criminal justice systems* (4th ed., pp. 92–104). Charles Thomas. Springfield.

Legal Services Society. (2011). *The Gladue primer*. LSS. British Columbia.

Malvaso, C. G., Cale, J., Whitten, T., Day, A., Singh, S., Hackett, L., ... Ross, S. (2022). Associations between adverse childhood experiences and trauma among young people who offend: A systematic literature review. *Trauma, Violence, and Abuse*, *23*(5), 1677–1694.

Malvaso, C. G., Delfabbro, P. H., & Day, A. (2017). The child protection and juvenile justice nexus in Australia: A longitudinal examination of the relationship between maltreatment and offending. *Child Abuse and Neglect*, *64*, 32–46. https://doi.org/10.1016/j.chiabu.2016.11.028.

Maruna, S., LeBel, T. P., & Lanier, C. S. (2004). Generativity behind bars: Some "redemptive truth" about prison society. In E. De St Aubin, D. McAdams, & T. Kim (Eds.), *Generative society* (pp. 131–152). American Psychological Association. Washington.

McGee, T., & Farrington, D. (2019). Developmental and life-course theories of crime. *Oxford research encyclopedia of criminology and criminal justice*. Retrieved from https://oxfordre.com/criminology/view/10.1093/acrefore/9780190264079.001.0001/acrefore-9780190264079-e-250.

McLachlan, K. (2021a). *'I cannot dismiss from my mind your traumatic and tragic upbringing': Judges' use of Defendant Trauma in Sentencing* [Unpublished Doctoral Thesis]. Adelaide: University of South Australia.

McLachlan, K. J. (2021b). Same, same or different? Is trauma-informed sentencing a form of therapeutic jurisprudence? *European Journal of Current Legal Issues*, *25*(1), 738.

Menzies, K. (2019). Understanding the Australian Aboriginal experience of collective, historical and intergenerational trauma. *International Social Work*, *62*(6), 1522–1534.

Moffitt, T. E. (1993). Adolescence-limited and life-course-persistent antisocial behavior: A developmental taxonomy. *Psychological Review*, *100*(4), 674–701.

Harris, M. & Fallot, R. D. (2001). Envisioning a trauma-informed service system: A vital paradigm shift. *New Directions for Mental Health Services*, *89*, 3–22.

Productivity Commission. (2021). Youth justice services. In Productivity Commission (Ed.), *Report on Government Services, 2019 Part F: Community Services*, Chapter 17. Canberra: Australian Government.

Sampson, R. J., & Laub, J. H. (2003). Life-course desisters—Trajectories of crime among delinquent boys followed to age 70*. *Criminology*, *41*(3), 555–592.

R v Constant [2016] SASCFC 87.

R v Gladue [1999] 1 SCR 688.

Sentencing Act 2017. SA.

Substance Abuse and Mental Health Services Administration. (2013). *Essential components of trauma-informed judicial practice*. SAMHSA. Rockville.

Substance Abuse and Mental Health Services Administration. (2014). *SAMHSA's concept of trauma and guidance for a trauma-informed approach*. SAMHSA. Rockville.

Walsh, T., & Douglas, H. (2016). Sentencing parents: The consideration of dependent children. *Adelaide Law Review*, *37*, 135–161.

Warner, K., Davis, J., & Cockburn, H. (2017). The purposes of punishment: How do judges apply a legislative statement of sentencing purposes? *Criminal Law Journal*, *41*, 69–85.

Wexler, D. B. (2000). Therapeutic jurisprudence: An overview. *Thomas M. Cooley Law Review*, *17*(1), 125–134.

Willmot, P., & Jones, L. (2022). Introduction. In P. Willmot & L. Jones (Eds.), *Trauma-informed forensic practice* (pp. 1–11). London: Routledge. https://doi.org/10.4324/9781003120766

Chapter 12

Understanding Pathways to Inform Prevention

A Programme of Research on Child Maltreatment and Youth Offending Behaviour

Catia Malvaso

The association between childhood maltreatment and criminal behaviour is striking. Depending on the sample and measures used, studies demonstrate that up to 90% of incarcerated young people have experienced maltreatment (Goodkind et al., 2012). Despite providing some initial insight into the overlap between these groups, retrospective cross-sectional studies are unable to provide a life-course view of when, how, and for whom maltreatment might be implicated in pathways that lead to offending. Life-course studies are needed to establish causal associations and, importantly, to identify underlying mechanisms linking maltreatment to offending. Research utilising prospective longitudinal cohort studies, the premier approach to studying criminal pathways in developmental and life-course criminology (DLC), has been central in building an understanding of maltreatment-offending pathways. Findings from these studies have shown that although most young people who have been maltreated do not go on to offend, their likelihood of experiencing subsequent criminal justice system contact is far higher than for non-maltreated groups (Malvaso et al., 2016).

It is clear then that the maltreatment-offending association is not deterministic, but is influenced by a complex interplay of individual, social, and contextual factors other than, and in combination with, maltreatment (Braga et al., 2017). This makes it difficult to ascertain which factor, or combination of factors, exerts the greatest influence on later offending behaviour, with few studies providing consistent insights into the mechanisms or potential causal processes underlying maltreatment-offending pathways. In particular, questions remain about the differential impacts on offending pathways of the type, timing, frequency, and severity of maltreatment experiences, as well as the effect of child protection system contact and interventions which are often used as a proxy for maltreatment (e.g., notifications or reports to child protection agencies, investigations and substantiations of reports, and placements in out-of-home care). Here it is particularly important to acknowledge that the impact of child protection system involvement itself is complex and may be distinct from the impacts of maltreatment experiences. As Font and Kennedy (2022) suggest in their recent article entitled "The centrality of

DOI: 10.4324/9781003294740-12

child maltreatment to criminology," far more attention needs to be directed towards understanding the impacts of child protection system contact and out-of-home care placement on offending pathways.

Very few studies have focused on the implications of the maltreatment-offending association for prevention, thus limiting progress in identifying ways to alter these developmental pathways. This may be attributed to the fact that the type of data needed to inform prevention initiatives has not previously been available. Whole-of-population data is required to identify when, how, and for whom maltreatment experiences lead to offending behaviour, and to overcome issues of small samples that preclude comparisons of different population groups. Without this population-level view, we are unable to produce locally relevant evidence of the size and characteristics of at-risk populations, severely limiting our ability to design and target prevention initiatives effectively. However, the data must also be detailed enough to provide a deeper understanding of the ways in which early developmental risk and protective factors influence behaviour over the life course. Since much of this detail will not be available in whole-of-population datasets, prospective longitudinal studies will continue to provide invaluable insights for prevention.

The prevention of both child maltreatment and youth crime is likely to have significant benefits both at individual and societal levels. Yet in Australia, most government expenditure is at the tertiary ends of implicated systems (as noted by Homel and colleagues, in Chapter 14), with about 60% of youth justice and child protection budgets spent on custodial-based supervision and out-of-home care services, respectively. Another important concern – and an opportunity for prevention – is the gross over-representation of First Nations children in these systems. While making up 5% of the general population, Aboriginal and Torres Strait Islander young people account for about 50% of the Youth Justice population (AIHW, 2022). And, as noted by Lockwood and colleagues in Chapter 7, Indigenous methodologies must be embedded in research in this area and community-driven responses to prevention are needed.

This chapter draws on an inter-disciplinary programme of research which has integrated criminological, psychological, and public health perspectives to generate the evidence needed to identify opportunities to prevent the initiation and continuation of offending behaviour over the life course. We discuss how whole-of-population linked administrative data, augmented by in-depth longitudinal cohort and survey studies, can be used to provide a comprehensive understanding of maltreatment-offending pathways. It is proposed that this can be achieved by following three key stages of epidemiological evidence generation: (1) *Description* of maltreatment-offending associations; (2) *Prediction* of which children who experience maltreatment subsequently enter the justice system; and (3) *Estimation* of the causal effect of child maltreatment on offending behaviour, including the investigation of potential mediators of this effect. A particular focus is on understanding changes over time and at different developmental stages. By identifying opportunities across the life course for the design and targeting of preventive interventions the goal of prevention can be placed front and centre.

Prevention research aims to counteract the effects of risk factors for offending, but the approach has been critiqued for not addressing the complex interplay between risk and protective factors underlying pathways to crime. As summarised by France and Homel (2014), "If pathways researchers tend to treat prevention problems as an afterthought, prevention researchers have not generally been very energetic in absorbing the pathways literature and theorising the prevention process in light of new findings about life course development" (p. 5). Accordingly, one of the challenges this chapter addresses is how DLC researchers can move beyond the study of static risk and protective factors by using evidence generated about changes across the life course to inform developmental crime prevention initiatives.

A first step is to synthesise evidence about pathways and key risk and protective factors from DLC longitudinal research with what can be learned from developmental prevention research about how and when the maltreatment-offending pathway can be most effectively disrupted. We then need to translate this evidence synthesis into effective policy to support the development of programmes that can be implemented in diverse community contexts and directed most efficiently to the families of children who are most at risk of offending. Finally, we need to evaluate programmes so that we can understand which children, families, and communities benefit most from interventions, identify new strategies for those who benefit least, and achieve a continuous cycle of quality improvement. By engaging in all these activities in parallel – evidence generation, synthesis, translation, and evaluation – we will be able to inform, scale up, and sustain developmental crime prevention investments.

Integrating Psychological, Criminological, and Public Health Perspectives to Generate Evidence and Inform Prevention: A South Australian Programme of Research on Maltreatment-Offending Pathways

The field of psychology has long recognised the pervasive effects of maltreatment on a child's development, including damage to neurological, physiological, and psychosocial functioning that can lead to a range of physical, mental, social, behavioural, and economic adversities later in life (Cicchetti & Toth, 1995). The effects of these experiences have also received significant attention in criminology (Farrington, 2007; Ireland et al., 2002; Stouthamer-Loeber et al., 2002), even though much of this research is found outside of criminology journals (Font & Kennedy, 2022). There is now also growing recognition that child maltreatment is a public health issue (O'Donnell et al., 2008), with epidemiological studies showing that child maltreatment is common, associated with detrimental outcomes across the life course, and that overloaded child protection agencies are often unable to respond to the growing volume of reports (Malvaso, Pilkington et al., 2020).

Bringing together criminology, psychology, and public health epistemologies facilitates a renewed focus on the scope and scale of the maltreatment-offending overlap; new insights into the developmental origins of offending pathways; and new ways of identifying opportunities for prevention and rethinking how and when interventions should occur. DLC research draws on both criminology and psychology in its focus on within-individual changes in behaviours that are multiply influenced by interconnections between different levels of a person's ecology including the individual (e.g., temperament), the social context (e.g., school and family factors), and the broader context (e.g., neighbourhood factors). Importantly, in Bronfenbrenner's (1979) bio-ecological systems theory the chronosystem encapsulates the changes in these interconnections over time. Similarly, life-course components of both DLC and epidemiology emphasise the timing of life events and transitions in altering developmental trajectories.

The basis of the South Australian programme of research has been to use whole-of-population, linked administrative data, augmented by in-depth, longitudinal cohort and survey studies, to provide a comprehensive understanding of maltreatment-offending pathways. While the research has been grounded primarily within a DLC framework, the use of different data sources has also meant drawing on methods and ideas from public health, epidemiology, and psychology. This chapter focuses on findings drawn from research utilising three data sources: the South Australian Better Evidence Better Outcomes Linked Data (SA BEBOLD) platform; the Cambridge Study of Delinquent Development (CSDD); and the smaller in scale but detailed survey of adverse childhood experiences (ACEs) and trauma among young people under Youth Justice supervision in SA. These data sources have been used to generate new evidence about the maltreatment-offending association.

The SA BEBOLD platform is the richest source of linked administrative data on children and families in Australia.[1] It has been developed over a decade and includes whole-of-population data on approximately 500,000 children in SA born from 1991 onwards, their parents and carers (Pilkington et al., 2019). It includes data from most SA government departments, including but not limited to data relating to pregnancy and birth characteristics, education (including school enrolments and indicators of child and adolescent development, engagement, and wellbeing), health (including inpatient hospital and emergency department records), human services (including child protection, housing, and homelessness), and criminal justice (including youth justice and adult corrections). It has been used to profile child and family contact with different government agencies over their life course and has become a powerful asset for communicating the scope and scale of complex social problems, such as child protection and justice system contact.

The CSDD[2] is one of DLC's key research assets. It is a prospective longitudinal survey of the development of delinquency and antisocial behaviour in 411 South London boys, mostly born in 1953, from ages 8 to 61. It contains nine waves of participant interviews at multiple time points from ages 8 to 48, with a 7% attrition rate across this timeframe. Self-reported offending was measured up to age 48, and criminal records officially recorded until age 61. Interviews with parents and teachers were also conducted when the boys were aged between 8 and 15. Between 2004 and 2013, interviews with 84.4% of the biological children (aged 18 years+) of participants were completed and their criminal records were searched up to age 34 on average. The original sample is now called generation 2 (G2) to distinguish them from their parents (generation 1 or G1) and from their children (generation 3 or G3). The design and results of the CSDD have been described in multiple books and summary articles, the latest of which were published by Farrington (2021) and Farrington and Jolliffe (2022). The CSDD provides one of the very few opportunities to examine the consistencies or differences in risk factors across multiple generations. The inclusion of both self-reported delinquent and offending behaviour and official offence records is a particular strength that enables insight into behaviours that precede contact with, or do not come to the attention of, the justice system.

Finally, the ACEs and trauma study involved the collection of data through a set of self-report assessments administered through interviews with young people under Youth Justice supervision in SA in 2019–2020 (Malvaso, Day et al., 2022). These data were subsequently linked with administrative child protection and youth justice records to provide the most comprehensive understanding of the prevalence of ACEs, trauma symptoms, substance use, social and emotional behavioural problems, child protection contact patterns, and official records of offending behaviour in a representative sample of young people under Youth Justice supervision.

Findings from research utilising these three data sources are being used to inform a comprehensive understanding of maltreatment-offending pathways and opportunities for prevention and early intervention. In particular, the BEBOLD platform has been used to identify at-risk populations at a local level on which preventive interventions can be targeted, with detailed measures in the ACEs study used to better understand which factors should be targeted when intervening with populations who are already justice-involved. The CSDD provides insight into intergenerational risk factors which can be used to further generate and test hypotheses derived from DLC theory. This research has been bolstered by completing systematic, meta-analytic, and scoping reviews in order to synthesise evidence on specific topics, including adversity, trauma and offending (Malvaso, Cale et al., 2021), trauma-informed practice (Day et al., 2023), and selected interventions (Malvaso,

Pilkington et al., 2021). Together, these reviews assist in the curation of evidence to enable a considered view of what might work to prevent maltreatment-offending pathways.

Generating Evidence Following Three Key Stages of Epidemiological Enquiry

Research can be organised according to three goals: descriptive, predictive, or causal (or explanatory: Hernan et al., 2019). Describing, or providing a quantitative summary, of the maltreatment-offending overlap may be viewed as the first step towards understanding opportunities for prevention. This descriptive component is important because we need to know the size and characteristics of populations at-risk of engaging in offending behaviours in order to develop and target preventive interventions. For example, using the BEBOLD platform, we have shown that more than one in seven young people who have been placed in out-of-home care will go on to experience Youth Justice supervision (Malvaso et al., 2020). We have also shown that patterns of social and economic disadvantage measured at birth are far more evident for those children known to both the Youth Justice and Child Protection systems, compared to those in the general population. These patterns are even more pronounced among young people who have their first contact with the Youth Justice system early (between the ages of 10 and 13), both compared to the general population and to those who have their first Youth Justice system contact later (after age 14; Malvaso et al., under review). These results highlight that prevention opportunities can start very early in life and resources should be directed towards children and families experiencing significant disadvantage. We have also shown that 84% of young people born in 1991–1998 and under Youth Justice supervision have been notified to Child Protection, and a third have experienced placement in out-of-home care. This information is critical for service planning in Child Protection and Youth Justice, where the prevention goal is about preventing these transitions and ensuring that young people do not continue offending into adulthood.

While whole-of-population linked administrative data has been critical for understanding the numbers and characteristics of young people who go on to have contact with Youth Justice compared to those who do not, there are some limitations to these data (see Thompson et al., this volume). The type of detailed information needed to differentiate which children will go on to offend from those who will not is not always available. Through our ACEs study, we established that augmenting administrative data with psychologically meaningful information can provide the level of detail required to develop prevention and intervention strategies. In this study, 184 young people under Youth Justice supervision were interviewed and their responses were linked to administrative data. We found that not only were the majority of young people under supervision known to Child Protection, but almost all reported other experiences of adversity, including exposure to parental substance use, mental illness, incarceration, separation, and death. This information was then used to identify four distinct groupings of young people based on different combinations or clustering of multiple types of adversities experienced. However, a close inspection of the characteristics of young people in these four groups revealed more similarities than differences. That is, the majority of young people in each group experienced significant trauma symptoms (including posttraumatic stress, anxiety, depression, anger, and dissociation) and substance use problems indicative of clinical-level disorders. This information has been crucial in developing an emerging evidence base for trauma-informed approaches to understanding and responding to youth crime and has instigated local commitment and investment in the reimagining of SA Youth Justice.

Data from the BEBOLD platform has been used to assist in the second task of epidemiological inquiry: how well can we predict which children known to Child Protection will subsequently have contact with Youth Justice? This information is important because, in order to target early intervention and prevention efforts, at-risk groups need to be identified. Yet, few studies in this area have utilised formal risk prediction methods to assess accuracy in the early identification of, for example, children in out-of-home care before age 10 who are at risk for later Youth Justice system contact by age 18. We investigated this problem in a series of parametric models with different combinations of 42 predictors relating to socio-economic characteristics at birth and child protection contact patterns before age 10 (Malvaso, Santiago et al., 2022). The prevalence of Youth Justice supervision in our cohort was 13.9%, that is, around one in seven young people in out-of-home care before age 10 had at least one Youth Justice supervision by age 18. When we defined our "at-risk" population as those children whose probability of Youth Justice supervision was in the top 30%, our prediction model including all 42 predictors identified 32.3% of those who went on to experience Youth Justice supervision by age 18 (i.e., our true positives). This means our model improved classification of those children who go on to experience Youth Justice supervision from 13.9% of all eligible children to 32.2% of those in the highest 30% of risk.

While these results indicate that the potential for prevention is large, there are a number of ethical and practical considerations in using risk prediction models in this population. Although the goal of such methods is to identify target populations for early investment and prevention that may help to reduce the number of children transitioning from out-of-home care into Youth Justice, it is necessary first to define the interventions to estimate the true costs of inevitable false positive and negative predictions. For example, we would want to avoid unnecessarily labelling children as high risk if there are likely to be iatrogenic effects. In addition, as discussed in detail by Malvaso, McGee, Harris, and Craig in this volume, there is no point in screening for risk unless there is an effective intervention to offer. As Homel and colleagues discuss in Chapter 14 of this volume, effective, non-punitive, community-based interventions do exist and can be invested in for prevention. Evidence syntheses of the effectiveness of existing programmes can assist in the identification of strategies that we should invest in to support young people at different stages of these higher risk pathways.

Finally, estimating the causal effect of maltreatment (or child protection contact) on offending behaviour (or justice system contact), including the investigation of potential mediating factors, is crucial in contributing to an understanding of which factors should be targeted to alter maltreatment-offending pathways. Nevertheless, this is also the most difficult task. Comprehensive datasets and sophisticated models are needed to explain these complex associations and to identify underlying mechanisms linking maltreatment to offending. DLC's focus on within-individual changes has much to contribute in this regard (see Allen and Williams, this volume for a detailed discussion of innovative methods). Methods common to epidemiology that are also becoming increasingly popular in psychology and criminology offer new opportunities for causal inference (e.g., directed acyclic graphs, Roher, 2018) and for minimising bias due to confounding (e.g., inverse probability of treatment weighting; Cole & Hernan, 2008). As a first step, using the CSDD, we have shown that experiences such as physical punishment and ACEs in childhood are associated with offending behaviour in adolescence and adulthood even after controlling for a number of confounding factors and that these associations are similar across successive generations (Craig et al., 2021; Farrington & Malvaso, 2019). The next step is to better understand mediators of these associations, including individual factors such as self-control and social-emotional development. Again, evidence syntheses will be crucial for identifying whether there are effective programmes that can target causal mediators of interest to alter maltreatment-offending pathways.

Working Towards Prevention: From Evidence Generation and Synthesis to Translation, Implementation, and Evaluation

As stated at the beginning of this chapter, simply generating and synthesising evidence will not be enough to influence the development of prevention and intervention strategies. We also need to translate evidence from the research into practical advice for policy and practice reform. Only then can this evidence be used to design, implement, and evaluate preventive interventions. However, evidence translation requires close, collaborative partnerships between researchers and key government, non-government, and community stakeholders, including those with lived experience. Significant time and effort have been expended with a view to embedding this programme of research on maltreatment-offending pathways within key local agencies responsible for policy decisions and service delivery. This work has been built on the foundation of trusting relationships with staff at all levels, from case managers to policy officers, directors, and ministers, to ensure that findings are translated into reform. This has led to further investment from Youth Justice in SA to establish the agency's first research and service development partnership. Such partnerships progress towards a culture of evidence-driven decision-making and practice.

The next step that we are working towards is to ensure that future research is co-designed with key community stakeholders, particularly those with lived experience. The benefits of such an approach are clearly articulated by Williams and colleagues in the Transforming Corrections to Transform Lives Project (this volume). Our own ACEs study has set a precedent in SA that sensitive research can be conducted with justice-involved young people, since 87% of the 211 young people approached agreed to participate. Youth Justice staff were key to facilitating this research with more than 70 staff members later participating in a forum to discuss the potential implications of the findings from our study. This led to a commitment by the Youth Justice executive leadership to invest in trauma-informed approaches to service delivery. Community co-design in the Australian context is especially significant given that the specific needs of Aboriginal and Torres Strait Islander children and communities must be prioritised. From a research perspective, this means embracing First Nations epistemologies and methods and will require thinking about and doing research differently (Day & Malvaso, 2021).

Finally, if we are able to co-design and implement preventive interventions, we need to ensure that these are embedded in a continuous cycle of evaluation and quality improvement. Pilkington and colleagues (this volume) describe how linked administrative data platforms like BEBOLD can be used to leverage quasi-experimental programme evaluations and overcome issues associated with randomised controlled trials of programmes delivered in human services and justice systems. Implementation and interview studies will also be needed to provide qualitative evidence about which children and communities benefit most from interventions and to identify new strategies for those who benefit least.

Acknowledgements

While I am the sole author of this book chapter, I do not work alone and have benefited from close collaborative relationships with mentors and colleagues who have strongly influenced and shaped my work and ideas. In particular, I would like to acknowledge Professors Andrew Day, John Lynch, Paul Delfabbro, Ross Homel, Tara McGee, and David Farrington, my colleagues in BetterStart (in particular Dr Rhiannon Pilkington and Alicia Montgomerie), and collaborators in Youth Justice (in particular, Louisa Hackett), who have all been influential in the design and execution of this programme of research. This programme of research is supported through an Australian Research Council Discovery Early Career Researcher Award (DE200100679), as well as funding from the Australian Institute of Criminology, Criminology Research Grants (CRG 12/18-19) and the Channel 7 Children's Research Foundation (Grants 12719454 and 19700064).

Notes

1 BEBOLD is led by Professor John Lynch and BetterStart Health and Development in the School of Public Health at the University of Adelaide.
2 The CSDD began in 1961 and was originally directed by Professor Donald West, with Professor David Farrington taking over in 1982.

References

Braga, T., Goncalves, L. C., Basto-Pereira, M., & Maia, A. (2017). Unraveling the link between maltreatment and juvenile antisocial behavior: A meta-analysis of prospective longitudinal studies. *Aggression and Violent Behavior*, *33*, 37–50.

Bronfenbrenner, U. (1979). *The ecology of human development: Experiments by nature and design*. Harvard University Press.

Cicchetti, D., & Toth, S. L. (1995). A developmental psychopathology perspective on child abuse and neglect. *Journal of the American Academy of Child and Adolescent Psychiatry*, *34*(5), 541–565.

Cole, S. R., & Hernan, M. A. (2008). Constructing inverse probability weights for marginal structural models. *American Journal of Epidemiology*, *168*(6), 656–664.

Craig, J. M., Malvaso, C. G., & Farrington, D. P. (2021). All in the family? Exploring the intergenerational transmission of exposure to adverse childhood experiences and their effect on offending behavior. *Youth Violence and Juvenile Justice*, *19*(3), 292–307. https://doi.org/10.1177/15412040211003648.

Day, A., & Malvaso, C. G. (2021). Research adverse childhood experiences in the youth justice system: Reflections on methodology from members of a non-indigenous research team. *International Journal of Offender Therapy and Comparative Criminology*, *67*(6), 707–719.

Day, A., Malvaso, C. G., Butcher, L., O'Connor, J., & McLachlan, K. (2023). Co-producing trauma-informed youth justice in Australia? *Safer Communities*. https://doi.org/10.1108/sc-08-2022-0030.

Farrington, D. P. (2007). Origins of violent behavior over the life span. In D. Flannery, A. Flannery, & L. Waldman (Eds.), *The Cambridge handbook of violent behavior and aggression*. Cambridge: Cambridge University Press.

Farrington, D. P. (2021). New findings in the Cambridge study in delinquent development. In J. C. Barnes & R. Forde (Eds.), *The encyclopedia of research methods in criminology and criminal justice* (pp. 115–138). Wiley.

Farrington, D. P., & Jolliffe, D. (2022). Latest results from the Cambridge Study in Delinquent Development (CSDD). In R. Andersson & P. Wahlgren (Eds.), *A life in criminology: Festschrift to Jerzy Sarnecki* (pp. 45–55). Justice Forlag.

Farrington, D. P., & Malvaso, C. G. (2019). Physical punishment and offending in two successive generations. In Y. Robinson, W. Petherick, & I. Bryce (Eds.), *Child abuse: Evidence, prevention, management, and policy* (pp. 203–224). Cambridge, MA: Academic Press.

Font, S. A., & Kennedy, R. (2022). The centrality of child maltreatment to criminology. *Annual Review of Criminology, 5*, 371–396.

France, A., & Homel, R. (2014). *Pathways and crime prevention: Theory, policy and practice*. Oxon: Routledge.

Goodkind, S., Shook, J. J., Kim, K. H., Pohlig, R. T., & Herring, D. J. (2012). From child welfare to juvenile justice: Race, gender, and system experiences. *Youth Violence and Juvenile Justice*. https://doi.org/10.1177/1541204012463409.

Hernan, M. A., Hsu, J., & Healy, B. (2019). A second chance to get causal inference right: A classification of data science tasks. *Chance, 32*(1), 42–49.

Ireland, T. O., Smith, C. A., & Thornberry, T. P. (2002). Developmental issues in the impact of child maltreatment on later delinquency and drug use. *Criminology, 40*(2), 359–399.

Malvaso, C. G., Cale, J., Whitten, T., Day, A., Singh, S., Hackett, L., ... Ross, S. (2021). Associations between adverse childhood experiences and trauma among young people who offend: A systematic literature review. *Trauma, Violence, and Abuse*. https://doi.org/10.1177/15248380211013132.

Malvaso, C. G., Day, A., Cale, J., Hackett, L., Delfabbro, P., & Ross, S. (2022). Adverse childhood experiences and trauma among young people in the youth justice system. *Trends and Issues in Crime and Criminal Justice, 651*, 1–19.

Malvaso, C. G., Delfabbro, P., & Day, A. (2016). Risk factors that influence the maltreatment-offending association: A systematic review of prospective and longitudinal studies. *Aggression and Violent Behavior*, 1–15. https://doi.org/10.1016/j.avb.2016.06.006.

Malvaso, C. G., Pilkington, R., Lynch, J., Montgomerie, A., Hunkin, H., & Chittlieborough, C. (2021). *The effect of multi-systemic Therapy and Functional Family Therapy in addressing child and adolescent delinquent and/or antisocial behaviour and childhood maltreatment*. Prospero.

Malvaso, C. G., Pilkington, R., Montgomerie, A., Delfabbro, P., & Lynch, J. (2020). A public health approach to preventing child maltreatment: An intelligent information infrastructure to help us know what works. *Child Abuse and Neglect, 106*. https://doi.org/10.1016/j.chiabu.2020.104466.

Malvaso, C. G., Santiago, P., Montgomerie, A., Pilkington, R., & Lynch, J. (2022). *Out-of-home care to youth justice transitions: Using risk prediction to inform prevention*. Edinburgh: International Population Data Linkage Network.

Malvaso, C. G., Santiago, P., Pilkington, R., Montgomerie, A., Delfabbro, P. H., Day, A., & Lynch, J. (2020). *The intersection between the child protection and youth justice systems in South Australia*. Adelaide: BetterStart Child Health and Development Group, The University of Adelaide.

O'Donnell, M., Scott, D., & Stanley, F. (2008). Child abuse and neglect – Is it time for a public health approach? *Australian and New Zealand Journal of Public Health, 32*(4), 325–330.

Pilkington, R., Montgomerie, A., Grant, J., Gialamas, A., Malvaso, C. G., Smithers, L., ... Lynch, J. (2019). An innovative linked data platform to improve the wellbeing of children – The South Australian Early Childhood Data Project.

Australia's Welfare 2019 data insights. Australia's welfare series no. 14, Cat. no. Aus 226. Canberra: AIHW.

Rohrer, J. M. (2018). Thinking clearly about correlations and causation: Graphical causal models for observational data. *Advances in Methods and Practices in Psychological Science*, *1*(1), 27–42.

Stouthamer-Loeber, M., Wei, E., Homish, D. L., & Loeber, R. (2002). Which family and demographic factors are related to both maltreatment and persistent serious juvenile delinquency? *Children's Services: Social Policy, Research, and Practice*, *5*(4), 261–272.

Chapter 13

Why Exploring the Interplay of Prosocial and Antisocial Behaviour Matters for Developmental and Life-Course Criminology and for Strengths-Based Developmental Crime Prevention

Corrie Williams

Introduction

The exploration of prosocial behaviour within the field of developmental and life-course criminology (DLC) is a crucial area of study that has been largely overlooked. While prosocial behaviour is often assumed to be the opposite or absence of antisocial behaviour (Batson, 2011; Krueger et al., 2001), there is a lack of empirical evidence confirming this assumption. In this chapter, I will provide evidence of where prosocial behaviour features in DLC literature and argue that DLC scholars can fill this research gap by drawing on their knowledge of the development of antisocial behaviour and longitudinal research methods to better understand the interplay of prosocial and antisocial behaviours. By exploring the relationship between prosocial and antisocial behaviours, DLC scholars can provide insights into the longitudinal patterns of these behaviours and the factors that may influence them. This will serve to strengthen the theoretical and empirical foundation for strength-based developmental prevention interventions.

I begin this chapter with a discussion on strength-based developmental prevention interventions. I follow with a discussion on why it is important to define prosocial and antisocial behaviour as distinct constructs. I then discuss current knowledge about the intersection of prosocial and antisocial behavioural development, highlighting some issues for consideration before bringing together investigations of prosocial and antisocial behaviour in DLC research. I conclude with a list of questions about the interplay of antisocial and prosocial behaviour that DLC researchers need to consider in moving this research and policy agenda forward.

Strength-Based Developmental Prevention

The aim of the developmental crime prevention approach is to translate empirical evidence into interventions that prevent the onset of problems or

DOI: 10.4324/9781003294740-13

offending behaviour (Tonry & Farrington, 1995; Welsh & Tremblay, 2020). Strength-based approaches seek to do this developmental prevention in a way that emphasises strengths within the individual, interpersonally, and those within contexts such as schools and communities (Vandevelde et al., 2017). While developmental prevention approaches are not always strength-based, many aim to strengthen the social and emotional wellbeing of children to prevent them from becoming involved in crime (Homel, 2005). The CREATE model (described in Chapters 8 and 14 in this volume) is one such example of a developmental crime prevention approach that aims to promote positive development early in life, rather than wait to "treat" negative developmental outcomes after they emerge (Homel et al., 2015). Two of the main principles underpinning the CREATE model are that targeted programmes are embedded in a universal framework and are evidence-driven (Homel et al., 2015). These are important principles in strength-based approaches as the universal targeting of the development of positive behaviour in an evidence-based manner has the potential to reach as many children as possible without a focus on risks and deficits (Tobin & Sugai, 2005).

Universal programmes that focus on the building of prosocial behaviour may be appropriate for addressing the risk factors associated with the problem and offending behaviour without the need to specifically focus on risk (Byrne & Case, 2016; McAra & McVie, 2007; Zubrick et al., 2005). One of the current problems with existing programmes, however, is that there is a lack of evidence to suggest that the promotion of prosocial behaviour corresponds to a reduction in antisocial behaviour. In fact, evaluations of programmes that aim to promote prosocial behaviour reveal limited effects on the antisocial behaviour of young people (Ang & Hughes, 2002; Ciocanel et al., 2017; DuBois & Keller, 2017; Harrell et al., 2009; van der Stouwe et al., 2016). These programmes, however, are generally based on the evidence for what works to increase prosocial behaviour, in the absence of evidence that simultaneously explores prosocial and antisocial behaviour. The remainder of this chapter is dedicated to discussing how DLC researchers may bridge the gap in current research and strengthen the theoretical and empirical foundation for the preference for strength-based developmental prevention interventions.

Defining Prosocial and Antisocial Behaviours as Distinct Constructs

It is important for this chapter to establish that prosocial and antisocial behaviour are distinct constructs, rather than the opposite ends of a continuum. If prosocial behaviour is simply the absence or opposite of antisocial behaviour, then there is no need for DLC scholars to explore prosocial behaviour because developmental crime prevention approaches that are already shown to reduce antisocial behaviour should consequently increase prosocial behaviour. Equally on this assumption, strength-based developmental crime prevention efforts need not target antisocial behaviour because the focus can be shifted to the fostering of prosocial behaviour. In this section, I explore the idea that prosocial and antisocial behaviour are distinct constructs by exploring the history of prosocial behaviour research and the different behaviours that characterise prosocial and antisocial constructs.

Despite scholars often claiming that the term prosocial behaviour was coined as an antonym for antisocial behaviour (e.g., Batson, 2011; Krueger et al., 2001), there is limited evidence in the early literature on prosocial behaviour to confirm this (e.g., Gergen et al., 1972; Rosenhan & White, 1967; Wispé, 1972). Rather, the term prosocial behaviour was initially used to define "socially acceptable" forms of aggressive behaviour, such as that used to come to the aid of others but was later used to describe acts of charity or altruism (Wispé, 1972). This evolution of the prosocial terminology has resulted in a distinct body of research that focuses on the development of peoples' motivation to behave prosocially (e.g., altruism) and the different types of prosocial behaviour (e.g., charity) that come from this motivation (see conceptual reviews by Dunfield, 2014 and Pfattheicher et al., 2022). This body of research sits firmly within the subfields of social and developmental psychology and is mostly independent of the explorations of antisocial behaviour found within criminology. Thus, there have been limited simultaneous investigations of prosocial and antisocial behaviour and therefore limited evidence that prosocial behaviour is simply the absence or opposite of antisocial behaviour.

Evidence that prosocial and antisocial behaviour are distinct constructs can be gained from exploring the contemporary conceptual definitions. The most widely accepted definition of prosocial behaviour comes from developmental psychology and includes behaviours that promote positive social relationships – such as sharing, helping, and comforting (Eisenberg et al., 2015). In contrast, there is no one accepted definition of antisocial behaviour, with the term being used to cover a broad range of behaviours. One approach is to equate antisocial behaviours with conduct problems, defined as a persistent disruptive set of behaviours that include lying, cheating, and disobeying reasonable requests (Loeber, 1990). Another approach is to use antisocial behaviour as an umbrella term for offending behaviour such as shoplifting and vehicle theft (Moffitt, 2018). From both definitions, it could be proposed that a child or adolescent who engages in such disruptive or offending behaviour may also have difficulty engaging in behaviours that promote positive social relationships (Hay & Cook, 2007).

However, there is a lack of evidence to suggest that antisocial and prosocial behaviour are mutually exclusive. Rather, the evidence indicates that because prosocial and antisocial behaviour are developmentally, socially, and contextually dependent, it is possible for a child or adolescent to be both prosocial and antisocial. For example, a prosocial child may lie about sneaking a sweet treat because they have not developed the necessary cognitive skills to delay gratification (Talwar & Lee, 2008). Further, an adolescent may behave antisocially in the presence of certain peers but otherwise behave prosocially when those peers are not present (Wilks et al., 2018). These findings shed some light on why school-based interventions that only focus on prosocial behaviour do not always translate to reductions in the antisocial behaviour of young people (as demonstrated by Ciocanel et al., 2017). Although prosocial interventions may allow young people to gain and practice prosocial skills within the controlled settings in which the interventions take place, some young people may lack the prosocial opportunities required to practice these skills outside of the controlled intervention setting. However, to confirm the reasons behind the limited effects of prosocial behaviour interventions on antisocial behaviour, more research is needed on the relationship between prosocial and antisocial behaviour.

Of the limited research that does simultaneously explore prosocial and antisocial behaviour, the findings related to the strength and direction of the relationship of the two constructs are mixed. For example, some scholars suggest that there is no relationship (Kokko et al., 2006; Krueger et al., 2001), while others propose that there is at least a co-occurrence of high prosocial behaviour and low antisocial behaviour (e.g., Barker et al., 2010; Nantel-Vivier et al., 2014). Although these differences may be related to the varying operationalisations of antisocial behaviour (e.g., aggressive versus non-aggressive behaviour), the reason for differences in the outcomes of these studies is not yet fully understood. This unresolved issue is due to the lack of research that provides a deeper exploration of the longitudinal developmental patterns of prosocial behaviour and how these patterns relate to those associated with antisocial behaviour.

The Developmental Patterns of Prosocial and Antisocial Behaviours

Although the causal factors related to prosocial behaviour have been extensively studied through experiments, understanding how these factors relate to normative and non-normative developmental patterns of prosocial behaviour is limited by a lack of longitudinal explorations (Eisenberg et al., 2015). There have been some notable exceptions where scholars have explored prosocial behaviour longitudinally (e.g., Carlo et al., 2014). Further, there are examples of research where the longitudinal relationship between prosocial and antisocial behaviour has been explored (e.g., Barker et al., 2010; Nantel-Vivier et al., 2014; Padilla-Walker et al., 2018). These investigations, however, are limited in that they only compare the developmental trajectories of the two behaviours separately (Barker et al., 2010; Nantel-Vivier et al., 2014), are unidirectional (Carlo et al., 2014), and do not disentangle the relationship between the two from potential shared underlying factors

(Padilla-Walker et al., 2018). Before turning to how DLC scholars may address these current research gaps, I examine where DLC researchers may theoretically position their investigations of prosocial behaviour. I do this by comparing current theories of prosocial development to those of antisocial behaviour.

Positioning Prosocial Behaviour in Developmental and Life-Course Criminology Research

Historically, theories that sought to explain the development of prosocial behaviour have been "static," like theories of antisocial behaviour. Both have tended to focus on the categorisation of people as being either prosocial or antisocial (Hay & Cook, 2007). Contemporary theories, however, recognise that prosocial behaviour development is a dynamic process that starts in infancy and shifts in frequency depending on the stage of development (Eisenberg et al., 2015). Unlike theories of antisocial behaviour that explore patterns across the life course (e.g., Moffitt, 1993, 2018), prosocial behaviour developmental theories tend to focus on the period from infancy to preschool. There are two ways that DLC theorists could extend thinking beyond the early years.

First, DLC researchers could explore the specific manifestations of prosocial behaviour beyond the early childhood period using longitudinal methods. Hay and Cook (2007) propose that different developmental stages correspond to different manifestations of prosocial behaviour in early childhood. For example, these scholars suggest that prosocial behaviour is marked in infancy by simple gestures of sharing that progress to more verbalised expressions of sympathy by age three. Developmental psychologists have suggested that once a child has progressed to verbal expressions of prosocial behaviour these behaviours remain relatively stable, only increasing in frequency (Eisenberg et al., 2015). In contrast, Loeber, Stouthamer-Loeber, and Ahonen (2016) suggest that prosocial behaviour may not be stable, manifesting differently across childhood, depending on the presence or absence of antisocial behaviour. However, there is a paucity of longitudinal research to confirm these assertions.

Second, DLC scholars could draw on their understanding of how social processes influence longitudinal patterns of antisocial behaviour to explore if there are similar processes that influence prosocial behaviour, beyond the early childhood period. Examples of such work include Hay and Cook's ideas on selective prosocial behaviour and Moffitt's (1993, 2018) explanation for adolescent-limited antisocial behaviour. Drawing on learning theory, Moffitt suggests that those on an adolescent-limited pathway are selective in their antisocial responses, based on the potential outcomes of those responses. Like Hay and Cook (2007), Moffitt recognises the role of early childhood, cognitive and biological factors in promoting or limiting prosocial opportunity.

Both theories recognise that cognitive or biological factors require an interaction between the person and their social environment to influence prosocial or antisocial behaviour. However, unlike Hay and Cook, Moffitt (1993, 2018) considers both the early factors related to antisocial behaviour and the potential for these factors to become more or less predictive of antisocial behaviour across the life course, depending on the social motivations and opportunities that arise.

The social development model (Catalano & Hawkins, 1996) is one DLC paradigm that does explicitly explore prosocial behaviour. In particular, this paradigm recognises an important role of prosocial bonds and the availability of prosocial opportunities in preventing antisocial behaviour (Catalano & Hawkins, 1996). This model has been translated into developmental prevention efforts that aim to reduce antisocial behaviour by enhancing prosocial opportunities (Cambron and colleagues, 2019 review these programmes). To understand the role of prosocial behaviour in reducing antisocial behaviour, however, requires further knowledge of whether these prosocial opportunities do in fact directly translate to increases in prosocial behaviour and subsequent decreases in antisocial behaviour. These explorations have not yet been a focus of the social development model.

Bringing Together Investigations of Prosocial and Antisocial Behaviour in DLC Research: Challenges and Opportunities

Loeber, Stouthamer-Loeber, and Ahonen (2016, p. 95) suggested that one of the limitations of research into the discontinuity of antisocial behaviour is: "the lack of conceptualisation or measurement that can shed light on the degree to which desistance from conduct problems and delinquency is followed, if not greatly facilitated, by the acquisition or 'turning-on' of prosocial behaviours." I argue that by exploring the interplay of prosocial and antisocial behaviours, DLC scholars could close this gap by providing insights into the longitudinal relationship between prosocial and antisocial behaviours and the factors that may simultaneously increase one and reduce the other. There are two issues specific to the exploration of prosocial behaviour, however, that warrant some attention and further explanation before scholars jump into exploring prosocial behaviour from a DLC perspective. First, the current difficulties in measurement of key developmental processes in DLC research, including persistence and desistance, are likely to plague research on the development of prosocial behaviour. Second, there is insufficient evidence to conclude that increases in prosocial behaviour will always correspond to decreases (rather than increases) in antisocial behaviour. Let us examine each of these issues in turn.

The current measurement issues in the DLC field are too complex to discuss thoroughly in this chapter. Here, I summarise how these measurement issues are likely to plague research on the interplay of prosocial and antisocial behaviour and point the reader towards further information. Arguably, persistence and desistance in antisocial behaviour are two of the most difficult processes to measure in DLC. McGee and her colleagues (2021) argue that popular methods, such as group-based trajectory modelling, fail to capture persistence because they miss periods of intermittency and obscure individual patterns of antisocial behaviour. Similarly, these methods obscure the true dynamic process and factors that contribute to desistance and rarely consider desistance from all forms of antisocial behaviour, including early conduct problems (Bushway et al., 2001; Loeber et al., 2016). One solution is to explore within individual change in these behaviours across the life course using methods that allow an exploration of random variation (Allen and Williams in Chapter 4 explore a range of such statistical methods).

The second issue, that there is insufficient evidence to conclude that increases in prosocial behaviour will always correspond to decreases (rather than increases) in antisocial behaviour, is a recurring theme that requires much more attention. Frequently the argument that a better understanding of prosocial behaviour could benefit developmental crime prevention is met with questions about whether engaging in prosocial behaviour can be used as a means for the achievement of antisocial goals. Critics argue that youth who engage in antisocial gang activities or in bullying behaviour may also selectively engage in prosocial behaviours to maintain their status amongst their peers (as demonstrated in research by Higginson et al., 2018 and Warden & MacKinnon, 2003). These critics further suggest that implementing interventions that increase prosocial behaviours may have iatrogenic effects by facilitating antisocial behaviours. The logical response is to assert that these criticisms reinforce, rather than diminish, the need for more research on the interplay of prosocial and antisocial behaviour over time, including in the evaluation of developmental interventions designed to promote prosocial behaviours.

Future Research Questions

The discussion so far affords some insights into the theoretical foundations and considerations that DLC researchers could use to address the current gaps in understanding how prosocial and antisocial behaviours interrelate over time. Addressing these gaps has the potential to provide the social service sector with stronger empirical evidence to preference universal interventions that focus on ways to promote positive development early in life, over those that focus on risks and deficits.

The following questions may advance this agenda:

1. Are prosocial behaviours stable or are there age-graded changes? And if so, does antisocial behaviour influence the stability of, or age-graded changes in, prosocial behaviour?

2. Do similar or distinct factors predict lower antisocial behaviour and higher prosocial behaviour?
3. When do prosocial behaviour interventions lead to both increases in prosocial behaviour and decreases in antisocial behaviour? And for which children and youth in particular?
4. Are there different manifestations of prosocial behaviour across different periods of development and types of antisocial behaviour?

These questions provide much scope for DLC research to explore the interplay of prosocial and antisocial behaviours. The intention of this chapter is to inspire DLC researchers to investigate these questions and apply their findings to the construction of strength-based developmental crime prevention initiatives.

References

Ang, R. P., & Hughes, J. N. (2002). Differential benefits of skills training with antisocial youth based on group composition: A meta-analytic investigation. *School Psychology Review*, *31*(2), 164–185. https://doi-org/10.1080/02796015.2002.12086149

Barker, E. D., Oliver, B. R., & Maughan, B. (2010). Co-occurring problems of early onset persistent, childhood limited, and adolescent onset conduct problem youth. *Journal of Child Psychology and Psychiatry*, *51*(11), 1217–1226. https://doi.org/10.1111/j.1469-7610.2010.02240.x.

Batson, C. D. (2011). A history of prosocial behaviour research. In A. W. Kruglanski & W. Stroebe (Eds.), *Handbook of the History of Social Psychology*. Taylor & Francis Group. Retrieved from http://ebookcentral.proquest.com/lib/griffith/detail.action?docID=1046911.

Bushway, S. D., Piquero, A. R., Broidy, L., Cauffman, E., & Mazerolle, P. (2001). An empirical framework for studying desistance as a process. *Criminology*, *39*(2), 491–516. https://doi.org/10.1111/j.1745-9125.2001.tb00931.x.

Byrne, B., & Case, S. (2016). Towards a positive youth justice. *Safer Communities*, *15*(2), 69–81. https://doi.org/10.1108/SC-11-2015-0036.

Cambron, C., Catalano, R. F., & Hawkins, J. D. (2019). The social development model. In D. P. Farrington, L. Kazemian, & A. R. Piquero (Eds), *The Oxford handbook of developmental and life-course criminology* (pp. 224–247).

Carlo, G., Mestre, M. V., McGinley, M. M., Tur-Porcar, A., Samper, P., & Opal, D. (2014). The protective role of prosocial behaviors on antisocial behaviors: The mediating effects of deviant peer affiliation. *Journal of Adolescence*, *37*(4), 359–366. https://doi.org/10.1016/j.adolescence.2014.02.009.

Catalano, R. F., & Hawkins, J. D. (1996). *The social development model: A theory of antisocial behavior* (pp. 149–197). In J. D. Hawkins (Ed.), *Delinquency and crime: Current theories* (pp. 149–197). Cambridge: Cambridge University Press.

Ciocanel, O., Power, K., Eriksen, A., & Gillings, K. (2017). Effectiveness of positive youth development interventions: A meta-analysis of randomized controlled trials. *Journal of Youth and Adolescence*, *46*(3), 483–504. https://doi.org/10.1007/s10964-016-0555-6

DuBois, D. L., & Keller, T. E. (2017). Investigation of the integration of supports for youth thriving into a community-based mentoring program. *Child Development*, *88*(5), 1480–1491. https://doi.org/10.1111/cdev.12887.

Dunfield, K. A. (2014). A construct divided: Prosocial behavior as helping, sharing, and comforting subtypes. *Frontiers in Psychology*, *5*(958). https://doi.org/10.3389/fpsyg.2014.00958.

Eisenberg, N., Spinrad, T. L., & Knafo-Noam, A. (2015). Prosocial development. In M. E. Lamb & R. M. Lerner (Eds.), *Handbook of child psychology and developmental science: Socioemotional processes* (pp. 610–656). Hoboken: John Wiley & Sons https://doi.org/10.1002/9781118963418.childpsy315

Gergen, K. J., Gergen, M. M., & Meter, K. (1972). Individual orientations to prosocial behavior. *Journal of Social Issues*, *28*(3), 105–130. https://doi.org/10.1111/j.1540-4560.1972.tb00035.x.

Harrell, A. W., Mercer, S. H., & DeRosier, M. E. (2009). Improving the social-behavioral adjustment of adolescents: The effectiveness of a social skills group intervention. *Journal of Child and Family Studies*, *18*(4), 378–387. https://doi.org/10.1007/s10826-008-9241-y.

Hay, D. F., & Cook, K. V. (2007). The transformation of prosocial behavior from infancy to childhood. In C.A Brownell & C.B. Kopp, *Socioemotional development in the toddler years: Transitions and transformations* (pp. 100–131). New York: The Guilford Press.

Higginson, A., Benier, K., Shenderovich, Y., Bedford, L., Mazerolle, L., & Murray, J. (2018). Factors associated with youth gang membership in low- and middle-income countries: A systematic review. *Campbell Systematic Reviews*, *14*(1), 1–128. https://doi.org/10.4073/csr.2018.11.

Homel, R. (2005). Developmental crime prevention. In N. Tilley (Ed.), *Handbook of crime prevention and community safety* (pp. 71–106). London: Taylor & Francis Group.

Homel, R., Freiberg, K., & Branch, S. (2015). CREATE-ing capacity to take developmental crime prevention to scale: A community-based approach within a national framework. *Australian and New Zealand Journal of Criminology*, *48*(3), 367–385. https://doi.org/10.1177/0004865815589826.

Kokko, K., Tremblay, R. E., Lacourse, E., Nagin, D. S., & Vitaro, F. (2006). Trajectories of prosocial behavior and physical aggression in middle childhood: Links to adolescent school dropout and physical violence. *Journal of Research on Adolescence*, *16*(3), 403–428.

Krueger, R. F., Hicks, B. M., & McGue, M. (2001). Altruism and antisocial behavior: Independent tendencies, unique personality correlates, distinct etiologies. *Psychological Science*, *12*(5), 397–402. https://doi.org/10.1111/1467-9280.00373.

Loeber, R. (1990). Development and risk factors of juvenile antisocial behavior and delinquency. *Clinical Psychology Review*, *10*(1), 1–41. https://doi.org/10.1016/0272-7358(90)90105-J.

Loeber, R., Stouthamer-Loeber, M., & Ahonen, L. (2016). Key behavioral aspects of desistance from conduct problems and delinquency. In J. Shapland, S. Farrall, A. Bottoms (Eds.), *Global Perspectives on Desistance: Reviewing What We Know and Looking to the Future* (pp. 85–98). London: Taylor & Francis Group.

McAra, L., & McVie, S. (2007). Youth justice? The impact of system contact on patterns of desistance from offending. *European Journal of Criminology*, *4*(3), 315–345. https://doi.org/10.1177/1477370807077186.

McGee, T. R., Whitten, T., Williams, C., Jolliffe, D., & Farrington, D. P. (2021). Classification of patterns of offending in developmental and life-course criminology, with special reference to persistence. *Aggression and Violent Behavior*, *59*, 101460. https://doi.org/10.1016/j.avb.2020.101460.

Moffitt, T. E. (1993). Adolescence-limited and life-course-persistent antisocial behavior: A developmental taxonomy. *Psychological Review*, *100*(4), 674–674. Retrieved from http://psycnet.apa.org/journals/rev/100/4/674/.

Moffitt, T. E. (2018). Male antisocial behaviour in adolescence and beyond. *Nature Human Behaviour*, *2*, 177–186.

Nantel-Vivier, A., Pihl, R. O., Côté, S., & Tremblay, R. E. (2014). Developmental association of prosocial behaviour with aggression, anxiety and depression from infancy to preadolescence. *Journal of Child Psychology and Psychiatry and Allied Disciplines*, *55*(10), 1135–1144. https://doi.org/10.1111/jcpp.12235.

Padilla-Walker, L. M., Memmott-Elison, M. K., & Coyne, S. M. (2018). Associations between prosocial and problem behavior from early to late adolescence. *Journal of Youth and Adolescence*, 961–975. https://doi.org/10.1007/s10964-017-0736-y.

Pfattheicher, S., Nielsen, Y. A., & Thielmann, I. (2022). Prosocial behavior and altruism: A review of concepts and definitions. *Current Opinion in Psychology*, *44*, 124–129. https://doi.org/10.1016/j.copsyc.2021.08.021.

Rosenhan, D., & White, G. M. (1967). Observation and rehearsal as determinants of prosocial behavior. *Journal of Personality and Social Psychology*, *5*(4), 424–431.

Talwar, V., & Lee, K. (2008). Social and cognitive correlates of children's lying behavior. *Child Development*, *79*(4), 866–881. https://doi.org/10.1111/j.1467-8624.2008.01164.x.

Tobin, T. J., & Sugai, G. (2005). Preventing problem behaviors: Primary, secondary, and tertiary level prevention interventions for young children. *Journal of Early and Intensive Behavior Intervention*, *2*(3), 125–144. https://doi.org/10.1037/h0100309.

Tonry, M., & Farrington, D. P. (1995). Strategic approaches to crime prevention. *Crime and Justice*, *19*, 1–20.

van der Stouwe, T., Asscher, J. J., Hoeve, M., van der Laan, P. H., & Stams, G. J. J. M. (2016). Social skills training for juvenile delinquents: Post-treatment changes. *Journal of Experimental Criminology*, *12*(4), 515–536. https://doi.org/10.1007/s11292-016-9262-2.

Vandevelde, S., Vander Laenen, F., Van Damme, L., Vanderplasschen, W., Audenaert, K., Broekaert, E., & Vander Beken, T. (2017). Dilemmas in applying strengths-based approaches in working with offenders with mental illness: A critical multidisciplinary review. *Aggression and Violent Behavior*, *32*, 71–79. https://doi.org/10.1016/j.avb.2016.11.008.

Warden, D., & MacKinnon, S. (2003). Prosocial children, bullies and victims: An investigation of their sociometric status, empathy and social problem-solving strategies. *British Journal of Developmental Psychology*, *21*(3), 367–385. https://doi.org/10.1348/026151003322277757.

Welsh, B. C., & Tremblay, R. E. (2020). Early developmental crime prevention forged through knowledge translation: A window into a century of prevention experiment. *Journal of Developmental and Life-Course Criminology*. https://doi.org/10.1007/s40865-020-00145-5.

Wilks, M., Kirby, J., & Nielsen, M. (2018). Children imitate antisocial in-group members. *Developmental Science*, *21*(6), e12675. https://doi.org/10.1111/desc.12675.

Wispé, L. G. (1972). Positive forms of social behavior: An Overview. *Journal of Social Issues*, *28*(3), 1–19. https://doi.org/10.1111/j.1540-4560.1972.tb00029.x.

Zubrick, S. R., Ward, K. A., Silburn, S. R., Lawrence, D., Williams, A. A., Blair, E., ... Sanders, M. R. (2005). Prevention of child behavior problems through universal implementation of a group behavioral family intervention. *Prevention Science*, 6(4), 287–304. https://doi.org/10.1007/s11121-005-0013-2.

Chapter 14

Building Capacity for Sustainable, Scalable, Place-Based Youth Crime Prevention

Ross Homel, Sara Branch, and Kate Freiberg

Introduction

The primary prevention of youth crime is not much practised in Australia. The main purpose of this chapter is to describe the sort of infrastructure linking the worlds of developmental research and practice that needs to be built as part of the process for remedying this lamentable policy lacuna. While innovative intermediary systems that build on developmental/life-course criminological research will not in themselves guarantee lower youth crime rates in the absence of policy settings that hold decision-makers to account for achieving measurable population-level impact, they will furnish frontline professionals with the kinds of tools and supportive arrangements that they will need when governments finally respond sensibly to public demands for safer communities and prioritise science over the "snake oil" of tough-on-crime rhetoric.

The absence of primary youth crime prevention from the Australian policy landscape persists nearly a quarter of a century after publication of a ground-breaking federal government report that made a powerful case for investment in national community-based developmental crime prevention and early intervention policies and initiatives (Developmental Crime Prevention Consortium, 1999). The report was deeply grounded in developmental science, systematically reviewing both the international literature on what worked in developmental crime prevention and a sample of projects and programmes operating across Australia that appeared to address at least a few of the risk and protective factors for youth crime. The great majority of the 46 projects reviewed were well implemented by dedicated staff and showed great promise. However, none had the primary prevention of youth crime (stopping offending before it starts) or even crime reduction (early intervention with at-risk groups of children) as an explicit aim. Moreover, the funding for most was short term and inadequate, and only a few programmes could clearly establish evidence for their impact on any risk or protective factors. Unfortunately, despite huge growth in both developmental science and in the number and range of programmes and services for

DOI: 10.4324/9781003294740-14

families and children now being delivered across Australia, our judgement is that the report's findings remain broadly accurate as a description of the field today. The report therefore failed in its primary objective of inspiring the development and implementation of a wide variety of community-based youth crime prevention initiatives based explicitly on developmental theory, concepts, and empirical research.

This problem is not restricted to Australia. In most countries primary prevention is the poor relation to treatment and detention through the youth justice system (tertiary prevention) and to early intervention through the attempted diversion of at-risk children to prosocial pathways (secondary prevention). Expressing this in more contemporary prevention science terminology, the lion's share of funding goes to "indicated interventions" for children and young people managing significant adversity and caught up in the youth justice system. Such interventions may of course be iatrogenic, especially if they are based on formal youth justice processing (Petrosino et al., 2010). Considerable sums of money are also committed to "selected interventions" through the social service, youth justice, and child protection systems for children deemed at-risk of dropping out of school, abusing drugs, committing crimes, or being maltreated by their families. A tiny proportion of a jurisdiction's budget is typically dedicated to "universal interventions" directed at a whole population or at all members of a specified collectivity like a local community or a cluster of schools (Homel & Thomsen, 2017).

The Policy Challenge

Turning this situation around will require, most fundamentally, a shift in the public policy imagination away from reliance on "expensive and demonstrably ineffective deep end services" (McCarthy & Kerman, 2010, p. 167) towards a focus on youth and child wellbeing at the whole-of-population level. Sound science, integrated with community participation or control, must become the cornerstones of best practice, underpinned by a culture committed to continuous system improvement through clear measurement of agreed outcomes and responsiveness to changing community needs. Such a radical transformation in social service system thinking and practice, we argue, requires the building of bridges across the chasm currently separating the worlds of science and service. Putting this another way, our argument is that we (that is, we developmental/life-course researchers with an interest in seeing our research get used by policy people and practitioners) need to build *linking or intermediary mechanisms and environments* through which respectful relationships between community members, policy people, frontline professionals, and researchers can be developed and sustained (Nutley et al., 2007). Such relationships are a prerequisite for building human capital and technological infrastructure that is specifically grounded in developmental research, furnishing frontline professionals with the tools and supports that make possible both the translation of scientific findings and methods into routine service delivery and, conversely, the incorporation of lived experience into developmental and prevention science (van Wanrooy, 2022).

We recognise that many new and long-established organisations are already seeking to address various aspects of this agenda for system transformation. These organisations range from third sector centres for research, advocacy, and action[1], through government information exchanges that seek to connect research evidence with practice in the human services, to for-purpose private sector businesses that support communities and agencies to make better use of data[2]. Much of the work carried out by these organisations is imaginative and innovative, grounded in the needs of practitioners, and is technically sophisticated. One might describe these organisations as an "intermediary ecosystem" which is highly dynamic, closely attuned to emerging policy and practice imperatives, with new organisations with new capabilities regularly being formed to meet newly perceived needs.

Critical as these developments are, our judgement is that this ecosystem is currently largely (but by no means entirely) disconnected from the world of developmental/life-course research and from prevention science[3]. This does not mean that many individual university researchers, especially those from disciplines with clinical skills (social work, medicine and health sciences, psychology), are not active in building tools, professional skills, and resources for a wide range of research translation activities. However, these tools and resources are mostly restricted to specific research programmes, with translational innovations not yet finding their way into the wider intermediary ecosystem. Stating the problem more plainly, with one exception that we will discuss shortly, there is no widely available, easily accessible system for connecting practitioners working with children and families, usually in challenging community environments, with the practical fruits of innovative developmental research.

There are several serious consequences of this disconnect between university research and service delivery. One consequence is that organisations sometimes commit considerable time and resources to addressing problems de novo for which there is a well-developed developmental literature. The other side of the same coin is that sometimes organisations are not even conscious that a problem or issue exists, such as the extreme difficulty of achieving genuine collaboration in an equal partnership that entails the surrender of significant organisational resources in pursuit of a commonly agreed goal (Homel et al., 2019). As Bruder (2005, p. 31) observed, "In the history of service integration one is struck by its nobility of intent, its tenacity of purpose and its ineffectiveness in implementation." Simply put, organisations are often unaware of their need for research-based tools and expert knowledge to achieve what seems, on the surface, to be a straightforward goal.

Perhaps the most serious consequence of the disconnect between "town and gown" is the absence of theory-driven practice or at least the absence of unifying conceptual schemas that guide the cycle of service delivery and evaluation. This means that the intermediary infrastructure required for sustained, population-level impact on youth crime and other adolescent behavioural health problems exists only in fragmentary form, with the fragments collectively falling short of the logical sequence of stages that developmental/life-course research and preventive practice require. Putting this in more concrete terms, the need to *evaluate the impact of services* for children and families has long been accepted. The importance of using, where possible, *evidence-based or evidence-informed interventions* has been more recently widely acknowledged. And community agencies that work with children and families have long recognised that without *good-quality data on the needs of children* in the communities that they work in, they are "flying blind." What is missing from routine service delivery, we contend, is a methodology that binds all these ingredients, and others, into a coherent set of community-controlled practices grounded in developmental research and directed at sustained population-wide impact within a framework of continuous quality improvement and iterative learning based on rigorous measurement of inputs and outcomes.

To make the discussion of our ambitious and comprehensive proposal tractable, we restrict our focus to place-based initiatives in disadvantaged communities with intended collective impact (Hart & Connolly, 2022; Homel et al., 2015). We also focus on building the specific intermediary structures required to get developmental/life-course research and prevention science translated into community practices that change pathways and measurably reduce youth offending. While there is no one correct way of doing this, in the following section we briefly describe an approach to forging an intermediary system that we developed during the Creating Pathways to Child Wellbeing in Disadvantaged Communities Project (the *CREATE Project*: Homel et al., 2015). In this project we explicitly built on, and adapted, the methods of *Communities That Care*, recognising its unique status as a place-based collective impact strategy with population-level impact on youth crime (Fagan et al., 2019).

Pathways to Scale: Communities That Care and CREATE

The road to scale runs through public systems (McCarthy & Kerman, 2010). What this means is that only state or national governments have the personnel, the bureaucratic apparatus, the resources, and the mandate to deliver services that can reach, year in year out, the whole population or a high proportion of sub-populations with specific needs or vulnerabilities. The problem is that, at least in Australia, government services for children, youth, and families delivered by non-government community agencies mostly cannot be demonstrated to have improved any outcomes at all for children, young people, or caregivers, especially at a population or whole-of-community level. In other words, government-funded, place-based, social service programmes have scale, but little demonstrated impact (Wilks, Lahausse, & Edwards, 2015).

Once again, this failure of Australian government services to demonstrate impact is not unique. A rapid systematic review of the international scientific evidence has shown that only two universal prevention initiatives, both developed in the United States outside of government, have achieved population-level impact on child and youth outcomes (Paul Ramsay Foundation, 2022). We focus here on one of these approaches, Communities That Care (CTC), a long-established, place-based, population health model for reducing the prevalence of adolescent "behavioural health problems" including antisocial behaviour, substance abuse, and crime (Fagan, Hawkins, Catalano, & Farrington, 2019). Importantly the CTC approach was developed in light of the social development model of adolescent development (that is, the CTC model is theory-based), but the developers also drew heavily on insights from a range of community-based participative research (CBPR) projects in formulating their measures and overall methodology. CBPR activities involving active collaboration between scientists and community members remain a prominent feature of the CTC approach. The CTC model is therefore thoroughly developmental in form and in practice, operating through a coherent cycle of five stages (Box 14.1).

Box 14.1. Communities That Care

Key Elements

- Mobilisation of community residents, human service professionals, and local leaders into community coalitions, which are supported and sustained at the local level
- Technical assistance and support are provided by a central organisation
- Planning is based on epidemiological data on adolescent risk and protective factors collected from an adolescent survey
- Coalitions can choose from a selection of evidence-based interventions
- Interventions are delivered by organisations under the auspices of the coalition
- Has been implemented in a range of countries including Australia

Cycle of Five Stages

Getting Started – Assessing community readiness and identifying key stakeholders

Getting Organised – Training key leaders, building and training the coalition
Developing a Profile – From community-level risk and protective factors reported by young people
Creating a Plan – Targeting priority risk and protective factors with tested interventions
Implementing and Evaluating – Train implementers, sustain collaborations, evaluate, reflect on outcomes and processes, and get ready to go round the cycle again

The population impact of the CTC system model is supported by a randomised controlled trial across 24 communities in the United States (Hawkins et al., 2014; Oesterle et al., 2015), by a state-wide effectiveness trial in Pennsylvania (Feinberg et al., 2010), and by numerous implementations around the world and in communities mainly in the southern parts of Australia, particularly Victoria (Rowland et al., 2022). In all of these evaluations, meaningful population- or community-level reductions in crime and other adolescent behavioural health problems have been demonstrated.

The unfortunate news is that very few people in Australia working on place-based social policy or in the community services sector have ever heard of CTC. The reasons for this are something of a mystery, given that other US-developed evidenced-based programmes like Multisystemic Therapy and Nurse-Family Partnerships have been implemented in Australia with government support (Porter & Nuntavisit, 2016; Segal et al., 2018). Perhaps the mystery of the CTC science-policy disconnect is partly explained by the fact that CTC is not just a programme but an "operating system" based on mobilising and empowering community members to act through multiple programmes tailored to the needs of their own young people. Governments may fund CTC initiatives and local government personnel may serve as active participants, but on the whole CTC can largely bypass government agencies and be very successful, depending on the energy and fund-raising capacities of local coalitions. This feature of CTC is a huge strength for proponents of democratic participation at a level of subsidiarity that best suits the problem at hand (Hart & Connolly, 2022), but is also a major weakness if the aim is to scale impact to a national or state-wide level, for which as we have argued comprehensive government participation is critical.

The conundrum posed by the evidence for CTC's potential for population-wide youth crime reduction combined with its policy invisibility in Australia was one of the main motivations for the development of the CREATE Project (Box 14.2) (Branch et al., 2019). The questions posed by the CREATE developers were twofold. The first question was whether an adapted form of the

CTC prevention support infrastructure (its measures, methods, and technical assistance regime) could be built into the routine practices of Communities for Children (CfC), an Australian programme that delivers services for children aged 0–12 years and their families (and can include children up to 18 years of age) through local agency partnerships coordinated by an independent non-government organisation (the Facilitating Partner) funded by the Commonwealth Government[4]. The rationale for the selection of CfC as a "prevention delivery system" (Wandersman et al., 2008) was that it has already achieved a degree of scale by operating in 52 socially disadvantaged communities in Australia since 2005 (Homel et al., 2015). In addition, the partnership model of delivery at the local level made the CfC framework similar in form to that of CTC, albeit more "top-down" than the grassroots, community mobilisation approach of CTC. The second question that we attempted to address was whether implementation of this infrastructure in a small sample of CfC communities could be shown through a quasi-experimental design to improve child wellbeing[5].

Box 14.2. The CREATE Model for Place-Based Collective Impact

CREATE Operating Principles

Collaborative practice – Through community partnerships or coalitions

Relationships-based – Strong connections between service providers and between providers and service consumers, but even more critically between organisations, horizontally within a community and vertically up to head offices

Early action in developmental pathways – prevention

Accountability of providers and consumers through shared, transparent, and measurable goals

Training of the workforce to access and use translational tools and resources effectively

Evidence-based services fitted to context

CREATE Support Infrastructure

1. Collective Change Facilitators – skilled system intermediaries
2. User-friendly science-based electronic resources that support integrated measurement, reporting, and action. These include:
    - A validated measure of child wellbeing for children aged 6–12 years derived from an engaging touch screen game, Rumble's Quest (described in Chapter 9)

- A validated measure of Parent Empowerment and Efficacy (PEEM) (Freiberg et al., 2014)
- A multidimensional online tool for self-directed use by community coalitions to measure, report, and review their own coalition function processes (Homel et al., 2019)
- Principal-led participatory action modules to enable school-family community partnerships
- An online Economic Support and Reporting Tool (ESRT) for analysing and supporting the economic efficiency of coalition-level action to achieve specified improvements in child outcomes

Cycle of Five Stages

Coming Together – Establishing, maintaining, and strengthening community collaborations/coalitions
Deciding Together – Collecting and interpreting community-level data on child risk and protective factors as a basis for action
Planning Together – Selecting evidence-based programmes that address priority child risk and protective factors
Doing Together – Implementing selected programmes through the coalition
Reviewing Together – Reviewing effectiveness through evaluations of individual

The two central pillars of the CREATE support infrastructure are user-friendly science-based electronic resources and skilled system intermediaries whom we call *collective change facilitators* (Branch et al., 2022). Both types of "boundary spanners," the electronic and the human, help optimise the research translation conditions required for community-based participative research and co-creation processes to flourish (Wood & Zuber-Skerritt, 2022) and for new measurement instruments, scientific tools, methodologies, and evidence-based resources to be developed that are responsive to local contexts, empower local people, and are suitable for use by frontline professionals as well as by community members and sometimes relatively untrained practitioners.

The CREATE operating model is underpinned by six principles encapsulated in the CREATE acronym (Box 14.2). Like CTC, CREATE operates through a coherent change cycle which can also be viewed as its theory of change. Like CTC the CREATE change cycle is designed to operate as a system for continuous quality improvement, especially regarding collaborative practices and impact on community-level child outcomes, both of which can be expected to improve most during the second and later cycles. As part of CREATE we built integrated measurement, reporting, and action support systems incorporating: Rumble's Quest, a valid and robust measure of child social-emotional wellbeing (Freiberg et al., in press); an instrument for assessing the health of a community collaboration (Homel et al., 2019); a validated measure of parent efficacy and empowerment (Freiberg et al., 2014); resources for school principals; and an online tool for supporting the economic efficiency of coalition-level action.

These technology-based support resources both parallel and extend the kinds of technical resources offered through CTC and were built with an eye to scalability through the Communities for Children programme or through primary schools. For example, Rumbles Quest (described in Chapter 9) was trialled and implemented in schools and measures risk and protective factors for children aged 6–12 years. It complements CTC's Youth Survey for adolescents from Grade 6 onwards, enabling schools and community coalitions to plan interventions for primary-aged children with more data-guided precision than might be possible relying only on the CTC survey. Similarly, the survey of coalition functioning parallels survey instruments extensively analysed by CTC researchers to assess factors contributing to impact on youth behavioural health outcomes and to the sustainability of coalitions (Feinberg et al., 2008). It was developed in partnership with CfC coalitions to ensure that it was a robust and useful instrument under Australian conditions.

Critical to the success of the CREATE online supports was the work of Collective Change Facilitators (CCF). Although all the electronic tools were integrated with extensive user-friendly resources designed to promote self-directed, iterative use across multiple change cycles, we realised from the outset that many service organisations, community coalitions, and schools would need extensive support from trained system intermediaries who spoke the language of both research and practice. We conceptualised the CCF role as going beyond technical assistance, the dominant model for such positions in the prevention science literature, to emphasise:

> the CCF as a critical friend who guides community coalitions to develop the goals, roles, procedures and relationships necessary for healthy coalition functioning. ... *They should always see themselves, and importantly be seen by others, as being close to, but separate from, the community coalition.*
>
> (Branch et al., 2022, p. 208; emphasis in original)

We placed particular emphasis on both initial training and ongoing professional development activities with a view to forming *a learning community* to support the development of the CCF role. Our evaluation of the CCF role led us to conclude that collective change facilitation should be viewed as an important new profession that could be incorporated into backbone organisations for collective impact projects. However, to be effective CCFs need unimpeded *access* to frontline staff and managers so that they can build relationships with the people who have the power to make adequate *time* available for the many aspects of the CCF role and to create the *safe settings* "in which exploration and learning could lead to more reflective and data-informed practices" (Branch et al., 2022: p. 216).

Looking to the Future

Despite financial and in-kind support from both government and non-government partners for the development of the CCF role and for the electronic tools and supports, the CREATE prevention support system is not yet mainstream within any government place-based collective impact initiatives, the settings for which it was specifically designed. In many respects it therefore shares the current policy isolation of CTC. It seems clear that the adage "build it and they will come" does not at present apply in the Australian context for system infrastructure approaches such as CTC and CREATE, even with clear evidence of community-wide impact as in the case of CTC or when government is an active partner in the building process as in the case of CREATE. The critical shift in the public policy imagination away from deep-end services to the primary prevention of youth crime has manifestly not yet occurred.

Nevertheless, the mounting evidence internationally and in Australia for the population-level impact of CTC, combined with the huge demand in the social services sector for training and resources to support data-guided action and evidence-based practice, suggests that eventually the policy tide will turn. One barrier to progress appears to be a lack of accountability by decision-makers at multiple levels for the achievement through place-based initiatives of measurable population-level reductions in youth crime and improvements in child wellbeing. These policy barriers may however be steadily eroded if DLC researchers and prevention scientists can accumulate further evidence for impact on youth outcomes through innovations in translational or intermediary systems tailored to communities' needs. Successful community implementations can help to build a constituency which demands government support for approaches that work (in contrast to tough on crime policies which do not) and that place control at the local level, thereby creating a political environment within which CTC and the CREATE prevention support systems, as well as other innovative translational resources that are rooted deeply in prevention science and developmental/life-course criminology research, could at last find their place in the sun.

Notes

1 The 'third sector' refers to the work of the voluntary sector, nongovernmental organisations, or non-profit organisations. These organisations are distinct from

private sector businesses but to some extent overlap. For example, some businesses operate solely for social benefit, reinvesting all profits to improve their capabilities. Third sector organisations are also not part of the public sector (i.e., the state), but may well depend on government funding for their survival.

2 Examples of third sector centres include the *Dartington Service Design Lab* in the United Kingdom, which is a research and service design charity dedicated to improving outcomes for children and young people (https://www.dartington.org.uk), and the *Centre for Just Places* established by Jesuit Social Services Australia to support place-based approaches to social and ecological problems through research, collaboration, engagement and knowledge exchange (https://jss.org.au/what-we-do/centre-for-just-places/). An example of a government information exchange is *Child Family Communities Australia* (https://aifs.gov.au/projects/child-family-community-australia), which provides evidence-based resources and interactive assistance for professionals working to protect children, support families, and strengthen communities across Australian jurisdictions. An example of a private company is *Seer Data and Analytics*, whose aim is to make the fruits of data science available to empower communities and improve lives through data-driven decision making (https://seerdata.ai).

3 The Australian Research Alliance for Children and Youth (https://www.aracy.org.au) is one notable exception. Established in the early 2000s by famous child health researcher and 2003 Australian of the Year Professor Fiona Stanley AC, ARACY has from its inception striven to connect researchers with the worlds of policy and practice. Another exception is Communities That Care Ltd (https://www.communitiesthatcare.org.au), discussed in this chapter.

4 https://www.dss.gov.au/our-responsibilities/families-and-children/programs-services/family-support-program/family-and-children-s-services

5 This objective was unfortunately thwarted by the 2020 Covid lockdowns across Australia.

References

Branch, S., Freiberg, K., & Homel, H. (2019). Strengthening the prevention delivery system for children in disadvantaged communities through infrastructure development. *Developing Practice*, *53*, 54–73.

Branch, S., Freiberg, K., Homel, R., & Stubbs, C. (2022). The importance of access, time and space – Developing the collective change facilitator role as part of a multi-partner research program. In L. Wood (Ed.), *Community-based research with vulnerable populations: Ethical, inclusive and sustainable frameworks for knowledge generation* (pp. 205–220). London: Springer Nature Ltd. ISBN: 978-3-030-86401-9.

Bruder, M. (2005). Service coordination and integration in a developmental systems approach to early intervention. In M. Guralnick (Ed.), *The developmental systems approach to early intervention* (pp. 29–58). London: Paul H. Brookes.

Developmental Crime Prevention Consortium. (1999). *Pathways to prevention: Developmental and early intervention approaches to crime in Australia (Summary Report, Full Report and Appendices)* (400 pages). Canberra: Australian Government Publishing Service. Retrieved from https://www.researchgate.net/publication/304737879_Pathways_to_Prevention_Developmental_and_Early_Intervention_Approaches_to_Crime_in_Australia.

Fagan, A.A., Hawkins, J.D., Catalano, R.F. & Farrington, D.P. (2019). *Communities That Care: Building community engagement and capacity to prevent youth behavior problems*. New York, Oxford University Press.

Feinberg, M. E., Bontempo, D. E., & Greenberg, M. T. (2008). Predictors and level of sustainability of community prevention coalitions. *American Journal of Preventive Medicine, 34*(6), 495–501. https://doi.org/10.1016/j.amepre.2008.01.030.

Feinberg, M. E., Jones, D., Greenberg, M. T., Osgood, D. W., & Bontempo, D. (2010). Effects of the communities that care model in Pennsylvania on change in adolescent risk and problem behaviors. *Prevention Science, 11*(2), 163–171. https://doi.org/10.1007/s11121-009-0161-x.

Freiberg, K., Homel, R., & Branch, S. (2014). The Parent Empowerment and Efficacy Measure (PEEM): A tool for strengthening the accountability and effectiveness of family support services. *Australian Social Work, 67*(3), 405–418. https://doi.org/10.1080/0312407X.2014.902980.

Freiberg, K., Homel, R., Branch, S., Allen, J., McGee, T., Vasco, D., & Haskard, K. (2023). The development and psychometric properties of a scalable digital measure of social and emotional wellbeing for middle childhood. *Applied Developmental Science*. https://doi.org/10.1080/10888691.2023.2208753.

Hart, A., & Connolly, J. (2022). Commonwealth place-based policies for addressing geographically concentrated disadvantage: A typology and critical analysis. *Australian Journal of Public Administration, 81*(1), 145–162. Retrieved from https://onlinelibrary.wiley.com/doi/epdf/10.1111/1467-8500.12498.

Hawkins, J. D., Oesterle, S., Brown, E. C., Abbott, R. D., & Catalano, R. F. (2014). Youth problem behaviors 8 years after implementing the communities that care prevention system: A community-randomized trial. *JAMA Paediatrics, 168*(2), 122–129.

Homel, R., Branch, S., & Freiberg, K. (2019). Implementation through community coalitions: The power of technology and community-based intermediaries. *Commentary, special issue on Implementation and Adaptation: Measurement and Monitoring Systems of the Journal of Primary Prevention, 40*(1), 143–148. First online. https://doi.org/10.1007/s10935-019-00541-8.

Homel, R., Freiberg, K., & Branch, S. (2015). CREATE-ing capacity to take developmental crime prevention to scale: A community-based approach within a national framework. *Australian and New Zealand Journal of Criminology, 48*(3), 367–385. https://doi.org/10.1177/0004865815589826.

Homel, R., & Thomsen, L. (2017). Developmental crime prevention. In N. Tilley & A. Sidebottom (Eds.), *Handbook of crime prevention and community safety* (2nd ed., pp.57–86). New York: Routledge.

McCarthy, P. & Kerman, B. (2010). Inside the belly of the beast: How bad systems trump good programs. *Administration and Policy in Mental Health and Mental Health Services Research, 37*, 167–172. https://doi.org/10.1007/s10488-010-0273-4

Nutley, S. M., Walter, I., & Davies, H. T. O. (2007). *Using evidence: How research can inform public services*. Bristol: The Policy Press.

Oesterle, S., Hawkins, J. D., Kuklinski, M. R., Fagan, A. A., Fleming, C., Rhew, I. C., … Catalano, R. F. (2015). Effects of communities that care on males' and females' drug use and delinquency 9 years after baseline in a community-randomized trial. *American Journal of Community Psychology, 56*(3–4), 217–228. https://doi.org/10.1007/s10464-015-9749-4.

Paul Ramsay Foundation. (2022). *Australian research roundtable: Promoting early life relational health to strengthen wellbeing within and across generations*. Darlinghurst NSW, Australia: The Paul Ramsay Foundation.

Petrosino, A., Turpin-Petrosino, C., & Guckenburg, S. (2010). Formal system processing of juveniles: Effects on delinquency. *Campbell Systematic Reviews, 1*(1). https://doi.org/10.4073/csr.2010.1.

Porter, M., & Nuntavisit, L. (2016). An evaluation of multisystemic Therapy with Australian families. *Australian and New Zealand Journal of Family Therapy, 37*(4), 443–462. https://doi.org/10.1002/anzf.1182.

Rowland, B., Kelly, A. B., Mohebbi, M., Kremer, P., Abrahams, C., Abimanyi-Ochom, J., ... Toumbourou, J. W. (2022). Evaluation of communities that care: Effects on municipal youth crime rates in Victoria, Australia: 2010–2019. *Prevention Research, 23*(1), 24–35. https://doi.org/10.1007/s11121-021-01297-6.

Segal, L., Nguyen, H., Gent, D., Hampton, C., & Boffa, J. (2018). Child protection outcomes of the Australian Nurse Family Partnership Program for Aboriginal infants and their mothers in Central Australia. *PLOS One, 13*(12), e0208764. https://doi.org/10.1371/journal.pone.0208764.

Van Wanrooy, B. (2022). *Lived experience and research: Complementary or competitors in the policy process?* Analysis & policy observatory, October 18, 2022.

Wandersman, A., Duffy, J., Flaspohler, P., Noonan, R., Lubell, K., Stillman, L., ... Saul, J. (2008). Bridging the gap between prevention research and practice: The interactive systems framework for dissemination and implementation. *American Journal of Community Psychology, 41*(3–4), 171–181.

Wilks, S., Lahausse, J., & Edwards, B. (2015). *Commonwealth place-based service delivery initiatives: Key learnings project (Research Report No. 32)*. Melbourne: Australian Institute of Family Studies. Retrieved from https://aifs.gov.au/sites/default/files/publication-documents/rr32_0.pdf.

Wood, L., & Zuber-Skerritt, O. (2022). Community-based research in higher education: Research partnerships for the common good. In L. Wood (Ed.), *Community-based research with vulnerable populations: Ethical, Inclusive and Sustainable Frameworks for Knowledge Generation* (pp. 3–30). London: Springer Nature Ltd. ISBN: 978-3-030-86401-9.

Chapter 15

Commentary

Developmental and Life-Course Criminology Has Come of Age!

David P. Farrington

Introduction

I am delighted to welcome this book, which shows that Developmental and Life-Course Criminology (DLC) has come of age and points the way to further exciting developments! However, before commenting on some of the chapters, I will discuss what DLC is all about. I will focus on advances in knowledge so far and on desirable further developments. For an account of the history of DLC, see Piquero (2023).

Key Issues in DLC

DLC is essentially the study of the development of offending and antisocial behaviour by individuals throughout life. There is a focus on onset, continuation, and desistance and on the influence of risk and protective factors at different ages on offending at different ages. There is some ambiguity about the meaning of protective factors; some researchers view them as opposite to risk factors (e.g., high IQ as opposed to low IQ), while other researchers view them as factors that interact with and nullify the influence of risk factors (see e.g., Farrington & Ttofi, 2011). There is also some interest in reasons and motives for offending at different ages, and in sequences of offences (see e.g., Basto-Pereira & Farrington, 2019). DLC is in addition very interested in the effects of life events (e.g., getting married: Theobald & Farrington, 2009) on the development of offending. A further important topic is the intergenerational transmission of offending (see, e.g., Farrington et al., 2017).

In order to investigate these topics, prospective longitudinal studies are needed, and 20 major longitudinal studies were reviewed by Farrington (2021c). Unfortunately, most studies of risk factors are based on between-individual comparisons, which make it difficult to establish whether factors have causal effects or whether they are merely correlated with offending (e.g., because they are measuring a similar underlying theoretical construct to offending). Since the concept of a cause is based on the idea that changes within individuals in X (a presumed causal factor) are followed by

DOI: 10.4324/9781003294740-15

changes within individuals in offending, it is important to carry out within-individual analyses to study causes. For example, in the Pittsburgh Youth Study, Farrington and colleagues (2002) found that peer delinquency was the strongest correlate of delinquency according to between-individual correlations, but that changes within individuals in peer delinquency over time did not predict changes in delinquency over time. In contrast, changes within individuals in poor parental supervision, low parental reinforcement, and low involvement of the boy in family activities did predict changes in delinquency over time. Therefore, they concluded that these latter three variables were possible causes of delinquency, but that peer delinquency was not. It seems likely that, because of co-offending, peer delinquency may be measuring the same underlying construct as delinquency itself.

In order to investigate within-individual changes, frequent assessments of risk factors and of offending are needed within longitudinal studies. The most usual risk factors that are measured are individual, family, peer, school, and socio-economic factors. There should also be more efforts to study biological, neighbourhood, and situational influences on offending, and more efforts to study protective factors. DLC has advanced knowledge enormously about the development of offenders, but there also needs to be an emphasis on studying the commission of offences (i.e., on how the potential to offend becomes the actuality of offending). Moreover, multiple cohort studies are needed to distinguish between age, period, and cohort effects (see, e.g., Fabio et al., 2006; Farrington, 1990) and investigate the influence of historical contexts. It is also important to establish the extent to which results are widely replicable and generalisable in different contexts and with different samples.

Another method of advancing knowledge about causes is to include experimental interventions within a longitudinal study. For example, if a parent training programme was followed by a reduction in delinquency in a randomised experiment (see, e.g., Piquero et al., 2016), or in a high-quality quasi-experiment, this would suggest that parental child-rearing had a causal effect. Unfortunately, relatively few longitudinal-experimental studies have been carried out (see, e.g., Farrington et al., 2010), and there have been relatively few attempts to follow up individuals after randomised experiments for long periods (Farrington, 2021a). Longitudinal-experimental studies could investigate short-term and long-term effects of interventions and developmental sequences linking them. It is also important to study the effectiveness of developmental prevention methods (see, e.g., Farrington, 2021b). In addition, it would be desirable to study interactions between types of individuals and types of effects of interventions.

Finally, there have been great advances in DLC theories to explain major findings (see e.g., McGee & Farrington, 2016). However, most theories yield qualitative rather than quantitative predictions. For example, they predict that major risk factors lead to offending, but they do not predict exact numbers. However, Barnett and colleagues (1987, 1989) developed and tested a simple mathematical model of offending, and more recently MacLeod and Farrington (2022) developed and tested quantitative predictions in the Cambridge Study in Delinquent Development (CSDD) and Pittsburgh Youth Study. Ideally, there should be more efforts to derive and test quantitative predictions from major DLC theories.

Commentary on the Chapters

Because of space limitations, I can only comment in some detail on a small number of chapters which address key DLC topics in this important book. Chapter 2 by Carleen Thompson and her colleagues is very interesting in arguing that many challenges to DLC research can be solved by using linked administrative data, which can produce quicker results than long-term prospective longitudinal studies. In particular, they contend that linked administrative data can assist in establishing the generalisability of results, the effects of historical contexts, and within-individual influences. They further point out that linked administrative data can assist in studying rare events and rare crimes and can assist in translating results into effective policies, because of the collaboration with government agencies. Their arguments are very persuasive.

Commendably, in Chapter 4 Jacqueline Allen and Corrie Williams discuss different methods of studying within-individual changes, including latent growth models, trajectory mixture models, multi-level hierarchical linear models, cross-lagged panel models, and dynamic structural equation models. Clearly, most psychologists and criminologists would need statistical assistance in applying many of these techniques. The authors end by raising two important issues. First, it is important to study the dynamic interplay between individuals and situations at different developmental stages that push a child on to a high-risk pathway (with multiple risk factors). Second, it may be important to understand the influence of life events such as marriage, not as a discrete event, but rather as part of a longer dynamic process. This chapter is highly thought-provoking.

I was particularly impressed by the two chapters that were first authored by Catia Malvaso (Chapters 10 and 12) because they address important DLC issues. Chapter 10, written in collaboration with Danielle Harris, Tara McGee, and Jessica Craig, focuses on Adverse Childhood Experiences (ACEs), which have become very important in the medical and health literature. These typically describe traumatic experiences before age 18, such as physical abuse or witnessing family violence, that influence later health and wellbeing. They have not been studied a great deal in the criminological literature, but Craig and colleagues (2017, 2021) showed that a high ACE score at age 8–10 predicted later offending in the CSDD. In order to investigate the extent to which ACEs predict delinquency, it seems important to measure them long before age 18.

Malvaso and her colleagues point out that ACEs are a very incomplete list of risk factors for offending. Sutton (2022) also made this point and presented a much more complete matrix of risk and protective factors at different ages for later offending. Malvaso and her colleagues also state that ACEs do not really guide interventions, because generally they do not describe causal or explanatory factors. The ACE score is commonly used as a screening tool, but the systematic review by Malvaso et al. (2022) concluded that it was unclear whether ACEs were simply correlates or coinciding vulnerabilities in a high-risk population, rather than causal or explanatory factors. Therefore, Malvaso and her colleagues conclude that the use of ACEs as a screening tool is likely to be ineffective.

Malvaso and colleagues (2022) also pointed out that the majority of studies of ACEs were cross-sectional and often based on retrospective reports. They argued that DLC researchers were well-positioned to address many key issues in ACE research (e.g., when, how, and for whom exposure to ACEs leads to offending), because of their use of prospective longitudinal studies. Moreover, DLC researchers could more adequately draw implications for the prevention of offending and explain how ACEs fitted into DLC theories of offending. Overall, knowledge about ACEs could be greatly advanced by new prospective longitudinal studies that measured ACE items and later offending (as well as medical and health problems).

In Chapter 12 Catia Malvaso focuses on child maltreatment, which made up five of the ten classic ACEs described by Felitti et al. (1998). She describes three studies: a large-scale study of linked administrative data on about 500,000 children in South Australia, the CSDD, and a small-scale but detailed survey of ACEs and trauma among young people under Youth Justice supervision in South Australia. She addresses three important DLC issues: (1) describe the maltreatment-offending associations; (2) predict which children will offend later, out of those experiencing maltreatment; (3) estimate the causal effect of maltreatment on offending, and potential mediators of this effect. She also discusses how to translate evidence into policy. Overall, this is a very good model of how to conduct DLC research.

The two chapters first authored by Corrie Williams (Chapters 9 and 13) are also very important in advancing DLC knowledge and practice. The first of these chapters, by Corrie Williams, Susan Dennison, Tara McGee, and Janet Ransley, describe the Transforming Corrections to Transform Lives (TCTL) project, which targets the important DLC issue of the intergenerational transmission of offending. This project aims to help imprisoned mothers and their children, and it is informed by extensive DLC research on risk factors for recidivism and intergenerational transmission. Typically, the imprisoned mothers are seen in focus groups, and the researchers act as a channel of communication between the mothers and correctional and child protection agencies. This chapter describes how DLC researchers can move beyond traditional approaches and understand the needs of the mothers and children and the barriers to support among the agencies.

In her single-authored chapter, Corrie Williams addresses the very important (but somewhat neglected) DLC issues of prosocial behaviour and strengths-based developmental crime prevention. She points out that DLC researchers have been mostly concerned with antisocial behaviour, but prosocial behaviour is not just the other end of the continuum from antisocial behaviour. Rather, prosocial behaviour is concerned with sharing, helping, and comforting. Unfortunately, most research on prosocial behaviour is based on infancy and pre-school children and is cross-sectional in nature. Therefore, DLC researchers could make great contributions to knowledge by investigating prosocial behaviour later than early childhood in prospective longitudinal studies. She correctly identifies the Social Development Model as the major DLC theory that aims to explain the development of both prosocial and antisocial behaviour; it has been very successful in reducing antisocial behaviour in the Seattle Social Development Project (SSDP), which is a very important developmental prevention project (Catalano et al., 2021).

In Chapter 14, Ross Homel, Sara Branch, and Kate Freiberg describe another important developmental prevention project: CREATE (Creating Pathways to Child Wellbeing in Disadvantaged Communities). This is based on an extremely important and influential project: Communities That Care (CTC: Fagan et al., 2019). CTC aims to reduce delinquency and drug use by implementing particular prevention strategies that have demonstrated effectiveness in reducing risk factors and/or enhancing protective factors. Like the SSDP, CTC is based on the Social Development Model. There is great emphasis in CTC in enhancing protective factors and building on strengths, partly because this is often more attractive to communities than the more negative approach of tackling risk factors. Ross Homel and his colleagues explain that the CREATE project was embedded within the well-established federally funded programme called Communities for Children, which aimed to increase the wellbeing of children from birth to age 12 in 52 disadvantaged communities. This is a very interesting case history of applying primary prevention in the Australian context.

The other chapters that I have not chosen to discuss in detail are also very interesting. David and Danielle Harris review data visualisation techniques using visual artists; Li Eriksson and her colleagues review the Life Event Calendar methodology; Krystal Lockwood and her colleagues review the use of this methodology with Aboriginal and Torres Strait Islander peoples; Kate Freiberg and Ross Homel describe Rumble's Quest, which is a digital game-based assessment of social and emotional wellbeing in middle childhood; and Katherine McLachlan analyses the trauma-informed sentencing of adult defendants in South Australia, based on sentencing remarks made by judges.

In conclusion, I am very happy to recommend this book to anyone who is interested in knowing about DLC, and especially in the practical application of DLC knowledge in developmental prevention techniques. The book is very important in grappling with important issues such as establishing causal influences, and it is very helpful in demonstrating the use of large-scale administrative data and the simultaneous collaboration with governmental agencies. Also, I am very pleased to see the application of internationally famous prevention techniques, such as CTC, in the Australian context. Hopefully, this book will encourage more application of effective techniques to prevent offending. That would be in everyone's interests!

References

Barnett, A., Blumstein, A., & Farrington, D. P. (1987). Probabilistic models of youthful criminal careers. *Criminology*, *25*(1), 83–107.

Barnett, A., Blumstein, A., & Farrington, D. P. (1989). A prospective test of a criminal career model. *Criminology*, *27*(2), 373–388.

Basto-Pereira, M., & Farrington, D. P. (2019). Advancing knowledge about lifelong crime sequences. *British Journal of Criminology*, *59*(2), 354–377.

Catalano, R. F., Hawkins, J. D., Kosterman, R., Bailey, J. A., Oesterle, S., Cambron, C., & Farrington, D. P. (2021). Applying the social development model in middle childhood to promote healthy development: Effects from primary school through the 30s and across generations. *Journal of Developmental and Life-Course Criminology*, *7*(1), 66–86.

Craig, J. M., Malvaso, C. G., & Farrington, D. P. (2021). All in the family? Exploring the intergenerational association of exposure to adverse childhood experiences and their effect on offending behaviour. *Youth Violence and Juvenile Justice*, *19*(3), 292–307.

Craig, J. M., Piquero, A. R., Farrington, D. P., & Ttofi, M. M. (2017). A little early risk goes a long bad way: Adverse childhood experiences and life-course offending in the Cambridge study. *Journal of Criminal Justice*, *53*, 34–45.

Fabio, A., Loeber, R., Balasubramani, G. K., Roth, J., Fu, W., & Farrington, D. P. (2006). Why some generations are more violent than others: Assessment of age, period and cohort effects. *American Journal of Epidemiology*, *164*(2), 151–160.

Fagan, A. A., Hawkins, J. D., Catalano, R. F., & Farrington, D. P. (2019). *Communities that care: Building community engagement and capacity to prevent youth behavior problems*. New York: Oxford University Press.

Farrington, D. P. (1990). Age, period, cohort, and offending. In D. M. Gottfredson & R. V. Clarke (Eds.), *Policy and theory in criminal justice: Contributions in honour of Leslie T. Wilkins* (pp. 51–75). Aldershot: Avebury.

Farrington, D. P. (2021a). Long-term follow-ups of criminological experiments. *Victims and Offenders*, *16*(7), 996–1010.

Farrington, D. P. (2021b). The developmental evidence base: Prevention. In D. A. Crighton & G. J. Towl (Eds.), *Forensic psychology* (3rd ed., pp. 263–293). Chichester: Wiley.

Farrington, D. P. (2021c). The developmental evidence base: Psychosocial research. In D. A. Crighton & G. J. Towl (Eds.), *Forensic psychology* (3rd ed., pp. 294–329). Chichester: Wiley.

Farrington, D. P., Loeber, R., & Welsh, B. C. (2010). Longitudinal-experimental studies. In A. R. Piquero & D. Weisburd (Eds.), *Handbook of quantitative criminology* (pp. 503–518). New York: Springer.

Farrington, D. P., Loeber, R., Yin, Y., & Anderson, S. J. (2002). Are within-individual causes of delinquency the same as between-individual causes? *Criminal Behaviour and Mental Health*, *12*(1), 53–68.

Farrington, D. P., & Ttofi, M. M. (2011). Protective and promotive factors in the development of offending. In T. Bliesener, A. Beelman, & M. Stemmler (Eds.), *Antisocial behavior and crime: Contributions of developmental and evaluation research to prevention and intervention* (pp. 71–88). Cambridge, MA: Hogrefe.

Farrington, D. P., Ttofi, M. M., & Crago, R. V. (2017). Intergenerational transmission of convictions for different types of offenses. *Victims and Offenders*, *12*(1), 1–20.

Felitti, V., Anda, R., Nordenberg, D., Williamson, D., Spitz, A. M., Edwards, V., ... Marks, I. (1998). Relationship of childhood abuse and household dysfunction to many of the leading causes of death in adults. *American Journal of Preventive Medicine*, *14*(4), 245–258.

MacLeod, J. F., & Farrington, D. P. (2022). *Testing criminal career theories in British and American longitudinal studies*. Cambridge: Cambridge University Press.

Malvaso, C. G., Cale, J., Whitten, T., Day, A., Singh, S., Hackett, L., ... Ross, S. (2022). Associations between Adverse Childhood Experiences and trauma among young people who offend: A systematic literature review. *Trauma, Violence, and Abuse*, *23*(5), 1677–1694.

McGee, T. R., & Farrington, D. P. (2016). Developmental and life-course theories of crime. In A. R. Piquero (Ed.), *The handbook of criminological theory* (pp. 336–354). Chichester: Wiley.

Piquero, A. R. (2023). "We study the past to understand the present; we understand the present to guide the future": The time capsule of developmental and life-course criminology. *Journal of Criminal Justice*, 85: 101932.

Piquero, A., Jennings, W. G., Diamond, B., Farrington, D. P., Tremblay, R. E., Welsh, B. C., & Gonzalez, J. M. R. (2016). A meta-analysis update on the effects of early family/parent training programs on antisocial behavior and delinquency. *Journal of Experimental Criminology*, *12*(2), 229–248.

Sutton, C. (2022). Editorial: Adverse childhood experiences are important but not the only risk to child development: Revisiting a full risk-resilience matrix. *Criminal Behaviour and Mental Health*, *32*(2), 67–74.

Theobald, D., & Farrington, D. P. (2009). Effects of getting married on offending: Results from a prospective longitudinal survey of males. *European Journal of Criminology*, *6*(6), 496–516.

Index